INDIAN NATURAL HISTORY

INDIAN NATURAL HISTORY

Dr. Anil Tandon

ANMOL PUBLICATIONS PVT. LTD.
NEW DELHI-110 002 (INDIA)

ANMOL PUBLICATIONS PVT. LTD.
Regd. Office: 4360/4, Ansari Road, Daryaganj,
New Delhi-110002 (India)
Tel.: 23278000, 23261597, 23286875, 23255577
Fax: 91-11-23280289
Email: anmolpub@gmail.com
Visit us at: www.anmolpublications.com

Branch Office: No. 1015, Ist Main Road, BSK IIIrd Stage
IIIrd Phase, IIIrd Block, Bangalore-560 085 (India)
Tel.: 080-41723429 • Fax: 080-26723604
Email: anmolpublicationsbangalore@gmail.com

Indian Natural History

First Edition, 2010

ISBN 978-81-261-4605-5

PRINTED IN INDIA

Printed at Mehra Offset Press, Delhi.

Contents

Preface

Natural history is the scientific research of plants or animals, leaning more towards the observational than experimental methods of study, and encompasses more research. Grouped among the natural sciences, Natural history is the systematic study of any category of natural objects or organisms.

The textbook explains more about the modern natural history historically from studies in the ancient Greco-Roman world and then the medieval Arabic world through to the scattered European Renaissance scientists working in near isolation, today's field is more of a cross discipline umbrella of many specialty sciences that like geobiology have a strong multi-disciplinary nature combining scientists and scientific knowledge of many specialty sciences. This textbook is specifically written for the students of UPTU University who are pursuing their graduation or post graduation.

Author

Chapter 1

The Orient List View

OVERVIEW

History of India and its civilization dates back to at least 6500 BC which perhaps makes the oldest surviving civilization in the world. India has been a meeting ground between the East and the West. Through out its history many invaders have come to India but Indian religions allowed it to adapt to and absorb all of them. All the while, these local dynasties built upon the roots of a culture well established. India has always been simply too big, too complicated, and too culturally subtle to let any one empire dominate it for long.

Based on archeological findings, Indian history can be broadly divided into five phases:

- *Saraswati (Harappan) civilization*: 6500 BC - 1000 BC or also called 'Vedic period' in history of India.
- *Golden period of Indian History*: 500 BC - 800 AD
- *Muslim influence in India*: 1000 AD- 1700 AD
- *British period in India*: 1700 AD - 1947 AD
- *Modern India*: 1947 - till date

VEDIC PERIOD AND GOLDEN PERIOD OF INDIAN HISTORY

ANCIENT INDIAN HISTORY (VEDIC PERIOD)

Earliest historical evidence from Mehargarh (north-west Indian sub-continent) shows beginning of civilization in India at around 6500 B.C. It is the earliest and largest urban site of the period in the world. This site has yielded evidence for the earliest domestication of animals, evolution of agriculture, as well as arts and crafts. The horse was first domesticated here in 6500 B.C. There is a progressive process of the domestication of animals, particularly cattle, the development of agriculture, beginning with barley and then later wheat and rice, and the use of metal, beginning with copper and culminating in iron, along with the development villages and towns. It has been suggested by some historians that an 'Aryan Invasion' of Indian subcontinent took place around 1500-1000 B.C. However, current archeological data do not support the existence of an Indo Aryan or European invasion into South Asia at any time in the pre or proto-historic periods. The people in this tradition were the same basic ethnic groups as in India today, with their same basic types of languages.

Two important cities were discovered: Harappa on the Ravi river, andMohenjodaro on the Indus during excavations in 1920. The remains of these two cities were part of a large civilization and well developed ancient civilization, which is now called by historians as 'Indus Valley Civilization', or 'Saraswati Civilization'. Later Harappan (Sarasvati) civilization 3100-1900 BC shows massive cities, complex agriculture and metallurgy, sophistication of arts and crafts, and precision in weights and measures.

They built large buildings, which were mathematically-planned. The city planning in those ancient cities is comparable to the best of our modern cities. This civilization had a written language and was highly sophisticated. Some of these towns were almost three miles in diametre with thousands of residents. These ancient municipalities had granaries, citadels, and even household toilets. In Mohenjodaro, a mile-long canal connected the city to the sea, and trading ships sailed as far as Mesopotamia. At its height, the Indus civilization extended over half a million square miles across the Indus river valley, and though it existed at the same time as the ancient civilizations of Egypt and Sumer, it far outlasted them. This Sarasvati civilization was a centre of trading and for the diffusion of civilization throughout south and west Asia, which often dominated the Mesopotamian region.

Mehrgarh, Harappa, Mohenjodaro, Kalibangan and Lothal are peripheral cities of the great Sarasvati civilization with more than 500 sites along its banks awaiting excavation.

The year 4500 B.C. marks Mandhatr's defeat of Druhyus, driving them to the west into Iran. 4000-3700 B.C. was the Rig Veda period. In 3730 B.C. occurred the 'Battle of Ten' Kings - the age of Sudas and his sage advisors, Vasistha and Visvamitra. From 3600 to 3100 B.C. was the late Vedic age during which Yajur, Sama, and Atharva Vedas were composed. 3100 B.C. is the probable date of the Mahabharata, composed by Vyasa. At this time, a tectonic plate shift resulted in river Yamuna which was a tributary of river Saraswati shifted its course and Saraswati became smaller.

It was the beginning of 'Kali Yuga'. In 1900 B.C., another tectonic plate shift made Saraswati lose Sutlej. This dried up Sarasvati, causing massive exodus of people towards the Ganga valley in east, whence arose the classical civilization of India. Post-Harappan civilization 1900-1000 BC shows the abandonment of the Harappan towns owing to ecological and river changes but without a real break in the continuity of the culture. There is a decentralization and relocation in which the same basic agricultural and artistic traditions continue, along with a few significant urban sites like Dwaraka. This gradually develops into the Gangetic civilization of the first millennium BC, which is the classical civilization of ancient India, which retains its memory of its origin in the Saraswati region through the Vedas.

David Frawley and other modern scholars propose:

- 6500-3100 BC, Pre-Harappan, early Rig Vedic
- 3100-1900 BC, Mature Harappan 3100-1900, period of the Four Vedas.
- 1900-1000 BC, Late Harappan, late Vedic and Brahmana period

BUDDHA AND MAHAVIRA

The sequence of development in the literature does not parallel a migration into India but the historical development of civilization in India from the Sarasvati to the Ganges'. In the 5th century BC, Siddhartha Gautama founded the religion of Buddhism, a profoundly influential work of human thought still espoused by much of the world. In the same another religion called Jainism was founded byMahavira.

Around 500 BC, when the Persian kings Cyrus and Darius, pushing their empire eastward, conquered the ever-prized Indus Valley. The Persians were in turn conquered by the Greeks under Alexander the Great, who came as far as the Beas River, where he defeated king Porus and an army of 200 elephants in 326 BC. The tireless, charismatic conqueror wanted to extend his empire even further eastward, but his own troops (undoubtedly exhausted) refused to continue. Alexander returned home, leaving behind garrisons to keep the trade routes open.

GOLDEN PERIOD OF INDIAN HISTORY

Although Indian accounts to a large extent ignored Alexander the Great's Indus campaign in 326 B.C., Greek writers recorded their impressions of the general conditions prevailing in South Asia during this period. A two-way cultural fusion between several Indo-Greek elements-especially in art, architecture, and coinage—occurred in the next several hundred years. North India's political landscape was transformed by the emergence of Magadha in the eastern Indo-Gangetic Plain.

As the overextended Hellenistic sphere declined, a king known as Chandragupta swept back through the country from Magadha (Bihar) and conquered his way well into Afghanistan. This was the beginning of one India's greatest dynasties, the Maurya. In 322 B.C., Magadha, under the rule of Chandragupta Maurya, began to assert its hegemony over neighbouring areas. Chandragupta, who ruled from 324 to 301 B.C., was the architect of the first Indian imperial power-the Mauryan Empire (326-184 B.C.)—whose capital was Pataliputra, near modern-day Patna, in Bihar.

Situated on rich alluvial soil and near mineral deposits, especially iron, Magadha was at the centre of bustling commerce and trade. The capital was a city of magnificent palaces, temples, a university, a library, gardens, and parks, as reported by Megasthenes, the third-century B.C. Greek historian and ambassador to the Mauryan court. Legend states that Chandragupta's success was due in large measure to his adviser Kautilya, the Brahman author of the *Arthashastra* (Science of Material Gain).

There was a highly centralized and hierarchical government with a large staff, which regulated tax collection, trade and commerce, industrial arts, mining, vital statistics, welfare of foreigners, maintenance of public places including markets and temples, and prostitutes. A large standing army and a well-developed espionage system were maintained. The empire was divided into provinces, districts, and villages governed by a host of centrally appointed local officials, who replicated the functions of the central administration.

Ashoka, was the most trusted son of Bindusara and grandson of Chandragupta. During his father's reign, he was the governor of Ujjain and Taxila. Having sidelined all claims to the throne from his brothers, Ashoka was coroneted as an emperor. He ruled from 269 to 232 B.C. and was one of India's most illustrious rulers. Under the great king Ashoka the Mauryan empire conquered nearly the entire subcontinent, Ashoka extended the Maurya Empire to the whole of India except the deep south and the south-east, reaching out even into Central Asia.Ashoka's inscriptions chiseled on rocks and stone pillars located at strategic locations throughout his empire—such as Lampaka (Laghman in modern Afghanistan), Mahastan (in modern Bangladesh), and Brahmagiri (in Karnataka)—constitute the second set of datable historical records.

According to some of the inscriptions, in the aftermath of the carnage resulting from his campaign against the powerful kingdom of Kalinga (modern Orissa), Ashoka renounced bloodshed and pursued a policy of nonviolence or ahimsa, espousing a theory of rule by righteousness. His toleration for different religious beliefs and languages reflected the realities of India's regional pluralism although he personally seems to have followed Buddhism. Early Buddhist stories assert that he convened a Buddhist council at his capital, regularly undertook tours within his realm, and sent Buddhist missionary ambassadors to Sri Lanka. His rule marked the height of the Maurya empire, and it collapsed only 100 years after his death.

Under his reign Buddhism spread to Syria, Egypt, Macedonia, Central Asia, Burma. For propagation of Buddhism, he started inscribing edicts on rocks and pillars at places where people could easily read them. These pillars and rocks are still found in India, spreading their message of love and peace for the last two thousand years. To his ideas he gave the name *Dharma*. Ashoka died in 232 BC. The capital of Ashoka pillar at Sarnath is adopted by India as its national emblem. The "Dharma Chakra" on the Ashoka Pillar adorns our National Flag.

KUSHAN DYNASTY

After the disintegration of the Mauryan Empire in the second century B.C., South Asia became a collage of regional powers with overlapping boundaries. India's unguarded northwestern border again attracted a series of invaders between 200 B.C. and A.D. 300. The invaders became "Indianized" in the process of their conquest and settlement. Also, this period witnessed remarkable intellectual and artistic achievements inspired by cultural diffusion and syncretism.

The Indo-Greeks, or the Bactrians, of the northwest contributed to the development of numismatics; they were followed by another group, the Shakas (or Scythians), from the steppes of Central Asia, who settled in western India. Still other nomadic people, the Yuezhi, who were forced out of the Inner Asian steppes of Mongolia, drove the Shakas out of northwestern India and established the Kushana Kingdom (first century B.C.-third century A.D.). The Kushana Kingdom controlled parts of Afghanistan and Iran, and in India the realm stretched from Purushapura (modern Peshawar, Pakistan) in the northwest, to Varanasi (Uttar Pradesh) in the east, and to Sanchi (Madhya Pradesh) in the south. For a short period, the kingdom reached still farther east, to Pataliputra.

The Kushana Kingdom was the crucible of trade among the Indian, Persian, Chinese, and Roman empires and controlled a critical part of the legendary Silk Road. Kanishka, who reigned for two decades starting around A.D. 78, was the most noteworthy Kushana ruler. He converted to Buddhism and convened a great Buddhist council in Kashmir. The Kushanas were patrons of Gandharan art, a synthesis between Greek and Indian styles, and Sanskrit literature. They initiated a new era called Shaka in A.D. 78, and their calendar, which was formally recognized by India for civil purposes starting on March 22, 1957, is still in use.

THE CLASSICAL AGE - GUPTA EMPIRE AND HARSHA

Gupta Age

Under Chandragupta I (320-335), empire was revived in the north. Like Chandragupta Maurya, he first conquered Magadha, set up his capital where the Mauryan capital had stood (Patna), and from this base consolidated a kingdom over the eastern portion of northern India. In addition, Chandragupta revived many of Asoka's principles of government. It was his son, however, Samudragupta(335-376), and later his grandson, Chandragupta II (376-415), who extended the kingdom into an empire over the whole of the north and the western Deccan. Chandragupta II was the greatest of the Gupta kings and called Vikramaditya.

He presided over the greatest cultural age in India. From Pataliputra, their capital, he sought to retain political preeminence as much by pragmatism and judicious marriage alliances as by military strength. The greatest writer of the time wasKalidasa. Poetry in the Gupta age tended towards a few genres: religious and meditative poetry, lyric poetry, narrative histories (the most popular of the secular literatures), and drama. Kalidasa excelled at lyric poetry, but he is best known for his dramas. The Indian numeral system—sometimes erroneously attributed to the Arabs, who took it from India to Europe where it replaced the Roman system—and the decimal system are Indian inventions of this period. Aryabhatta's expositions on astronomy in 499 A.D. gave calculations of the solar year and the shape and movement of astral bodies with remarkable accuracy. In medicine, Charaka and Sushruta wrote about a fully evolved medical system. Indian physicians excelled in pharmacopoeia, caesarean section, bone setting, and plastic surgery including skin grafting.

The Guptas fell prey, however, to a wave of migrations by the Huns, a people who originally lived north of China. Beginning in the 400's, the Huns began to put pressure on the Guptas. In 480 AD they conquered the Guptas and took over northern India. Western India was overrun by 500 A.D., and the last of the Gupta kings, presiding over a vastly diminished kingdom, perished in 550 A.D. Over the decades Huns gradually assimilated into the indigenous population and their state weakened.

HARSHA VARDHANA

The northern and western regions of India passed into the hands of a dozen or more feudatories. Gradually, one of them, Prabhakar Vardhana, the ruler of Thanesar, who belonged to the Pushabhukti family, extended his control over all other feudatories. Prabhakar Vardhan was the first king of the Vardhan dynasty with his capital at Thanesar now a small town in the vicinity of Kurukshetra in the state of Haryana. After the death of Prabahakar Vardhan in 606 A.D., his eldest son, RajyaVardhan, became king of Kananuj. Harsha ascended the throne at the age of 16 after his brother Rajya Vardhana was killed in a battle against Malwa King Devigupta and Gauda King Sasanka..

Harsha, quickly re-established an Indian empire. From 606-647 AD, he ruled over an empire in northern India. Harsha was perhaps one of the greatest conquerors of Indian history, and unlike all of his conquering predecessors, he was a brilliant administrator. He was also a great patron of culture. His capital city, Kanauj, extended for four or five miles along the Ganges River and was filled with magnificent buildings. Only one fourth of the taxes he collected went to administration of the government. The remainder went to charity, rewards, and especially to culture: art, literature, music, and religion.

The most significant achievements of this period, however, were in religion, education, mathematics, art, and Sanskrit literature and drama. The religion that later developed into modern Hinduism witnessed a crystallization of its components: major sectarian deities, image worship, *bhakti* (devotion), and the importance of the temple. Education included grammar, composition, logic, metaphysics, mathematics, medicine, and astronomy. These subjects became highly specialized and reached an advanced level.

Because of extensive trade, the culture of India became the dominant culture around the Bay of Bengal, profoundly and deeply influencing the cultures of Burma, Cambodia, and Sri Lanka. In many ways, the period during and following the Gupta dynasty was the period of "Greater India," a period of cultural activity in India and surrounding countries building off of the base of Indian culture.

The history of the Kingdom of Kanauj after the death of Harshavardhana can be said to have been uncertain till the year 730 AD, when Yashovarman is said to have ruled till 752 AD. This was followed by the Ayudha dynasty which comprised three kings. The first was Yajrayudha who is said to have ruled in about 770 AD. After Ayudhs, Prathihara King Nagabhatta II annexed Kannauj. North and north west part of India after Harsha Vardhana was mostly controlled by Pratihara Kings while Central India and part of South was mostly under Rashtrakutas dynasty (753-973 AD). Pala Kings (750-1161 AD) ruled the Eastern part of India (present Bengal and Bihar).

PALA AND SENA: 730-1197 A.D.

The Pala empire was founded in 730 AD. They ruled over parts of Bengal and Bihar. Dharmapala (780-812 AD) was one of the greatest kings of the Pala dynasty. He did much to restore the greatness of Pataliputra. The Nalanda university was revived under their rule. The Palas had close trade contacts and cultural links with South-East Asia.

In the early twelfth century, they were replaced by the Sena dynasty. In early 13th century, Tughan Khan defeated the Sena king, Laxman. After this defeat the Nalanda University was destroyed.

PRATIHARAS 750-920 AD

The greatest ruler of the Pratihara dynasty was Mihir Bhoja. He recovered Kanauj (Kanyakubja) by 836, and it remained the capital of the Pratiharas for almost a century. He built the city Bhojpal (Bhopal). Raja Bhoja and other valiant Gujara kings, faced and defeated many attacks of the Arabs from west. Between 915-918AD, attack by a Rashtrakuta king, to the weakening of the Pratihara Empire and also who devastated the city of Kannauj. In 1018 AD, Mahmud of Gazni sacked Kannauj then ruled by Rajyapala Pratihara. The empire broke into independent Rajput states.

RASHTRAKUTAS 753-973 A.D.

Dantidurga laid the foundation of Rashtrakuta empire. The Rashtrakuta's empire was the most powerful of the time. They ruled from Lattaluru (Latur), and later shifted the capital to Manyaketa (Malkhed).

Amoghavarsha (814-880AD) is the most famous Rashtrakuta kings. His long reign was distinguished for its royal patronage of Jainism and the flourishing of regional literature. Indra III, great-grandson of Amoghvarsha defeated the Pratihar king Mahipala. Krishana III was the last great king of Rashtrakuta dynasty. Rashtrakutas were great patrons of art and architecture. Krishana I, built the Kailasa Temple at Ellora. The caves at Gharapuri (Elephanta near Mumbai) were also built by this dynasty.

THE INDIAN RULERS

During the Kushana Dynasty, an indigenous power, the Satavahana Kingdom (first century B.C.-third century A.D), rose in the Deccan in southern India. The Satavahana, or Andhra, Kingdom was considerably influenced by the Mauryan political model, although power was decentralized in the hands of local chieftains, who used the symbols of Vedic religion and upheld the *varnashramadharma*. The rulers, however, were eclectic and patronized Buddhist monuments, such as those in Ellora (Maharashtra) and Amaravati (Andhra Pradesh).

Thus, the Deccan served as a bridge through which politics, trade, and religious ideas could spread from the north to the south. Further south were three ancient Tamil kingdoms-Chera (on the west), Chola (on the east), and Pandya (in the south)—frequently involved in internecine warfare to gain regional supremacy. They are mentioned in Greek and Ashokan sources as lying at the fringes of the Mauryan Empire.

Peninsular India was involved in an eighth-century tripartite power struggle among the Chalukyas (556-757) of Vatapi, the Pallavas (300-888) of Kanchipuram, and the Pandyas (seventh through the tenth centuries) of Madurai. Their subordinates, the Rashtrakutas, who ruled from 753 - 973 AD, overthrew the Chalukya rulers. Although both the Pallava and Pandya kingdoms were enemies, the real struggle for political domination was between the Pallava and Chalukya realms.

THE SATVAHANA DYNASTY

The Satvahanas (also known as Andhras) established their kingdom in the Deccan after the decline of Maurya Empire. The kingdom was in the present Maharashtra state. The founder of the Satvahana dynasty was Simuka in 40 B.C. Satakarni I was the most distinguished ruler of this dynasty. Satakarni I allied with powerful Marathi chieftain and signaled his accession to power by performing ashvamedhas (horse-sacrifice). After his death, the Satvahana power slowly disintegrated under a wave of Scythian invasion. The Satvahana dynasty lasted until the 3rd century AD.

PALLAVA DYNASTY

They established a capital at Kanchipuram (Tamil Nadu state) and came to hold sway in the south. They were defeated by the Guptas in about 360 AD but continued to rule until the

Cholas finally conquered their lands. They ruled from the 4th century to the 9th century although some remnants survived till 13th century. The dynasty was at its peak under Mahendra-Varman I (600-630 AD), when architecture flourished, notably in temples such as Mahabalipuram.

During the 7th and the 8th centuries, this dynasty ruled over a region extending from centre of Andhra Pradesh far to the Kaveri River; Later, in the 9th century, the Pallava themselves were definitely conquered by the Chola from Tanjore and became their vassals.

PANDYA (AROUND 200S B.C TO 1378 AD)

They were the longest ruling dynasty of Indian history. They ruled the southern most part of India and the capital of the Pandya kings was Madurai (Tamil Nadu). First Indian Ambassador from Pandya Dynasty is sent to Rome. (26 BC). The dynasty extended its power into Kerala (southwestern India) and Sri Lanka during the reigns of kings Kadungon (ruled 590- 620 A.D), Arikesar Maravarman (670-700 A.D), Varagunamaharaja I (765-815A.D), and Srimara Srivallabha (815-862 A.D). Pandya influence peaked in Jatavarman Sundara's reign 1251-1268 A.D. After forces from the Delhi sultanate invaded Madurai in 1311, the Pandyas declined into merely local rulers.

CHALUKYA DYNASTY 425 - 753 AD AND 973 - 1190 AD

After Satvahan, the next great empire in the Deccan was the Chalukya empire. Pulakesin I, first ruler of the Chalukya dynasty. Pulakesin II was the greatest ruler of the Chalukya dynasty. He consolidated his authority in Maharashtra and conquered large parts of the Deccan.

His greatest achievement was his victory against Harshvardhan in 620. However, Pulakesin II was defeated and killed by the Pallava king Narasimhavarman in 642. His capital Vatapi was completely destroyed. His son Vikramaditya was also as great a ruler. He renewed the struggle against Pallavas and recovered the former glory of the Chalukyas. In 753A.D, his great grandson Vikramaditya II was overthrown by a chief named Dantidurga. Chalukyas constructed many temples at Aihole. Some Ajantha caves were also built during this period.

During Rashtrakutas rule, the Chalukyas were a minor power. For 200 years, they survived the Rashtrakutas. In 973 AD Tailap Chalukya of the Kalyani branch gained power and restored the Chalukyan rule. They gained supremacy for about 200 years to be partitioned into: Yadavs of Deogiri, Kaktiyas of Warangal and Hoysalas of Belur.

YADAVAS OF DEVAGIRI

Yadavas extended their authority over a large territory. Their capital was situated at Chandor (Nasik district). They built the *Deogiri fort* in 11th century. Marathi language received the status of a court language in Yadava rule. The Yadava king Singhana was great patron of learning *Sant Dnyaneshwar* belonged to this age. In 1294, Alla-ud-din Khilji laid four sieges to Deogiri. Finally, the Yadavas were defeated and the strong fort of Deogiri fell into the hands of Muslim rulers. The riches of Deogiri were looted. By 1310 the Yadav rule came to an end.

KAKATIYAS OF WARANGAL

Telgu language and literature flourished under Kakatiyas. They also built many forts. The last king Prataprudra defeated Allaudin Khilji when he was first attacked in 1303. In 1310, after another war, he agreed to pay heavy tributes to Malik Kafur (Alladin's general.) In 1321 Ghias-ud-din Tughlaq marched with a large army, and took Prataprudra as a prisoner to Delhi. Prataprudra died on the way to Delhi. Thus ended the glorious rule of Kaktiyas.

HOYSALAS OF BELUR-HALEBID

King Sala was the founder of Hoysala dynasty. Hoysalas built as many as 1500 temples. The style of their architecture became famous as the Hoysala style. Most famous are the temples of Belur and Halebid with intricate carvings. Allaudin Khilji, defeated this kingdom between 1308-1312.

MUSLIM PERIOD IN INDIAN HISTORY

There were many causes for Muslim conquest but the major reason was the spread of Islam. The Muslim dominated Kabul, the Punjab, and Sind, before intruding in to India. The wealth in India lured the Muslim rulers. Further the inter-rivalry between the kingdoms in India paved the way for their entry in to India.

EARLY MUSLIM INVASIONS

The very first Muslim attack on India in Sindh in the year 715 A.D by Arabs led by Mohammad Bin Qasim. They had displaced Raja Dabir who ruled Sindh from his capital Deval (near modern Karachi).

They even unsuccessfully tried to attack Malwa. After this invasion, which was limited to Sindh, for a period of 300 years, kings like Raja Bhoja and other Gurjara Kings thwarted further Muslim attacks. The next invasion was by Turk Sabuktagin. He had established himself in Khorasan and extended his kingdom to Kabul and Ghazni. In 986 AD he came into conflict with Raja Jaipal of Bathinda. In 991 A.D. Raja Jaipal allied with other Hindu king including Rajyapala the Prathira king of Kannauj and Dhanga the ruler of the distant Chandela kingdom but they too were defeated.

Mahmud of Ghazni

The elder son of Sabuktagin, Mahmud of Ghazni assumed the throne in 997 AD. He was very conscious of the wealth he could achieve from further conquests into India. He was also a religious fanatic who aimed to spread Islam. Mahmud is said to have invaded India seventeen times between 1001 -1027 AD. King Jaipal and later his son Anandpal resisted Mahmud but were defeated.

Between 1009 A.D and 1026 A.D he invaded Kangra, Thaneshwar, Kanauj, Mathura, Gwalior, Kashmir and Punjab. In 1025 A.D Mahmud invaded Somnath and looted its temple on the coast of Saurashtra or Kathiwar. Enormous treasure of the fortified temple was looted. His last invasion was in about 1027 AD. He died in 1030 AD.

Mohammad Ghori

The next important Muslim ruler who had made his influence in Indian history known was Muhammad Ghori. Muhammad Ghori is said to have invaded India seven times. Mohammad Ghori invaded Multan in about 1175-76AD. In 1178 A.D he attempted the conquest of Gujarat. He was strongly resisted by Bhimdev II who inflicted a crushing defeat on him. In 1191 AD Mohammad Ghori met Prithvi Raj Chauhan in the first battle of Tarain.

Mohammad Ghori was severely wounded and outnumbered. He was defeated and left the battlefield. In the very next year in 1192 AD both the armies met again at Tarain. This time Mohammad cleverly defeated Prithvi Raj Chauhan. In 1194 AD Mohammad Ghori invaded and defeated and killed the ruler of Kannauj Jaichand and also captured Benares. Gwallior, Gujarat and Ajmer were also occupied by 1197 AD. Mohammad Ghori died in 1206AD.

THE SLAVE DYNASTY

Mohammad Ghori had left Qutab-ud-din Aibek who was a slave from Turkistan in charge of the Indian affairs. Qutab-ud-din's general Muhammad Khilji successfully plundered and conquered the fort of Bihar in 1193 AD. In about 1199-1202AD Muhammad Khilji brought Bengal under his authority. Qutab-ud-din died in 1210AD. He had laid the foundation of a new dynasty called the Slave dynasty in 1206AD. In 1211 A.D. Iltumish (son in law of Qutub-ud-din) ascended the throne. He spent his days in retrieving the lost territories of Qutab-ud-din, and also added Malwa and Sind. He defeated Rajput rulers of Ranthambor, Ajmer, Jalor, Nagor, Gwalior. Kannauj, Banaras and Badaun were under his dominion. During his period Qutab Minar in Delhi was completed.

Iitutmish's daughter Razia Begum came to power 1236 AD after a brief power struggle and ruled till 1240 AD when she was killed. Nasir-uddin Mahmud the youngest son of Iltumish came into power after another power struggle. He ruled for twenty-five years. The affairs of the state were left to his father-in-law and minister Ulugh Khan Balban. After the death of Nasir-ud-din Mahmud in 1226 AD the power was taken over by Balban who was an able administrator. He maintained a strict attitude towards the Hindus and kept them under strong suppression with the help of his military power. He was one of the greatest military rulers of the Slave dynasty. Balban died in 1287 AD.

THE KHILJI DYNASTY

Following the death of Balban the Sultanate became weak and there were number of revolts. This was the period when the nobles placed Jalaluddin Khilji on the throne. This marked the beginning of Khilji dynasty. The rule of this dynasty started in 1290 AD. Alauddin Khilji a nephew of Jalaluddin Khilji hatched a conspiracy and got Sultan Jala-lud din killed and proclaimed himself as the Sultan in 1296. In 1297 AD Alauddin Khilji set off for conquering Gujarat.

In 1301 A.D. Ramthambhor was captured and the Rajput Hamir Deva was murdered. In 1303 A.D. he conquered Chittor killing Rana Rattan Singh. His queen Rani Padmini with the other women committed Jauhar. In 1305 A.D. Alauddin Khilji captured Malwa, Ujjain, Mandu, Dhar and Chanderi but failed to capture Bengal. By 1311 A.D. he captured nearly the whole of North India. His General Malik Kafur captured a large part of south India. During his reign Mongols invaded the country several times but were successfully repulsed. From these invasion Allauddin Khilji learnt the lessons of keeping himself prepared, by fortifying and organizing his armed forces. Allaudin Khilji died in 1316 A.D.

There was lot of infighting after Alauddin Khiljis death and Mubarak Khan the third son of Alauddin Khilji ascended the throne as Qutb-ud-din Mubarak in the year 1316 AD. The rule of Qutb-ud-din Mubarak was an utter failure. Ultimately Qutb-ud-din Mubarak was murdered by Khusru Khan and Khilji dynasty ended.

THE TUGHLAQ DYNASTY

In 1320, Ghazi Tughlaq, the governor of the northwestern

provinces took the throne under the title Ghiyasuddin Tughlaq after killing Khusru Khan. In 1325 the Sultan met an accidental death and was succeeded by his sonMuhammad bin Tughlaq. During his reign, the territorial expansion of Delhi Sultanate reached its farthest limits.

His empire covered the regions from Peshawar in the north and Madurai in the South, and from Sindh in the west to Assam in the east. The capital was transferred from Delhi to Devagiri. However, it had to be shifted back within two years, as there were no adequate arrangements in the new capital.

Muhammad also introduced copper and brass coins as "token coins" and ordered that these coins should be considered at par with the silver and gold coins in value. This resulted in forged coins and as a result token currency was withdrawn. The Sultan's ambitions plan of invading Himachal and the devastation of his army owing to inhospitable climate was another blunder by Mohammed-bin -Tughlaq. Administrative blunders, military failures and revolts weakened Muhammad bin Tughlaq. He died in 1351 of illness while trying to suppress revolt in Gujrat.

His cousin Feroz Tughlug who became Sultan in the year 1351 AD succeeded Muhammed-bin- Tughlaq. Feroz Tughlak did not contribute much to expand the territories of the empire, which he inherited. In 1360 he invaded Jajnagar to destroy the Jagan nath Puri temple. In 1326 AD he met with success in his expedition to Sindh, before this he had led an invasion Nagarkot with an idea to destroy the Jwalamukhi temples. The Sultan was not tolerant towards people with different religion. Feroz Tughluq also introduced reforms in the field of irrigation and also constructed buildings with architectural skill.

He reformed the currency system. After him the dynasty began to disintegrate. The last Tughluq ruler Mahmud Nasir-uddin ruled from 1395-1413 AD. The invasion of Mongol ruler Timur in1398 A.D. sealed the fate of the Tughluq dynasty. Muhammad fled and Timur captured the city and destroyed many temples in north India. Thousands of people were killed and Delhi was plundered for fifteen days, Timur returned to

Samarkhand carrying away a large amount of wealth with him. Muhammad Tughlaq re-occupied Delhi and ruled till 1413 A.D.

THE SAIYYID

Then came the Saiyyid dynasty founded by Khizr Khan. The Sayyids ruled from about 1414 AD to 1450 AD. At a time when the provinces were declaring themselves independent the first task of Khizr Khan was the suppression of the revolts. Last in Saiyyid dynasty was Muhammad-bin-Farid. During his reign there was confusion and revolts. The empire came to an end in 1451 AD with his death.

THE LODHI DYNASTY

Behlol Lodhi who was in service during Khizr Khan rule founded the Lodhi dynasty. Behlol Lodhi an Afghan was proclaimed the Sultan in 1451AD. After his death his son Sikandar Lodi proved to be a capable ruler who brought back the lost prestige of the Sultan. He maintained friendly relations with the neighbouring states. He brought Gwalior and Bihar under his rule. He was a religious fanatic but encouraged education and trade. His military skill helped him in bringing the Afghan nobles under his control.

Sikandar Lodi was succeeded by Ibrahim Lodi who is said to have been the last great ruler of the Lodi dynasty. Ibrahim Lodi came to the throne in 1517 AD. He conquered Gwalior, and came into conflict with Rana Sanga the ruler of Mewar who defeated him twice.

His relations with the Afghan nobles became worse and this led to several conflicts with him. The discontented Afghan chiefs invited Babur the ruler of Kabul to India. Babur with an army of 10,000 defeated Ibrahim Lodi who had an army of 100,000 in the first battle of Panipat in 1526. Ibrahim Lodhi was killed in a fierce fight. With this defeat the Delhi Sultanate was laid to rest.

The History of India added a new outlook with the coming of Babur. This was the beginning of the Mughal dynasty in Indian History

MUGHAL DYNASTY (1526 - 1707 A.D)

Mughal dynasty started with Babur ascending the throne of Agra in 1526 A.D. In the beginning his rule in India Babur had to face the problems of the Rajputs and the Afghan chiefs. He battled Rana Sanga of Mewar in 1527 A.D. in the battle of Kanwah. Rana lost the battle. The defeat of Rana Sanga shook the power of the Rajputs. Babur's Empire extended from Bhera and Lahore to Bahraich and Bihar and from Sialkot to Ranthambhor. Like his predecessor Muslim Sultans Babur continued with policy of plundering and destroying Hindu temples and killing people. Babur died in 1530 AD. Humayun the eldest of his four sons succeeded him and ascended the throne of Agra in 1530. Humayun was faced with numerous difficulties. He had to reorganize his army that comprised of mixed races. He faced problems from his brothers, and nobles.

The Afghans though defeated by Babur were not vanquished. Sher Khan the King of Bengal defeated Humayun in the battle of Chausa in 1539 A.D. In 1540 A.D., he again defeated Humayun at Kanauj, and went on to capture Delhi and Agra. Thus Sher Khan re-established the Afghans rule in Delhi. Humayun was compelled to flee from India.

SHER SHAH AND THE SUR DYNASTY

Sher Shah's reign barely spanned five years (1540 - 1545), but is a landmark in the history of the Sub-continent. Sher Shah was a capable military and civilian administrator. He set up reforms in various areas including those of army and revenue administration. Numerous civil works were carried out during his short reign. After the death of Sher Shah in 1545 his son Islam Shah ruled up to 1553 A.D. Then Muhammad Adil Shah came to power. Muhammad Adil was not a capable ruler. His minister Hemu became important and virtually controlled the kingdom. As a result of the onslaught by Ibrahim Shah and Sikander Shah the Sur Empire was broken up.

RETURN OF HUMAYUN (1555 A.D.)

In the mean time Humayun took support of Persian Shah.

He managed to win over Kabul and Kandhar after a power struggle with his brother Kamran in 1949. He occupied Lahore and Dipalpur in 1555.A.D. By July 1555 Humayun reached Delhi where he spend his time in administration of his kingdom. In 1556 Humayun died in an accidental fall.

After the death of Humayun the history of India saw the rule of greatest of the Mughal rulers:

AKBAR THE GREAT (1556-1605)

Akbar inherited the throne of the Mughal Empire at the age of 14 years after the death of Humayun. His uncle Bairam Khan advised him. In 1556 Akbar met Hemu on the battlefield of Panipat (second battle of Panipat) and defeated his large army. With the defeat of Hemu, the Mughals had established their sway over Delhi and Agra.

Akbar followed a policy of reconciliation with the Rajputs and won their support by establishing matrimonial alliances. In 1562 he married the eldest daughter of Raja Bihal mal of Jaipur. In 1584 his son Salim was married to the daughter of Raja Bhagwan Das. In 1567 he marched against Chittor. In 1568 the Mughals captured Chittor. By 1569 Ranthambhor and Kalinjar was also captured.

He met the Rajput ruler Maharana Pratap in the battle of Haldighati in 1576. After a fierce battle Akbar defeated Maharana Pratap. Akbar conquered Bengal, Gujrat, Kashmir, Kabul by 1589 A.D. and Sind and Kandhar by 1595 A.D. Moving towards the Deccan Akbar attacked Ahmednagar. Chand Bibibravely defended this but she could not hold on longer and Ahmednagar fell in 1596.

It is said that Akbar followed generally a tolerant policy towards Hindus. Mughal emperor Akbar 'ordered the massacre of about 30,000 captured Rajput Hindus on February 24, 1568 AD, after the battle for Chittod, a number confirmed by Abul Fazl, Akbar's court historian.

He tried to establish a national religion called Din-i-illahi that was to be pleasing both the Hindus and Muslims. This was politically motivated and Din-i-illahi failed miserably. Akbar introduced the Mansabdari system that systematized the civil and military administration. He was also a patron of art and literature and Nav Ratans (Nine Gems) in his court are famous. They included great singer Tansen, poet Mulla-do-pyaja, and Ministers like Birbal and Todarmal. Akbar was not only a conqueror by an able administrator and was the greatest of the Mughal emperors.

His son Muhammad Salim also called Jahangir succeeded Akbar. In 1605 Akbar proclaimed him as the ruler. Salim was deeply influenced by the charms of his queen Nur Jahan whom he married 1611 and left the task of administration entirely on her at times. Jahangir won several wars but could not reach the glory of his father Akbar.

Jahangir died in 1627 A.D and was succeed by Shah Jahan was ruled from 1627 to 1658 A.D. Shahjhan's period is best known for construction of Taj Mahal and other great monuments. His love for his queen Mumtaz Mahalwas immense. After her death in 1631, he built the Taj Mahal in memory of her. In the years 1631-32 he was involved in wars with the Portuguese. He shared the Kingdom of Ahmednagar with the Sultan of Bijapur in 1636. After settling the problems he faced in the Deccan he retired to Agra in 1636 where he was later imprisoned by his son and successor Aurangzeb. In 1657 a war of succession started owing to the illness of Shah Jahan between Dara, Shah Suja, Aurangzeb, and Murad. Aurangzeb being the ablest of the three sons succeeded Shah Jahan. He ruled from 1658-1707. Aurangzeb was the last great Mughal ruler who took the Mughal Empire to its greatest glory. Aurangzeb possessed an empire that extended from Ghazni to Bengal and from Kashmir to the Deccan. But he was a religious fanatic and destroyed large number of temples and forcefully converted thousands of Hindus to Islam giving them a choice between Islam and death.

The imposition of Jizya on the Hindus in 1679, which was an anti Hindu policy, resulted in the rise of the Rajput in a revolt in 1769. This struggle continued till 1681 when Aurangzeb made peace with the Rajputs. The other sect affected by the Anti-Hindu policy of Aurangzeb was the Satnamis. Aurangzeb crushed their revolt. Next was the revolt of the Jats of Mathura, which was an opposition to the policy and oppression under Aurangzeb. Though they were suppressed in the early period they carried on the struggle till the death of Aurangzeb. The revolt of the Bundela Rajputs and the Sikhs were other significant effects of Aurangzeb's anti Hindu policy. The Sikhs whose temples were destroyed were hurt. The killing of Guru Teg Bahadur their 9th guru was more hurting. They swore the destruction of the Mughals. Under the 10thGuru Govind Singh, and after his death in 1708 A.D the struggle was carried on.

Aurangzeb faced stiff resistance from the Marathas under Shivaji and remained unsuccessful in subduing the Marathas. It was in about 1600 that the Mughals established contacts witht the English ever since the visit of Sir Thomas Roe. In 1616 the English were permitted to build a factory at Masulipattam. Aurangzeb died in 1707. Bahadur Shah I who was the eldest of the three surviving sons of Aurangzeb succeeded him. The vast Mughal Empire, which the biggest of all the empires existing then, was divided among the three sons. Bahadurr Shah I who was known, as Prince Muazzam had to face the problems from the Marathas, Rajputs and the Sikhs. Mughal rule in Delhi continued under a number of weak rulers after death of Bahadur Shah I in 1712 A.D. and the great Mughal Empire disintegrated. The Mughal rule in Delhi while under Muhammad Shah witnessed the invasion of Nadir Shah in 1739. This invasion sealed the fate of Muhammad Shah. This was followed by the invasion of Ahmad Shah Abdali, the general of Nadir Shah.

As the Mughal Emipre broke down there was rise of great Maratha power, Sikhs and arrival of British East India Company. Last of the titular Mughal King Bahadur Shah II took part in the revolt of 1857 against the English. After the failure of this revolt he was imprisoned and deported to Rangoon where he died in 1862. This marked the end of the Mughal dynasty.

VIJAYNAGAR KINGDOM

In order to check the progress of Islam in the

south Harihar and Bukkafounded an independent kingdom in the region between the river Krishna and Tungabhadra in 1336. The capital of this kingdom was at Vijayanagar on the banks of the river Tungabhadra. The kingdom was known as the Kingdom of Vijayanagar. Harihar was the first ruler of the kingdom. After his death, his brother Bukka succeeded. He died in 1379 and was succeeded by his son Harihar II.

Harihar II was given the title of Maharajadhiraja. During his reign, the whole of Southern Deccan came under the authority of Vijayanagar.

This also included present Karnataka, Tamil Nadu and Kerala states. Harihar II died in 1404 A.D. This dynasty was known as Sangama dynasty. The dynasty ruled for about 150 years till 1486, when one of their chiefs Narasimha Saluva deposed the last ruler of Sangama dynasty and seized the throne.

The ruler of Saluva dynasty did not last long. His two sons succeeded Narasimha Saluva. During the reign of the second son Immadi Narasimha in 1505 A.D, the Taluva chief Vira Narasimha usurped the throne and thus laid the foundation of the Taluva dynasty.

Krishnadeva Raya (1509-1529): Vira Narasimha ruled for four years and in 1509 A.D. was succeeded by his younger brother Krishnadeva Raya. The Vijayanagar kingdom reached the pinnacle of its glory during the reign of Krishnadeva Raya. He was successful in all the wars he waged. He defeated the king of Orissa and annexed Vijaywada and Rajmahendri. He defeated the Sultan of Bijapur in 1512 and took the possession of the Raichur Doab. The Vijayanagar kingdom extended from Cuttak in east to Goa in the west and from the Raichur Doab in the north to the Indian Ocean in the south.

Krishnadeva Raya encouraged trade with the western countries. He was not only a great warrior, but was also a playwright and a great patron of learning. Telugu literature flourished under him. Painting, sculpture, dance and music were greatly encouraged by him and his successors. He endeared himself to the people by his personal charm, kindness, and an ideal administration.

The decline of the Vijayanagar kingdom began with the death of Krishnadeva Raya in 1529. The kingdom came to an end in 1565, when Ramrai was defeated at Talikota by the joint efforts of Adilshahi, Nizamshahi, Qutubshahi and Baridshahi. After this, the kingdom broke into small states.

MUSLIM RULERS IN DECCAN

Nizam-ul-Mulk Bahri founded the Nizam Shahi dynasty. In 1490 AD his son Malik Ahmad defeated the army of Mahmud Bahmani and established himself independent. He assumed the title of Ahmad Nizam Shah and after him the dynasty was named Nizam Shahi dynasty. The next ruler was Burhan Nizam Shah was the next ruler who ruled for forty-five years. The state was later annexed in Mughal Empire in 1637 during the reign of Shah Jahan.

THE ADIL SHAHI SHAHI DYNASTY OF BIJAPUR

Yusuf Adil Khan, the governor of Bijapur who declared his independence in 1489, founded the Adil Shahi dynasty. Ismail Shah succeeded Adil shah but being a minor he was helped by Kamal Khan. He lost his life in a conspiracy and was succeeded by Ibrahim Adil Shah and ruled till 1557 AD. Ali Adil Shah succeeded Ibrahim Adil Shah. Following a policy of alliance he married Chand Bibi the daughter of Hussain NIzam Shah of Ahamadnagar. In the year 1564 - 1565 AD the four sultans allied at Talikota against the Vijayanagar Empire and defeated and annexed it. Adil shah was killed in 1579 AD. The throne was passed on to Ibrahim Adil Shah II who was a minor. His mother Chand Bibi looked after him while ministers ruled the kingdom. In 1595 AD the Ahmadnagar monarch was killed in a fight between Bijapur and Ahmednagar. In 1680 AD Aurangzeb annexed Bijapur.

THE QUTAB SHAHI SHAHI DYNASTY OF GOLKANDA

The Qutab Shahi dynasty was a part of the Bahmani Empire that was called Golkonda. Sultan Quli Qutab Shah who was formerly the governor of the eastern province declared his independence in 1518 AD. And started the The Qutab Shahi dynasty. Qutab Shah met with his death in 1543 AD and his son Jamshed ruled till 1550 AD. The throne was held by Ibrahim till 1580 AD and later his son Muhammad Quli ruled till 1611 AD. Aurangzeb finally annexed the state in 1687 AD.

BAHAMANI KINGDOM OF DECCAN

During the region of Muhammad-bin-Tughluq a series of revolts between the periods 1343 - 1351 AD helped in formation of numerous independent provinces. An officer of the Delhi Sultan named Hassan assumed the title of Bahman Shah and after occupation of Daulatbad in the Deccan proclaimed independence.

He was also known as Alauddin I, the founder of the Bahmani dynasty. Alauddin I was succeeded by Muhammad Shah I. He waged wars against the Hindu rulers of Vijayanagar and Warangal. With his policy of subjugation he subdued countless number of rival Hindu rulers, and accumulated vast treasures. A number of successful Sultans followed him till 1482 A.D. Shihab-ud-din Mahmud succeeded to the throne in 1482 AD and ruled till 1518 AD.

During his reign the provincial governors declared their independence and Bahmani Kingdom started to break up. Kalim-ullah Shah (1526 - 1538 AD) was the last ruler of Bahamani Kingdom.

List of Bahmani Kingdom Rulers

Gulbarga as capital -75 years

1. Ala-ud-din Hasan Bahman Shah 1347 - 1358 AD
2. Muhammad I 1358 - 1375 AD
3. Ala-ud-din Mujahid Shah 1375 - 1378 AD
4. Daud Shah I 1378 - 1378 AD
5. Muhammad II 1378 - 1397 AD
6. Ghiyas-ud-din Tahmatan Shah 1397 - 1397 AD
7. Shams-ud-din Daud Shah II 1397 - 1397 AD
8. Taj-ud-din Firoz Shah 1397 - 1422 AD

Bidar as capital -116 years

1. Shihab-ud-din Ahmad Shah I 1422 - 1436 AD
2. Ala-ud-din Ahmad Shah II 1436 - 1458 AD
3. Ala-ud-din Humayun Shah 1458 - 1461 AD
4. Nizam-ud-din Ahmad Shah III 1461 - 1463 AD
5. Shams-ud-din Muhammad Shah III 1463 - 1482 AD
6. Shihab-ud-din Mahmud 1482 - 1518 AD
7. Ahmad Shah IV 1518 - 1520 AD
8. Ala-ud-din Shah 1520 - 1523 AD
9. Wai-ullah Shah 1523 - 1526 AD
10. Kalim-ullah Shah 1526 - 1538 AD

THE IMAD SHAHI DYNASTY OF BERAR

This consisted of the northern part of the Bahamani Kingdom. The Imad Shahi Dynasty of Berar lasted for four generations till 1574 AD.

THE BARID SHAHI DYNASTY OF BIDAR

The Barid Shahi Sultans governed the Barid Shahi dynasty. Qasim Barid the minister of Mahmud Shah Bahamani established it in 1492 AD. This dynasty lasted till 1619 AD when Bijapur annexed it.

POLICY OF MUSLIM RULERS IN INDIA

The general policy of most of the rulers during the 700 years of Muslim occupation of India was to systematically replace the fabric of Hindu society and culture with a Muslim culture. They tried to destroy Indian religions language, places of knowledge (universities e.g Nalanda were totally destroyed by Muslims). They destroyed and desecrated places of thousands of temples including Somnath, Mathura, Benaras, Ayodhaya, Kannauj, Thaneswar and in other places. There was wholesale slaughter of the monks and priests and innocent Hindus with the aim to wipe out the intellectual bedrock of the people they overran.

The Muslims could not subjugate India with ease and were never able to rule it entirely. There was a valiant and ceaseless struggle for independence by Hindus to deliver India from Muslim tyranny. The Rajputs, Jats, Marathas and Sikhs led this struggle in North India. In the South this struggle was embodied in the Vijayanagar Empire. This struggle culminated when the Marathas ended the Muslim domination of India.s

HISTORY OF INDIA

India's extraordinary history is intimately tied to its geography. A meeting ground between the East and the West, it has always been an invader's paradise, while at the same time its natural isolation and magnetic religions allowed it to adapt to and absorb many of the peoples who penetrated its mountain passes. No matter how many Persians, Greeks, Chinese nomads, Arabs, Portuguese, British and other raiders had their way with the land, local Hindu kingdoms invariably survived their depradations, living out their own sagas of conquest and collapse. All the while, these local dynasties built upon the roots of a culture well established since the time of the first invaders, the Aryans. In short, India has always been simply too big, too complicated, and too culturally subtle to let any one empire dominate it for long.

True to the haphazard ambiance of the country, the discovery of India's most ancient civilization literally happened by accident. British engineers in the mid-1800's, busy constructing a railway line between Karachi and Punjab, found ancient, kiln-baked bricks along the path of the track. This discovery was treated at the time as little more than a curiosity, but archaeologists later revisited the site in the 1920's and determined that the bricks were over 5000 years old. Soon afterward, two important cities were discovered: Harappa on the Ravi river, and Mohenjodaro on the Indus.

The civilization that laid the bricks, one of the world's oldest, was known as the Indus. They had a written language and were highly sophisticated. Dating back to 3000 BC, they originated in the south and moved north, building complex, mathematically-planned cities. Some of these towns were almost three miles in diametre and contained as many as 30,000 residents. These ancient municipalities had granaries, citadels, and even household toilets. In Mohenjodaro, a mile-long canal connected the city to the sea, and trading ships sailed as far as Mesopotamia. At its height, the Indus civilization extended over half a million square miles across the Indus river valley, and though it existed at the same time as the ancient civilizations of Egypt and Sumer, it far outlasted them.

The first group to invade India were the Aryans, who came out of the north in about 1500 BC. The Aryans brought with them strong cultural traditions that, miraculously, still remain in force today. They spoke and wrote in a language called Sanskrit, which was later used in the first documentation of the Vedas.

Though warriors and conquerors, the Aryans lived alongside Indus, introducing them to the *caste* system and establishing the basis of the Indian religions. The Aryans inhabited the northern regions for about 700 years, then moved further south and east when they developed iron tools and weapons. They eventually settled the Ganges valley and built large kingdoms throughout much of northern India.

The second great invasion into India occurred around 500 BC, when the Persian kings Cyrus and Darius, pushing their empire eastward, conquered the ever-prized Indus Valley. Compared to the Aryans, the Persian influence was marginal, perhaps because they were only able to occupy the region for a relatively brief period of about 150 years. The Persians were in turn conquered by the Greeks under Alexander the Great, who swept through the country as far as the Beas River, where he defeated king Porus and an army of 200 elephants in 326 BC. The tireless, charismatic conqueror wanted to extend his empire even further eastward, but his own troops (undoubtedly exhausted) refused to continue. Alexander returned home, leaving behind garrisons to keep the trade routes open.

While the Persians and Greeks subdued the Indus Valley and the northwest, Aryan-based kingdoms continued developing in the East. In the 5th century BC, Siddhartha Gautama founded the religion of Buddhism, a profoundly influential work of human thought still espoused by much of the world. As the overextended Hellenistic sphere declined, a king known as Chandragupta swept back through the country from Magadha (Bihar) and conquered his way well into Afghanistan.

This was the beginning of one India's greatest dynasties, the Maurya. Under the great king Ashoka (268-31 BC), the Mauryan empire conquered nearly the entire subcontinent, extending itself as far south as Mysore. When Ashoka conquered Orissa, however, his army shed so much blood that the repentant king gave up warfare forever and converted to Buddhism. Proving to be as tireless a missionary as he had been as conqueror, Asoka brought Buddhism to much of central Asia. His rule marked the height of the Maurya empire, and it collapsed only 100 years after his death.

After the demise of the Maurya dynasty, the regions it had conquered fragmented into a mosaic of kingdoms and smaller dynasties. The Greeks returned briefly in 150 BC and conquered the Punjab, and by this time Buddhism was becoming so influential that the Greek king Menander forsook the Hellenistic pantheon and became a Buddhist himself. The local kingdoms enjoyed relative autonomy for the next few hundred years, occasionally fighting (and often losing to) invaders from the north and China, who seemed to come and go like the monsoons. Unlike the Greeks, the Romans never made it to India, preferring to expand west instead.

In AD 319, Chandragupta II founded the Imperial Guptas dynasty, which conquered and consolidated the entire north and extended as far south as the Vindya mountains. When the Guptas diminished, a golden age of six thriving and separate kingdoms ensued, and at this time some of the most incredible temples in India were constructed in Bhubaneshwar, Konarak, and Khahurajo. It was time of relative stability, and cultural developments progressed on all fronts for hundreds of years, until the dawn of the Muslim era.

Arab traders had visited the western coast since 712, but it wasn't until 1001 that the Muslim world began to make itself keenly felt. In that year, Arab armies swept down the Khyber pass and hit like a storm. Led by Mahmud of Ghazi, they raided just about every other year for 26 years straight. They returned home each time, leaving behind them ruined cities, decimated armies, and probably a very edgy native population. Then they more or less vanished behind the mountains again for nearly 150 years, and India once again went on its way.

But the Muslims knew India was still there, waiting with all its riches. They returned in 1192 under Mohammed of Ghor, and this time they meant to stay. Ghor's armies laid waste to the Buddhist temples of Bihar, and by 1202 he had conquered the most powerful Hindu kingdoms along the Ganges. When Ghor died in 1206, one of his generals, Qutb-ud-din, ruled the far north from the Sultanate of Delhi, while the southern majority of India was free from the invaders. Turkish kings ruled the Muslim acquisition until 1397, when the Mongols invaded under Timur Lang (Tamerlane) and ravaged the entire region. One historian wrote that the lightning speed with which Tamerlane's armies struck Delhi was prompted by their desire to escape the stench of rotting corpses they were leaving behind them.

Islamic India fragmented after the brutal devastation Timur Lang left in Delhi, and it was every Muslim strongman for himself. This would change in 1527, however, when the Mughal (Persian for Mongol) monarch Babur came into power. Babur was a complicated, enlightened ruler from Kabul who loved poetry, gardening, and books. He even wrote cultural treatises on the Hindus he conquered, and took notes on local flora and fauna. Afghan princes in India asked for his help in 1526, and he conquered the Punjab and quickly asserted his own claim over them by taking Delhi. This was the foundation of the Mughal dynasty, whose six emperors would comprise most influential of all the Muslim dynasties in India.

Babur died in 1530, leaving behind a harried and ineffective son, Humayun. Humayun's own son, Akbar, however, would be the greatest Mughal ruler of all. Unlike his grandfather, Akbar was more warrior than scholar, and he extended the empire as far south as the Krishna river. Akbar tolerated local religions and married a Hindu princess, establishing a tradition of cultural acceptance that would contribute greatly to the success of the Mughal rule. In 1605, Akbar was succeed by his son Jahangir, who passed the expanding empire along to his own son Shah Jahan in 1627.

Though he spent much of his time subduing Hindu kingdoms to the south, Shah Jahan left behind the colossal monuments of the Mughal empire, including the Taj Majal (his favourite wife's tomb), the Pearl Mosque, the Royal Mosque, and the Red Fort. Jahan's campaigns in the south and his flare for extravagant architecture necessitated increased taxes and distressed his subjects, and under this scenario his son Aurungzebe imprisoned him, seeking power for himself in 1658.

Unlike his predecessors, Aurungzebe wished to eradicate indigenous traditions, and his intolerance prompted fierce local resistance. Though he expanded the empire to include nearly the entire subcontinent, he could never totally subdue the Mahrattas of the Deccan, who resisted him until his death in 1707. Out of the Mahrattas' doggedness arose the legendary figure of Shivagi, a symbol Hindu resistance and nationalism. Aurungzebe's three sons disputed over succession, and the Mughal empire crumbled, just as the Europeans were beginning to flex their own imperialistic muscles.

The Portuguese had traded in Goa as early as 1510, and later founded three other colonies on the west coast in Diu, Bassein, and Mangalore. In 1610, the British chased away a Portuguese naval squadron, and the East India Company created its own outpost at Surat. This small outpost marked the beginning of a remarkable presence that would last over 300 years and eventually dominate the entire subcontinent. Once in India, the British began to compete with the Portuguese, the Dutch, and the French. Through a combination of outright combat and deft alliances with local princes, the East India Company gained control of all European trade in India by 1769.

How a tiny island nation, thousands of miles away, came to administer a huge territory of 300 million people is one of history's great spectacles. A seemingly impossible task, it was done through a highly effective and organized system called the Raj. Treaties and agreements were signed with native princes, and the Company gradually increased its role in local affairs. The Raj helped build infrastructure and trained natives for its own military, though in theory they were for India's own defence. In 1784, after financial scandals in the Company alarmed British politicians, the Crown assumed half-control of the Company, beginning the transfer of power to royal hands.

In 1858, a rumor spread among Hindu soldiers that the British were greasing their bullets with the fat of cows and pigs, the former sacred animals to Hindus and the latter unclean animals to Muslims. A year-long rebellion against the British ensued. Although the Indian Mutiny was unsuccessful, it prompted the British government to seize total control of all British interests in India in 1858, finally establishing a seamless imperialism. Claiming to be only interested in trade, the Raj steadily expanded its influence until the princes ruled in name only.

The Raj's demise was partially a result of its remarkable success. It had gained control of the country by viewing it as a source of profit. Infrastructure had been developed, administration established, and an entire structure of governance erected. India had become a profitable venture, and the British were loath to allow the Indian population any power in a system that they viewed as their own accomplishment. The Indians didn't appreciate this much, and as the 20th century dawned there were increasing movements towards self-rule. Along with the desire for independence, tensions between Hindus and Muslims had also been developing over the years. The Muslims had always been a minority, and the prospect of an exclusively Hindu government made them wary of independence; they were as inclined to mistrust Hindu rule as they were to resist the Raj. In 1915, Mohandas Karamchand Gandhi came onto the scene, calling for unity between the two groups in an astonishing display of leadership that would eventually lead the country to independence.

The profound impact Gandhi had on India and his ability to gain independence through a totally non-violent mass movement made him one of the most remarkable leaders the world has ever known. He led by example, wearing homespun clothes to weaken the British textile industry and orchestrating a march to the sea, where demonstrators proceeded to make their own salt in protest against the British monopoly. Indians gave him the name Mahatma, or Great Soul. The British promised that they would leave India by 1947.

Independence came at great cost. While Gandhi was leading a largely Hindu movement, Mohammed Ali Jinnah was fronting a Muslim one through a group called the Muslim League. Jinnah advocated the division of India into two separate states: Muslim and Hindu, and he was able to achieve his goal. When the British left, they created the separate states of Pakistan and Bangladesh (known at that time as East Pakistan), and violence erupted when stranded Muslims and Hindu minorities in the areas fled in opposite directions. Within a few weeks, half a million people had died in the course of the greatest migration of human beings in the world's history. The aging Gandhi vowed to fast until the violence stopped, which it did when his health was seriously threatened. At the same time, the British returned and helped restore order. Excepting Kashmir, which is still a disputed area (and currently unsafe for tourists), the division reached stability.

India's history since independence has been marked by disunity and intermittent periods of virtual chaos. In 1948, on the eve of independence, Gandhi was assassinated by a Hindu fanatic. His right-hand man, Jawarhalal Nehru, became India's first Prime Minister. Nehru was a successful leader, steering the young nation through a period of peace that was contrasted by the rule of Lal Bahadur Shastri, who fought Pakistan after it invaded two regions of India. Shastri died in 1966 after only 20 months in power, and he was succeeded by Nehru's daughter, Indira Gandhi.

With the name Gandhi (though no relation to Mahatma), Indira was a powerful, unchallenged leader, and opposition remained negligible until she abused her power by trying to suppress the press. When the rising opposition began to threaten her power, she called a state of emergency and continued to reform the nation, actually making some positive economic and political changes despite her questionable tactics.

Her most unpopular policy was forced sterilization, and she was eventually defeated at the polls in 1977 by Morarji Desai of the Jenata party. She won back power in'79, however, but was later assassinated in 1984 by a Sikh terrorist. Although India's political climate remains divisive, the country has attained apparent stability in recent years. Today, India seems poised to realise its potential as an international economic power.

Please note that I have not"reinvented the wheel." The following text was gathered in patches, condensed from"Historic India" a Times Life Book. It seemed best, for quick addition, to take much text as it was, to pick and choose the parts which might give a shortened history of the time, and gather enough facts in historic order, while giving a feel for the civilization. The maps are copies from"An Historical Atlas of the Indian Peninsula" by Oxford Uni Press, written by C. Colin Davies.

The land that has accepted such a great variety of unlike immigrants is huge- a peninsula so large that is often called a subcontinent-but few lands have had to reconcile so many different racial strains, so many unlike social patterns and such a sheer multitude of people. By the end of the fourth century BC India's population had already reached 100 million. Many of these people were descendants of invaders: and in later centuries other invaders came to India. Quickly or slowly, all the invaders and all their descendants became parts of the mosaic of historic India.

Many new arrivals came form the Hindu Kush mountain passes. At first they encountered a hilly region of the Punjab. Traveling southeast, they found the land leveling out and saw the vast Indo-Gangetic plain, which sweeps across the subcontinent in a great arc that, like the mountains that lie to the north, measure 2,000 miles from west to east and 150 to 200 miles north to south.

They soon shed their cold weather clothes for a few garments of cotton. Once in the Indo-Gangetic plain, some migrants went southwestward along the Indus River and found themselves in the region call the Sind— a cul-de-sac that is cut off from India;s heartland by the huge Thar Desert. Luckier ones moved southwestward, on the lush path that lies between the rambling Ganges river and the foot hills of the Himalayas. Continuing south westward, they would arrive at the Bay of Bengal, where the Ganges delta was eventually to provide the great natural ocean harbour of Calcutta.

Traveling south from the plain by an alternate route, some migrants followed the Chambal River to enter a different kind of land. They would be on the Deccan plateau, a harsh, infertile grassland sloping west to east and broken by scrub and clumps of trees.. East and west, at the borders of the Deccan, were more mountain ranges, the Ghats, so called for the passes (ghats) that penetrate them and narrow coastal plains.

There the peninsula is shaped like an arrowhead, pointing south to the sea. The migrants who ventured south of the fertile Indo-Gangetic plain, whether just onto the high plateau or all the way to the coast, found themselves in a hostile world. This land was difficult to invade or control, just getting into it was not easy task: a jungle like river valley of the Narmada and a high escarpment, the Vindhya Mountains cut the Deccan off from the Indo Gangetic plain.

Once the invader reached the plateau, they faced new difficulties. The monsoon winds—cool and dry in the winter, drenching in the summer made either farming or herding a risky business.

Only some straggling migrants continued southward through the Deccan, for innumerable rivers flowed from west to east across the land—rivers just wide enough to make the prospect of crossing look formidable.

Naturally enough most of the people who entered India at the northwest mt passes stopped north of the Deccan. South of the Deccan the land slopes downward to the sea, forming a low, temperate coastal plain. This is the land of the Dravidian people, whose ancestors were among the earliest migrants to India and whose physical characteristics and social customs still prevail.. Migrants from the north who later came to southern India never out numbered or overwhelmed the Dravidians.

By 1500BC, a long series of invasions had got under way. A main source of new peoples was Central Asia. India was always so strangely vulnerable to invasion, migrating people could come from anywhere and everywhere. From the north and from the west, Indo-Europeans, Persians, Scythians, Huns, Arabs, Turks, Mongols and uncountable others flowed in For thousands and thousands of years, migrants or marauders moved in and wandered to the fertile plains. Always pouring in were completely different kinds of people at completely different levels of culture. There were black and while and yellow races. There were nomads, traders and armies. There were large, refined societies with poets and troubadours, and there were tiny clans of still primitive root-grubbers. India found room for them all.

Hinduism did not absorb these people; it enfolded them. Any group with special customs could be dropped into India and, by living apart, live amicably side by side with those already there. The new group then became a caste of its own.

India's characteristic refusal to act as sort of a social blending-machine has always seemed peculiar to most non-Indian; to many her separation of groups and isolation of people by caste has seemed peculiarly inhuman, but the the caste system might have produced the only reasonable way for India to make an orderly process of growth. While inherently different groups could live their intimate lives distinctively and separately from the others, they could all at the same time contribute their work to the commonweal.

From the right and wildly heterogeneous mixture of people that is India burst repeated explosions of culture. Hindu art, literature and science made truly golden ages of the Mauryan Empire in the third century BC> Some 1200 years later, Muslim tradition, which was influenced but never overwhelmed by Hinduism- created yet another period of glory in the Mughal Empire.

Cultural Exchange Between Iran and India: An Ancient But Lasting Model Of Dialogue Among Civilizations Iran's part in Indian History

MAURYAN

In the Mauryan period the vitality of the Indian life is reflected in achievements in stone sculpture, as an art as old as the foundations of Hindus itself. Centuries later, during the Gupta period, the great religious sculpture of India, both Buddhist and Hindu, gave witness to Hinduism at its height. Gupta poetry and drama, written in India's classic Sanskrit language are considered peers of the finest Western literature, and it was Gupta science that the game the world the concept of zero and the so-called Arabic numerals.

In the time of the Mughal empire, India displayed an ability to combine its Hindu culture, which was by then ancient, with that of the Muslims, who for 8 centuries had been moving into the subcontinent. Cultural splendor is not the only product of India's diversity and separateness: political disunity has also been a constant and plaguing result. Hundreds of tiny states--kingdoms, principalities, the holdings of petty nobles-have proliferated to a degree that makes the fragmented Europe of medieval times seem positively monolithic...

Archaeologists now know that the beginnings of civilization in India are nearly as old as civilization itself. About 4000 BC., soon after the appearance of farming communities in Mesopotamia, men in the northwest corner of India made the great transitionfrom nomadic hunting gathering to agriculture. West of the Indus River, on the hills of Baluchistan and the rim of the Iranian plateau, such men began to settle on the land. By 3000 BC, they had developed a primitive village culture, a culture of farmers who lived in mud huts and practiced the animalistic worship of natural objects and forces.

Then, in a great and unexplained advance, these people developed one of the earliest of the worlds great civilizations.

Because the centres of this civilization were first found along the Indus River, some archaeologists call it the Indus Valley Civilization; other call it Harappan Culture, after one of its two capital cities. It flourished mightily for a thousand years from about 2500 BC to about 1500 BC, and then mysteriously disappeared.

This civilization covered a gigantic triangle with sides a thousand miles long. Archaeologists have found remains of more than 50 communities. To these communities came wheat, barely and a variety of fruits and earliest cultivated cotton in the world.

The seaports were magnificently equipped: the port of Lothal, on the Gulf of Cambay, contained an enclosed brick shipping dock over 700 feet long, controlled by a sluice gate and capable of loading ships at low and high tides. At such ports Harappan traders dealt in gold and copper, turquoise and lapis lazuli, timber from the slopes of the Himalayas. Harappan ships sailed up the Persian Gulf to Mesopotamia, carrying Indian ivory and cotton to the age old cities of Agade and Ur,in the Tigris-Euphrates Valley. And all of the wealth of farming of the two capitals, the cities of Mojenjo Daro and Harappa.

Both were Masterpieces of urban planning, consisting of a rectangle three miles in circumference, dominated by a fortified citadel as high as a modern five-story building. The citadel, containing a huge granary, a hall for ceremonial assemblies, a public bath which might have been a ritual bath, was apparently the centre of government and religion. Below it the city spread out in a rigidly mathematical gridiron patter, with avenues and streets running north and south, east and west.

Solidly built brick houses, shops and restaurants lined the streets, with windowless walls facing the streets themselves, entrances on narrow lanes, and rooms graciously arranged around open interior courtyards. Even sanitary arrangements in these buildings, the most elabourate in the world of that time, speak of the sophistication of the Indus Valley technology. Indoor baths and privies were connected by a system of drains and water chutes to sewers running beneath the main streets. Presenting a picture of middle-class prosperity with zealous municipal controls.

In the arts, the people excelled in brilliantly decorated wheel-turned pottery and small, beautifully executed figurines. Mother-Goddess, a seated male divinity, a sacred bull and pipal tree, and imaginative secular figures.. Animals toys, etc.

The richest store of Indus artifacts was assembled by the merchant class for commercial ends.

THE MAURYAN PERIOD

From what has been said above it is clear that any definite knowledge of South India does not reach back beyond the Mauryan period. What we do learn from the scanty sources of information accessible to us gives us but a glimpse into the political condition of India in the age of the Mauryas. Such glimpses as we get warrant the presumption that the states of the south must have had an anterior history of some length. Our knowledge of that history however does not carry us back beyond the period of the Mauryas. Thus the Buddhist chronicles of Ceylon which pretend to carry us back to the age of the Buddha himself are so meagre in point of that history before the age of Asoka that the conclusion seems inevitable that there was in Ceylon itself no real knowledge of its history anterior to the age of the great Buddhist emperor. We shall presently see that such information as we get from Tamil Literature does not take us any further back than this, and we are driven round again to the same conclusion that our knowledge of the history of the south dates back to the age of the Mauryas and no farther, although absence of information available to us does not inevitably mean absence of history in the region concerned.

The Main Source of Information, Tamil Literature

The main source of information for the period previous to the rise of the Pallavas into importance is Tamil Literature, of which we have a body with a character all its own. This body of works is known among Tamil Scholars by the collective designation,"Sangam works." This designation assumes the existence of a body 2 or an academy of scholars and critics, whose imprimatur was necessary for the publication of any work of literature in Tamil. The Tamil word"Sangam' is the Sanskrit"Sangha" and means ordinarily no more than an assembly. In this particular application, however it means a body of scholars, of recognised worth and standing in the world of letters, who were maintained by the contemporary kings and constituted themselves a board before whom every work seeking recognition had to be read. It is only when this body as a whole signified its approval that the work could go forth into the world as a Sangam work. It does not, however, mean that other works were not written and published.

There are some which have come down to us, which do not appear to have gone before the Sangam. The function of this body seems therefore to be merely to set up a standard of excellence for works which aspire to the dignity of Sangam works. Tamil Scholars recognise a body of works that are acknowledged to have passed this gauntlet of criticism among the Sangam works. Some others also are included in this group apparently as belonging to the same age and partaking of the same character. This is not done by scholars of today, nor is it a matter purely of present-day opinion. The commentators who lived five or six centuries before us, and more, also make this classification and treat the works accordingly. It is the tradition of the commentators that has come down to us and the whole position in respect of this classification rests upon the authority generally of these commentators.

Of these Sangams, tradition knows of three. The numbers of scholars in the first and the second, and the numbers of Pandya kings that took an active part in the work of these bodies, were according to this tradition very large. Although some of the works referred to as belonging to these Sangams, and mentioned as such, have come down to us in isolated quotations the actual existence of these bodies as stated in tradition would be difficult to postulate with the evidence accessible to us. It rather seems to be that this body of scholars was a permanently existing body, and did exist for a certain number of centuries continuously. In the work of these bodies there were periods of great output and periods of comparative barrenness. We have no means of ascertaining what exactly might have been the cause of this alternation. But such brilliant periods seem marked as the period of the first Sangam and of the second Sangam, not very far behind their historical successor, the third Sangam. What actually does make the tradition look very suspicious, is the extraordinary length of time that is given to each one of these periods. It is this impossible longevity in the traditional acc[illegible]nt that stamps the whole tradition connected with these two bodies as entirely false in the estimation of modern scholarship.

The third Sangam counts among its scholar members 49, and 3 Pandya rulers, who bore an honourable part in the work of the academy. The bulk of the works that have come down to us may be ascribed actually to this body, in our present state of knowledge of these three academies, as a whole. It would perhaps be better to assume that they refer to three brilliant epochs in the active work of a single academy which might have existed for a number of centuries. This body of antique literature contains embedded in it various details reminiscent of what to them must have been contemporary or other history, as also a considerable amount of information very interesting to us in regard to their own times.

GLIMPSES OR MAURYAN INVASION IN IT

In this mass of literature we get some allusions to the Mauryas and Mauryan invasions of South Indiawhich throw a new light upon this particular period of history. Among the number of poets whose works are found collected in this volume of literature there are three authors that refer to the Mauryan invasions specifically. One of them is the Brahman poet, Mamulanar, the much respected Brahman poet of the Agastya gotra belonging to the south country, the other is one Param-Korranar and the third is Kallil Attirayanar.

Mamulanar has got two references in respect of this particular matter, and the other two one each. The general character of these references is to a distant hill worn by the rolling: cars of the Mauryas beyond which a young lover might have gone in quest of wealth.

His love-lorn sweetheart at home, pining away in solitude for his return, is assured in various ways that even if he should have got past this hill he would keep his promise and return on the appointed day. That is the general purport of the passages 1 in the first two authors. This means that a particular hill marks the frontier limit of the Tamil land, going beyond which one gets into foreign land and unknown country, return from which in safety is problematical.

The hill under reference marks therefore some well-known frontier hill a considerable distance from the Tamil land across which the war chariots of the Mauryas had to be taken at considerable labour. A tribe of people, foreigners apparently, specifically called Kosar, advanced southwards so far as the Podiyil Hill and defeated some enemy there when the chieftain of Mohur declined to submit. In consequence the Mauryas marched upon the territory. In regard to this the points to be noted are that the Kosar, of whom 4 divisions are known in this body of Tamil literature, were somehow connected with the Mauryas. There is only one Mohur known to Tamil literature of which a chief of the name Palaiyan played an important part against various enemies, most conspicuous among them being Seih-Kuttuvan Sera.

It is to subjugate this Mohur which is a place about 7 miles north-east of the town of Madura with a fortified temple and some remnants of a comparatively old chieftaincy, that the Mauryas are said to have advanced after the failure of the Kosar. The other poem of this author refers to the southern invasion of the Mauryas. This time the Mauryas came led forward by the Vadukar, or pushing them in front. In this connection there is the same reference to the hill worn by the war chariots of the Mauryas.1 The second author merely refers to the Mauryas and the cutting down of the hill to make a roadway for the war chariots of the Mauryas. The third author refers similarly to the cutting down of the hill side to make way for the rolling cars. But the word Moriyar has a second reading Oriyar which the learned commentator on the work has adopted as the reading.

On this point it must be noted that a dispassionate and close examination of the passage shows clearly that the reading Moriyar would read very much better and would be very much more in keeping with the general sense of the passage than the reading Oriyar.

Having regard to the class of works concerned, the other passages under reference in connection almost with the same matter ought to be the best commentary on this doubtful passage. It therefore leaves no room for doubt that there is a Mauryan invasion or invasions under reference, and that in the course of this invasion they had to get across a difficult hill making a roadway for themselves. That this hill was at some considerable distance, from the point of view of the Tamilian, and to a love-lorn damsel of the Tamil land going across the hill is as much as Shakespeare's"her husband is to Aleppo gone."

The author Mamulanar refers in the first passage rather familiarly to the wealth of the Nandas. The same author in another1 passage refers to this wealth of the Nandas as having accumulated in Patali (Patna), but got hidden in the floods of the Ganges in times gone, by. The point of the reference in these cases is, as is borne out by a corresponding passage 2 of the same author in connection with the accumulated wealth of the Seras, that the Nandas had accumulated vast wealth and the accumulated wealth at one time came to be of no use to them having been hidden in the one case in the waters of the Ganges, in the other by being buried in the earth. We have then in Mamulanar an author who had heard of the wealth of the Nandas and who speaks of the southern invasions of the Mauryas.

By way of confirmation, the two other authors speak of the invasions of the south by the Mauryas also in equally clear terms excepting for a difference of reading in one of the two cases. We shall now proceed to consider who the Vadukar and the Kosar are, the two people that are brought into connection with these Mauryan invasions.

HINDUISM - THE VEDIC PERIOD

Ravaging the country as they came, nomads put an end to the culture and set the course of all later Indian history."Aryans", the noble ones, spoke a language used by great masses of barbarians who began to move out of the steppes of Central Asia about 2000 BC. Aryans introduced a pattern of life that was to persist for centuries. Intertribal warfare was common; temporary alliances must have been formed to attack the people of the Indus civilization. For such attacks, the Aryans flung themselves into battle on light, swift, horse-driven chariots, against people who had never seen anything faster than a bullock cart. Even the fortified citadels of the Indus cities succumbed to Aryan sieges.

The Aryans were wandering herdsmen. Their food and clothing came from cattle; cows and bulls were their measure of wealth; and though they eventually took to farming, they continued to feel that a man's dignity lay in his herds rather than in his crops. Such a people could not maintain or even comprehend a complex urban culture. Writing, craftsmanship, arts and architecture, these ornaments and achievements of the Indus Civilization died in Aryan hands. They did leave a great'artifact', literature of the period which is a collection of religious writing, a set of scriptures. Aryan priests built up an exhaustive record of their religious beliefs and practices., Composed in a complex poetic style already perfected in pre-Indian days. And passed along by memorization and recitation. This record grew slowly for a thousand years. Its four great books, the Vedas, have given their name to that period of Indian history.

The earliest and most important of the four Vedic books, the Rig Veda, consists over a thousand hymns, a heterogeneous collection of prayer, instructions for ritual, incantations, poems on nature, and such secular songs as a gamblers lament of his luck at dice. The other three books, more specialized in content are the Yajur Veda, the Sama Veda, and the Atharva Veda, which consist respectively of technical instructions for the priests, ritual formulas and magic spells. They provide not dates, no dynasties, no wars or peace treaties, no events or series of events that a historian can place in any precise chronology.

The Vedas picture a people of enormous pride, utterly convinced of their own racial and social superiority, for the local peoples of India, the non-Aryans, they had nothing but contempt and overwhelming scorn. These conquered peoples were completely segregated, forced to live in clusters outside the Aryan village boundaries and banned from Aryan religious rites. This also extended to the social order...

Some time after they had learned enough about agriculture to grow crops of their own, the Aryans began to move deeper into India. Their route ran southeast to the middle of the Indo-Gangetic plain, the area of modern Delhi. From there, they probably conquers and colonized their way to the Ganges itself, then followed the river southward to settle the area around Banares (Varanasi). As many as 600 years had passed before the Aryans began to penetrate the Deccan.

During this time the Aryan tribeș fought continually against each other and against the original inhabitants. The conquest of new lands and contacts with new people combined to bring profound changes to the Aryan way of life. Wandering tribes settled in small kingdoms; the tribal chiefs, once chosen by their peers, became power-hungry hereditary kings ruling from permanent capitals, And as kingdoms grew in territory and population, and the victors and vanquished fused,, the loose classes of Aryan society became more complex.

The kings claimed rank above all other nobles, the old class of the ordinary tribesmen, once the herdsmen among the original nomadic Aryans, became peaceful farmer, cattle breeders, artisans and tradesmen. Meanwhile the descendants of the non-Aryan peoples became a fourth class.

The greatest change of all took place among the priests, a change not so much of function as of status. In early Aryan society, the Priest class had held the second rank, below the nobles. Now they raised themselves up above the nobles, above the kings who had risen from the nobles class. They accomplished this feat by giving a new importance to religious ritual. They taught that if the rituals were not performed precisely, a catastrophe would ensue.. They became the most important creatures in their universe. Even the kings assented to the glorification to the priesthood.

By an odd coincidence in history, the Sixth Century BC was a century of remarkable intellectual discovery for nearly every ancient civilization. The answers they found in the Sixth Century BC, made India a centre of religious creativity. They drew on existing body of sacred teaching, but went beyond these to found an important heterodox sect, Jainism, and a religion of world importance Buddhism, both of which interacted with the older religion of the Brahman priests to catalyze the development of the Hindu religion.

Perhaps so many stimulating ideas arose simultaneously in these far-flung lands because men communicated with one another through trade; perhaps the coinciding genius was due solely to chance. Changing social and economic conditions may have played a role in all these places. In many parts of India at this time the trade and agriculture were thriving, cities were growing, large kingdoms were superseding the rule of old tribal families. The rise of commerce brought height standard of living and with it time to think.

The final and most significant portion of the resulting literature is a collection of philosophical speculations. This portion, begun around 700 BC, and called the Upanishads, contained many of the themes that inspired the originators of Jainism and Buddhism and provided the religious foundation for Hinduism. These too were passed on orally by sages to pupils. The Upanishads probe into the nature of the universe and the human oul, and the relation of each to the other. IN proposing that the human soul is one with the Supreme Spirit, the Brahman priest who composed the Upanishads had in effect, deified mankind.

That idea had far reaching consequence, By the middle of the sixth century, other men besides the Brahmans had begun to engage in philosophical explorations, and when they did, they built on the foundations laid in the Upanishads. New cults were formed, and out of hundreds of cults, two survived to alter Brahman traditions and endure as independed and significant sects. They were Jainism and Buddhism.

The founder of Jainism was a youth named Vardhamana. He was born about 540 BC into a setting of wealth, nobility and pride. His father was an Indian Lord, a powerful chieftain of the Jnatrika clan that lived south of Nepal. Vardhamana seems to have been drawn to asceticism early in his life, but to have resisted the call and lived in the manner of his aristocratic family until he was 30, when his parents died. Then he left home and all his worldly possessions to become a mendicant. He set out wearing one thin garment. Mahavira's(the great soul) regimen was harsh, but his teachings endured.

BUDDHISM

Siddhartha Gautama, like Mahavira, was the son of a lord of a tribe that lived in the foothills of the Himalayan Mountains. He was born sometime in the Sixth century BC. From that point on, legends take over.

As the son of a rich nobleman, he lived in a royal manner. He had the run of three palaces the entertainment of numerous dancing girls and a herd of elephants decked in silver ornaments. At 16 he married, but in his twenties, he was apparently stirred by a sort of divine discontent. The first discovery the Buddha made was that all men were born to suffer, and by meditation, could release oneself from earthly bonds... attaining Nirvana, the ultimate release from rebirth. (We might use this in the first MOD, as when the single city is destroyed, you are reborn within another of your factions protective area, and can start over.. from zero!)

MAURYAN DYNASTY

MAURYA

- Chandragupta (322-301)
- Bindusara (301-269)
- Ashoka (269-232)

- Kunala (232-225)
- Dasaratha (232-225)
- Samprati (225-215)
- Salisuka (215-202)
- Devadharma (202-195)
- Satamdhanu (195-187)

Some time around the year 320 BC, a young Indian warrior-king named Chandragupta Maurya set out to build an empire. He rose from ordinary people, and not from the nobility. During his lifetime, he extended his power from a bast in the central Ganges Valley east and west to the farthest limits of the Indo_Gangeic plain. His descendants, the emperor of the Mauryan Dynasty, held sway of still vaster areas, at his height, the Mauryan Empire was the first great Indian empire of historic times.

The western regions had a very different history from that of northeast India. In 531 BC, Cyrus the Great, the founder of the Persian empire, led an invading army across the Hindu Kush mountains in into India; by 518 one of his successors, Darius I had conquered the Indus Valley and the Punjab. Through these military victories, the northwest India became a province of the Persian Empire. For nearly 200 years the Persians ruled the region with an iron hand. According to the Greek historian Herodutus, that satrapy paid more tribute to Persian than any other division of the empire, and a contingent of Indian troops served under the Persian emperor Xerxes in his invasion of Greece in 479 BC. On the other hand, the peoples of northern India gained something from the Persian occupation. Sophisticated Persian styles in art and architecture were influential throughout the region. It was an educational centre to which came well born young men from such Indian kingdoms as the expansionist policies of Magadha were inspired by the Persian example.

It was not the Indians, however, who ended Persian rule in the area. In 331 BC, the Macedonian conqueror, Alexander the Great won a crucial victory against Persian forces near the Tigris river. Having destroyed Persian power at its source, Alexander drove eastward, and in 327 entered India to take possession of the Persian territorial there. His troops fought their way into the northwest, defeating both Persian and native Indian forces and planting settlements as they came. For a moment in history of Northwest India, it seemed that one foreign ruler would be permanently replaced by another.

Within two years, Alexander had left India and in 323, with his dream of ruling the world completely shattered, he died in Babylon, far to the west. It was the Indian subcontinent itself that defeated the would-be world conqueror. Alexander had come to India with the false notion that the subcontinent was a small peninsula, with its farther shore only a short distance beyond the Indus Rive. Once he crossed the Indus, however, he realised that unknown immensity's lay before him. What was more important, his troops, wearied in battles against local Indian forces, and terrified bye tales of fierce people and beast, refused to go farther.

Returning to Babylon, it weakened his army and broke his power. Alexander's departure created a great military and political vacuum. The small outposts and garrisons left behind by the Macedonians soon withered away and the Indian kings of the northwest, who had held no real power for centuries, were too weak to take command. A power vacuum had been formed and Chandragupta Maurya was eager to fill it. He assumed the Magadhan throne about two years after Alexander's retreat from Indian and began almost at once to move in on the northwest.

Within a decade, Chandragupta made himself master of the Punjab and the Indus Valley. In 305 BC. he met and defeated Seleucus Nicator, a successor of Alexander's who was attempting to recover the dead emperor's Indian province. Instead of regaining lost lands, Selucus had to give up lands of his own in the mountainous northwest- Baluchistan, and the regions of Kabul, Kandahar and Herat in what is not Afghanistan. Legends also suggest that he also gave his daughter to Chandragupta in marriage, while the Indian ruler made a regal gift of 500 elephants to the man he had defeated.

Chandragupta was now an emperor, rather than a king. From his capital at Pataliputra, on the site of the present day city of Patna, in north east India, he ruled an empire that included the plains of the Indus and Ganges River and the high country of the northwest. His son extended the borders southward, deep into the Deccan plateau and as far down the western coast as modern Mysore.

Ashoka, Chandragupta's grandson and third king of the dynasty brought the empire to its height.

The spy system was a gigantic secret service that both funneled information to the emperor and carried out his secret orders. The imperial army was magnificently equipped. At its height, it numbered 700,000, men with 9,000 elephants and 10,000 chariots. According to Megasthenes, its operations were supervised by a central War Council of 30 officials, who held responsibility for everything from food and transport to the maintenance of the proper servants to beat drums, carry gongs and perform a host of military ceremonies. It was reported that the troops had an easy time when not on the battlefield.

If Chandragupta represented the promise of an golden age, his grandson, the Emperor Ashoka, brought that promise to fulfillment. For the first time the state was led by a man who preached goodness, gentleness and non-violence.and who based his own policies on a high ethical code. By his example and actions, the emperor proved himself, the greatest and noblest ruler India had known till that time. This was suggested by the inscriptions in sites around the country. Taken together the edicts constitute and extraordinary revelation of the thoughts and decision of a great man.

But the edicts are the fruits of Ashoka's maturity. In his early years he seems to have let the conventional military and political apprenticeship of a potential heir to the throne. His accession to the throne, was violent. His great military achievement called Kalinga, on India's east coast, was bloody and merciless. The Kalinga campaign of 261 BC, proved to be a turning point in Ashoka's life. It was his last war. He became remorseful for the cruelties he inflicted. The emperor was converted to Buddhism.

During his reign, a council of theologians met at Pataliputra to codify the Buddhist canon, the laws and principle of a new formal religion. He made Buddhism a missionary faith. He sent emissaries to Egypt, Macedonia and the Near East, hoping in vain to convert them. He was more successful at home as Buddhism spread thorough India... though it never became the dominant religion and his son, converted the king of Ceylon. From there Buddhism spread to the lands of southeast Asia. Where it was to remain strong to the present time.

Less than 50 years after the Emperor's death, in 232 BC, the Mauryan Empire fell. His descendants quarreled over the succession and provincial governors revolted and gained independence for their regions. The Mauryan army lost its vigour and combativeness, and was not longer able to defend the empire against invasion or to control the native populations. Buddhist ideals no longer inspired government policy and the priestly Brahman class, once more advisers to kings, reasserted the old intolerance, the old belief in the separation of people.

"All sects deserve reverence for one reason or another, By thus acting, a man exalts his own sect and at the same time does service to the sect of other people."... Ashoka.

Corporate life was in vogue in India since Vedic times. The word gana meant community and head of the group, or corporate body, was known as'Ganapati'. This name came to be associated in later times with Elephant God or deity of learning also known as'Ganesha'. Mention of corporate bodies is found as back as 800 - 1000 B.C. Caravans (Sarthas, Sarthavahanas), of merchants which toured the entire sub-continent do find mention in good numbers in early centuries. Guilds were known as srenis or nigamas and these elected mercantile bodies controlled trade and commerce of various commodities.

These were great supporters of royal power. Guilds arranged wrestling matches and athletic games. Harivamsa, mentions a wrestling match between Krishna and Kamsa for which an arena was constructed with pavilions of different guilds and banners each bearing an emblem signifying their craft.

We get a clear idea of formation and function of guilds from Kautilya's Arthashatra (4th century B.C). In an ideal scheme of a city, sites were reserved for offices and quarters of guildsmen.

Taxes paid by guilds formed an important source of income to the state. Guilds of a cooperative nature were referred to as Samutthachara. These guilds supervised community projects of those times. The local interest was guarded by the elders of the guild. Various undertakings of the guilds helped amass huge fortunes and Kautilya prescribes methods of extracting money from these guilds in times of need by the state.

Sreshtin or Jyeshthaka was the elder. There used to be a treasurer (Bhandagarika) and a superintendent of accounts (karanika) who made regular entries in prescribed registers. The history, customs, professions and transactions of corporations were clearly notified. Various rules and regulations were laid down for the workmen of guilds and due concessions given. Representatives of guilds formed important members in royal meetings.

Joint guild of bankers, traders and transport merchants (Sarthavaha) existed with membership spread over a large number of towns and cities. In Karnataka, Aihole was a great centre of guilds controlled by five hundred swamis. Their branches were spread throughout South India. There were seals of merchants, caravan traders and their commodities. Chief artisans (Prathamakulika) and number of artisans indicate a systematic network of corporate activities in ancient India.

Qualifications of Guildsmen

There used to be executive officers called karyachintakas who were appointed by the king. They were supposed to possess honesty, ability, self-control, knowledge of law-books and selflessness. Lekhakriya (documentation) was important and Madhyastha or middleman stood probably as guarantee for the faithful conduct of a guild. There were rules regarding membership of a guild.

Srenimukhyas or Heads of guilds were prominent members in city administration. In Gupta age (2nd century to 5th century) Sreshtnis, Sarthavahas, Prathamakuliks (Head of a local guild) and Prathamakayastha (Head Accounts – Officer) figured prominently in town and district councils.

Different crafts and artisans formed guilds which educated the youngsters of each craft, spinning, weaving, oil-crushing, ship-building, and other industries. The rich guilds maintained armies which accompanied trade caravans. Srenibala or Ayudha srenis (Guilds of arms) existed. Mandasore inscription of Kumara Gupta (414 - 455 A.D.) refers to a guild of silk-weavers. Some members of this guild took to arms. Some were bankers, some supervised endowments and some patronized art and religion. The guilds also acted as courts of law, disputes among members were settled by their own (elected) executives and not by the State tribunals.

This Mandasore inscription (modern Mandasore in Malva M.P.) gives some interesting information about corporate mobility of the times. Originally they came from Sourashtra in Gujarat. Some members learnt archery and became fighters. Some took to religious life. Some became astrologers. Some became ascetics. But all joined in constructing a temple to Sun-god. Oilmen and artisans find mention.

This only shows that there was mobility and flexibility in vocations though the Guild is mentioned prominently as one of silk-weavers. In the words of Dr. R.C. Majumdar, the eminent historian, "The guild in ancient India was not merely the means for the development of arts and crafts. Through autonomy and freedom accorded to it by the law of the land, it became a centre of strength and abode of liberal culture and progress, which truly made it a power and ornament of the society

During the Mauryan Period the outer walls consisted of a colossal palisade made of huge tree trunk embedded deep in the ground. There were also thick walls of sun dried brick and later, walls of unmortared bricks. These ramparts were topped by serrated parapets, backed by flights of steps, and had a huge gateway. The ramparts were ringed by a series of moats serving as main sewers. A bridge crossed the moat at each entrance. Some cities had numerous rings of walls and moats. The town's main gateway was a building in itself, with massive towers flanking and overlooking the actual gates... Inside were arranged various official apartments, including those of the toll-collectors; the windows of the offices were furnished with balconies and fitted with latticework or finely cut wooden screens.

Interior stairways let to the upper storys: the municipal granary was on the top floor and light was provided by gable-windows whose carved beams were decorated with painting. The vaulted roofs were either thatched or covered with roughly baked curved tiles; the joists were curve and painted; the crest of the roof was ornamented with a line of tapering, rounded projections fashioned from wood or terra-cotta; the doorway and fore-part of the building were embellished with statues. The main entrance was high enough to allow entry to elephants carrying palanquins. At night the entrance was closed by heavy wooden doors, reinforced by iron bars. There were two smaller gates for foot traffic. Curfew was fixed for midnight. Secret passages in the country, were constructed, so that spies might ply their trade, and those in power make a quick getaway when needed.

Near the main gateway, facing east, there was always to be found a tall column standing by itself. Made of stone, wood or iron, and topped by a sculpted froup or by a wheel resting on a bill-shaped capital, recalling similar columns in Persepolis. This was a most important monument in the eyes of the Indians, a symbol of victory and hospitality, endowed with both imperial and cosmological significane, and forming part of the severigns'regalia'. They were often engraved with edicts, or indicated that the city enjoyed royal protection.

The town itself was encircled by a boulevard connected by a regular network of streets and landes crossing each other at right angles. Main streets were paved with cobblestones, and gutters ran alongside to carry off sewage water into the drainage trenches outside the town. The streets were wide enough to allow passage of 4 horse chariots.

Market

Every important town a great expanse of ground reserved for the daily markets at which the peasants from the surrounding countryside sold their produce and products. The various guilds also possesed hedquarters in the same district. The stalls lining the streets were separated from the living quarters by a courtyard, and were fronted by a veranda, as they are today.

Light carts were on the roads, they were 2 wheeled vehicles with roofs made of brightly coloured materials stretched over hoop-shaped ribs, funished inside with carpets on which the driver and passengers squatted, and equipped with screens to protect the riders from being viewed by passerbys.

Further toward the centre of the capital were situated the residential districts. The building here wer larger and better built. Several stories hich and even presented an even frontage of whipewashed wall along the sides of the avenues. These same districts also contained myany public buildings. These buildings included those devoted to the town's health services, such as hospitals and maternity homes, and sanatoriums for ages and sick animals. There were alms-houses for the poor and to beggars. Other buidings housed educational establishments in which the masters were lodged. Art galleries were open to the public and frequented by it particularly during the autumn. The area near the palace had residences of courtesans, professional musicians, and the royal offices. Here were to be found the resididence of the city administrator, the headquarters of the public scribe, the Treasure and all the other State secretariats; presided by a commissioner and a municipal council.

The kings country house served as a hunting reserve.

Religious structures:

- Shrines
- Holy Places
- Reliquary of Buddhist Saints, Stupa

Hindu Temples, robust buildings made from timbers, brick and stone, had interior courtyards paved with gravel surfaces, decorated with garlands of flowers and greenery. Gongs, clarinets, conches and cymbals were used by the sacred orchestra.

Health Care

There were 2 kinds of physician: independent doctores called into consultation privately and responsible financially if convicted of error; and official practitioners in hospitals subsidized by pious or royal foundations, where medical assistance was free.

Doctors made house calls, and were provided with a meal when they arrived.

Although there was an ingredient of magic in the treatments, the doctors had advanced the study of oto-rhino-laryngology, toxicology, opthamology, and pharmacy. Anotomical research, tho contrary to ritual regulations, had been pursured since Vedic times. Plastic surgery was provided for those with split lips or noses could be regrafted and torn lobes reattached to ears, all services which were also appreciated for post battlefield medicine.

Fashionable Existence

Courtesans were a common in daily life for the well to do. Common people used prostitutes, who also followed armies, and set up along the main road outside of the main army encampment.

Games and Gaming

Although games of chance were condemned by the Brahmanic code of conduct, where were played in all classes of society and chess was enormously popular. Chess was invented in India as a means to work out military strategy. It was played by four players who used two dice, four figures (king elephant, horse, and chariot or ship), the traditional units of the army. Young nobles met together daily to play several sessions of the game. Chess was played on specially designed boards or on a table with precious inlays. Dicing existed in various forms. They were made of gilded shells. Die were the size of a hazel nut and had five facets. Dice were played on the floor. This game entailed taking a handful of dice from a heap on any one of 24 premitted manners, at the same time announcing aloud the number of dice being thrown and the number remaining in the heap. The winner was the one who threw the number he had announced, at his first attempt; the rules demanding, in addition, that this number must be a multiple of four.

Gaming dens seemed to have abounded. They were subject to strict control by the State and contributed large sums to the treasury in the form of taxation, the hiring of premises and the dice themselves, since the players wer not allowed to make use nor own their own dice.

Artistic Diversions

Music held a great place in the daily life of the nobility. They all learned to play the bow-harp, and later the instrument was replaced by a form of lute. The bow harp was one of the most ancient instruments. Eventually even men, kings were required to master it. (coinage in Gupta Dynasty show the king holding the lute)

Painting was an essentian adjunct of elegant love-life, and also held an important place in everyday existence. It served the purposes of religious propaganda, and was used as a means of communication, and to memorialize an image of a loved one. They used 'pencils' for sketching, paint brushes made with bristles made of animal hair, and shells or pots containging colured powders, all arranged in a box. It was an appropriate gift to a bride from the bridegroom. Religious thermes were executed on long lengths of material with bamboo rollers at each end.

Sculpture was also appreciated and taught to the lesiure class. The aristocracy devoted particular attention to the various forms of literary expression. Many nobles composed poems or dramas in the elegant style in fashion at the roual court. Kings themselves devoted themselves to the arts of writing: The famous Drama Mrcchakatjka 'The little clay cart' has been attributed to Sudraka, 4th century AD.

Harsa, King of Thanesvar, wrote three interesting dramas. The Kings Samudragupta and Kumaragupta endowed themselves with the title 'King among poets'.

The theatre was at its preak of brilliance during the age of this study. The period between the first and eigth centuries AD saw the rise of India's greatest dramatic authors, some of them kings, other poets or brahmans. Dramas were constructed according to the precise rules which were codified in various teatises and which made drmatic writing an art designed specifically for the intelligentsia, making no appeal at all outside of the king, the nobility and cultured classes. Actors depended on the patronage of the king. Theatrical performances generally took place only during religious or princely festivals, great pilgimages and publick or private celebrations of some importance such as wedding.

Actors were recruited from the lowest castes. Their reputations were deplorable, and their wives wer generally considered to be over-generous in bestowing their favours. Those actors who graduated to leading roles were practically un-budeable from their particular range of parts. Female roles were usually played by women, but sometimes by men. Male roles included a lover, a buffoon, and a wit, while the female roles comprised lover and confidante. Junior rolse were shared among the other members of the company.

The troupe's manage was the theatres chief stage hand. He was called the 'rope holder' the producer, dramatic coach and star actor. There were no special theatre buildings and actors used the halls reserved for dancing and music which was attached to most palaces and temples. Sometimes they played in the temples.

The preparation of the 'theatre' was gaudily decorated. Sometimes wooden stages were erected at the end of a rectanglular room.

Life at Court

The royal chaplain held first place among the kingdom's great men. Even at courts of Buddhist kings, he was usually a Brahman. His post was usually hereditary and more than likely he was the king's tutor when he was a boy. He was the favourite partner for games of chance, supervised the running of the palace while the king was absent.

The Field Marshal was equally important, enjoyed heretitary rights.

- The Grand Treasurer
- Driver of the King's Chariot (up to the 7th century) also could be the bard.
- King's barber
- Kings cook
- Kings food taster
- The white parasol was the symbol of kingship.
- King's mahout

Two animals, the State Horse and the Kings Elephant demanded special attention, and were regarded as royal regaila.

- Harem
- Imported wine in use and very popular.
- Royal processions were proceeded by the palace orchestra

There was a change in the primary Military units over India's long existance.

One of the historical aspects of India is that it had a shortage of local horses. A breeding programme in the tropics did not provide the great numbers of them required for the chariot armies. (The Medieval period required them for cavalry) Nearly all of the horses were acquired from trading via the north or west, and for the southern kingdoms, by sea trade.

Elephants and elephant training were also key to vast armies of Elephants during the Mahabharata, and were also key to the historical aspect of the early and Medieval eras. These two elements (horse supply and elephants) would be key to any India Mod. I have made direct quotes more than likely, but have also condensed and paraphrased where the book has gone into more detail than is needed. It would take me quite a long time to indicate long quotes and paraphrasing, so if there are any questions, please ask me to find a more direct quote and its context. Design specifics: only limits were the military units, which would not go beyond a weak cavalry. There were no basic warriors. The basic military unit was the (short bow) archer... and led to the longbow.

Chariots were modeled on two patterns, either the biga with two horses, or the quadriga, with four horses. If its at all possible to get the animations made, that upgrading a 2 horse chariot would show an extra horsie... up to 4 horses.

"In the 4th century BC, the Indians placed their chief reliance in warfare on elephants tamed and trained for the purpose, in the epics the chief strength of the army consisted in chariots, as reported by Greek writers..

The general trend for early Indian armies was: Archer>Chariot>Elephant>Cavalry, with Chariots phasing out by early Medieval era.

One of the principal weapons of the Ancient Hindu armies were bowmen. They went through extensive training. Skill with the bow was necessary for promotion. It was an art form for the nobility, who had to master the bow, as they were the caste of the military.

In the Vedic period the army appears to have consisted of two divisions, the archers and the chariots. During the post-Vedic period the horse and elephant were incorporated in the corps... by the time of the Islamic kingdoms in India, there were no more chariots in the army. They had been gradually replaced by horsemen.

Another view of the organization of the armies was the six-fold division, which consisted of the hereditary troops, mercenaries, guild levies, soldiers supplied by feudatory chiefs or allies, troops captured or won over from the enemy, and forest tribes... this came from inscriptions dated from the 6th to 11th century AD.

Of the different classes of troops, ancient military opinion seems to have attached greatest importance to the hereditary troops. The mercenaries came next, then guild levies (drafted units), next the allied troops while the forest tribes were placed at the bottom. In a passage from the Mahabharata, the guild levies are considered as important as the mercenary troops...

guild levies did not receive any regular wages from the royal exchequer. There were wild tribes in central India who were often employed for military purposes by Hindu kings, as the same manner as American Indians were employed by the English and French in the wars in North America.

They brought their own war apparatus to the theater of war, but they fought for pay and plunder. Their services were considered helpful when the army had to pass through forests and defiles, morasses or mountains, or when it was the intention of the invader to ravage and devastate the enemy's country.

Huien Tsiang, a Chinese pilgrim in the 12th century reported... "On the even of his famous campaigns of conquest, king Harsa of Kanau, 606-647 AD possessed an army which comprised of 50,000 infantry, 20,000 cavalry, and 5,000 elephants. When he had finished his task, the cavalry are said to have been increased to 100,000, and the elephants to 60,000."

Infantry

They are described in the Mahabharata as a conglomerate mass. They were recruited from the lower classes, and followed the charioted knight, but at the knights death, they usually fled, or were slaughtered like sheep who had lost their shepherd. In fact, the epic foot soldiers seem to have been useful in order to secure a decorous setting for the display of knightly prowess.

They suffered the greatest number of casualties, but contributed little or nothing to the decision of battles. In this respect the very early Indian infantry bears a remarkable affinity to European infantry the the feudal age. Evidence of the classical authors later works on politics and military science, and early Mohammedan chronicles. All point to the conclusion that the infantry in ancient India never outgrew this subsidiary position in the military organization of the country. It seems that in the 15 to 16 centuries, there was no continued or systematic attempt in any part of the country to use the infantry as the kernel of armies or develop in that solidarity and defensive power... like that of the Roman legions. From the foregoing remarks it must not be thought that the infantry in ancient India were mere'residue'. As archers they seem to have been redoubtable fighters, and won the admiration of the Greeks. It is also probable that being the most numerous part of the army, they sometimes decided the fortunes of battles by sheer weight of their numbers. Moreover, in certain special forms of warfare, their services must have been of real importance.

Hautilya, declares that the best ground for the infantry is one which contains big stones and boulders or is thickly planted with trees, green or dry. Another source declares that even ground is best, another says forest and hilly regions. Another source says"his troops are mostly infantry, because the seat of his government is among the mountains." In defence of forts and strongholds, foot soldiers were especially relied upon. The equipment of the infantry varied from age to age and region to region, which are difficult to document.

Arrian says that Indian-footsoldiers in the 4th century BC. carried a bow made of equal length with the man who bore it."This they rest upon the ground, and pressing against it their left foot, thus discharge the arrow, having drawn the string far backwards; for the shaft they use is little short of being three yards long, and there is nothing which can resist an Indian archer's shot, neither shield, nor breastplate, nor any stronger defence if such there be. In their left hand they carry bucklers made of undressed ox-hide. Some are equipped with javelins instead of bows, but all wear a sword, which is broad in the blade, but not longer than 3 cubits. And this when they engage in close fight, they do so with reluctance and wield with both hands to fetch down a lustier blow." It appears that the bow was the principal weapon of the infantry of 4th century BC; but the sword and the javelin were also used. Archers did not have shields, because they needed both hands to fire their bows, but the other infantry were depicted with shields.

War Chariots

The use of war chariots were found in early history of Indian warfare. They were employed as early as the Vedic age.

In the epics, they constitute the most important arm. The car-warrior is the main strength of the epic army. So completely does he dominate in the battle scenes, so controlling is the role that he fills, that the period represented by the epics may well be designated as the Chariot age of Indian history.

Both Vedic and epic evidence, prove that chariots were more or less a monopoly of warriors belonging to the noble classes. The rank and file fought on foot. The chariot was followed by by two wheel guards, and attended by a retinue of foot men.

When we come down to the age of Alexander, we are struck by a profound change in the Indian military situation. The chariots were still in use, but no longer the most important arm. Unlike the average epic knight, king Porus came to the field of battle riding, not a chariot, but an elephant. Megasthenes reports.. "No one invested with kingly power ever keeps on foot a military force without a very great number of elephants and foot and cavalry."

He omits war chariots completely. (Circa 300 BC) Porus had some 300 chariots, but the elephants frightened the Macedonian horses and caused a rout. Chariots required perfect ground, or they became mired in the mud, rocks etc., and became useless, while the cavalry and elephants would be effective on most terrain. Chariots seemed to disappear after the Mauryan era. Vedic period saw light 2 horse chariots, and developed in time to those with 4 or more horses. Heavy Chariots could have 4 wheels or more, were drawn by at least 4 horses, and gradually supplanted the lighter ones.

Cavalry

There is no satisfactory record of the use of cavalry in battles of the Vedic period. In the epics the cavalry is recognized as a separate arm, but it is of no real value and is wholly unorganized."The mounted soldiers are recognized as a body apart from others, but do not act together. They appear as concomitants of the war cars, dependent groups, but separate horsemen appear everywhere. Their employment was much influenced by that of the elephants. A body of horsemen are routed by an elephant. The classical chronicles show that the Indian cavalry in the age of Alexander were no longer as inefficient and unskillful as in the epic age. They were gradually outgrowing the impotence of infancy and winning recognition as an arm of real value. In the third and fourth century BC, Indian states maintained larger cavalry forces.

The Indian cavalry could not withstand the attack of Alexander, but that was because of two reasons. First the Macedonian cavalry were better trained, better disciplined and better equipped. And, second, Alexander himself was a cavalry commander of superb genius. He understood the advantage of hurtling masses upon the enemy and breaking through with sheer momentum, using the horse and rider as projectiles.

There is little knowledge from the Gupta period about cavalry. In the tenth century AD, Somadeva says: "the cavalry represents the mobility of the army. With a king having strong cavalry even enemies at a distance easily come within his grasp". Never the less, it must be noted that the cavalry never came to occupy the front rank in the army organization of ancient India. It never came to form the core of the Indian army. It appears that place was taken by the elephant than the horse. As in the 4th century BC, so in the 11th and 12 century AD, the superiority of foreign horsemen once again decided the fate of India There are early Mohamedan chronicles to show that their most brilliant military triumphs in India were won by the skillful use of a numerous and well trained cavalry."

Horse Supply

One of the reasons that the Hindus never did or could evolve a cavalry system comparable in strength and efficiency to that of the Greeks or Mohammedans was the lack of good horses in India. Ancient writers are unanimous in regarding the horses of the north and the west as better than those of India proper. In the Mahabharata, the most famous horses come from the Sindu country..The imported horses excelled in speed and in not being shied by noise. This paucity of good horses within India proper often compelled powerful monarchs both in the north and in the south to get their supply of horses from foreign countries. Kingdoms closer to the source of horses were better armed, than those at a distance.

Southern Kingdoms even traded for horses by sea. "It was agreed that every year... should send to the Dear, 14,000 strong Arab horses obtained from the islands of Fars. Each horse is reconned at 220 dinars of red gold." Marco Polo said later.. "There is no possibility of breeding horses in this country."

The lack of good horses of indigenous breed must have proved a serious obstacle to the development of a first rank cavalry system in ancient India, I was indeed a fatal lack. Bitted and bridled, unsaddled mostly, they had some kind of armour.. shields of protection. There was no proficiency in mounted archery! There were few notes of any horse archery.. And that only in the Gupta period and it did not take hold.

Horse Training Skills

They were trained in: circular movement, jumping, gallop, movement following signals, tight circling, running and jumping simultaneously, kicking with forelegs, side movement.. All of which reminds me of the Spanish school in more recent history. Similar training moves were taught to the elephants.

Elephants

Elephants are mentioned in the Rig Veda as wild, terrible beasts. They were tamed and domesticated well before this time. They became the most important arm about the time of the Macedonian invasion. The classical chronicles make it clear that in his titanic struggle against Alexander, Parus pinned all his hopes on the elephants in his army. In the battle-array that he drew up on that fateful day, he posted the elephants along the front like bastions in a wall.

He seems to have thought that these monsters would terrify the foreign soldiers, and reneder the Macedonian cavalry unmanageable. Alexander, a shrewder judge of military affairs, instinctively realised the grave danger involved in such extensive employment of elephants in war.

Everywhere in India was the same implicit faith in the effectiveness of elephants. In the eastern kingdom of Magadha, there were about 4,000 trained war elephants. Shortly afterwards Candragupta Maurya increased the strength of the elephant corps to 9,000. The age of chariots had passed, that of elephants had begun. In the succeeding centuries, the importance of elephants went on mounting higher and higher in Indian military estimation. A medieval author goes so far as to declare that "an army without elephants is as despicable as a forest without a lion, a kingdom without a king, or as valour unaided by weapons."

It may be pointed out here that it was not in India alone that elephants were used in war. Classical authors tell us that after his conflict with Chandragupta Maurya, Selucas Nikator ceded to the Indian emperor the three satrapies of Herat, Kandahar and Kabul and received in exchange a gift of 500 war-elephants. A few years later (301 BC), when fighting against Antigonus, the Sirian king brought these elephants into the field and it is to their instrumentality, that contemporary opinion ascribed his victory at Ipsos. Many centuries later, Sultan Mahmud carried off from India a large number of trained elephants and used them in his wars against the Turks and Tansoxiana.

As a matter of fact, elephants, though dangerous, were of real value in ancient and medieval warfare. Used with caution, and as a subordinate arm, they sometimes turned the scale of victory at the decisive moment. The Hindus erred not in the use of elephants, but in the emphasis they put upon that use. Ancient writers have valued the functions of war elephants. The most important of these functions were: acting as the vanguard of a marching army, preparing roads, camping grounds, and landing ghats in rivers, clearing away such impediments as small trees and shrubs, battering down walls, gates and towers, breaking up or scattering of trampling down the hostile force. Another writer stated that elephants were specially useful in all confused battles. Elephants were sometimes of more harm than benefit. If wounded, they were liable to get beyond control and escape at top speed Once taken by terror, they could turn and trample their own men. The elephant was usually ridden by several warriors, one of which was the mahout.. Megasthenes says that in his time the usual practice was for a war-elephant was to carry three fighting men. The elephantry fought with both missile and short-arm weapons. In the Mahabharata elephant warriors were described as armed with knives, daggers, stones and other weapons, but from the Gupta period onwards, their principal weapons appear to have been bows and arrows.

Elephants were equipped from early times. In the Mahabharata, they are referred to as armed with spikes and iron harness, and wearing a girth about the middle, neckchains, bells, wreathes, nets, umbrellas and blankets. Adorned with ornaments and bells, they could also have a howdah on the back. In the middle ages, they were covered with iron or brass plates.

Naval Warfare

The old notion that the Hindus were essentially a land locked people, lacking in spirit of adventure and the heart to brave the seas, is now dispelled. Researchers have proved that from very early times the People of India were distinguished by nautical skill and enterprise, that even in the Harappan period, they went out on trading voyages to distant shores and established settlements and colonies in numerous lands, islands skirting the Indian Ocean and Mesopotamia. The question as to whether they ever developed a navy to fight battles on rivers and seas is a baffling problem.

Ancient writers sometimes speak of fighting galleys as constituting a part of the royal military establishment. They kept pirates from controlling the sea lanes, hiding from customs agents and protecting merchant vessels. It is agreed that these duties would be performed by armed vessels belonging to the state. There are more direct literally references to ships employed as instruments of war. One mentioned the navy as one of the'limbs' of a complete army. Another says"by regular practice one becomes an adept in fighting from chariots, horses, elephants and boats, and a past master in archery. In describing the various classes of boats, is specified one class with a prow cabin that was useful for naval warfare. They were also shown on coins as having two masts and a rather unusual jib

The earliest known case belongs to the time of Candragupta Maurya. Megathenes informs us that the Mauryan War Office had a naval department with an admiral at its head and a committee of five to assist him. Asoka's rock edict mentioned that he maintained diplomatic relations not only with Ceylon, but with the Hellenistic monarchies of Syria, Egypt, Cyrene, Macedonia and Epirus."

Three areas of Indian that had nautical skill and enterprise were in Bengal, the valley and delta of the Indus, and the extreme south of the Deccan Peninsula.

The people of Bengal were famous for their nautical resources very early in history. Sources indicate that harbours and dockyards were well-known in the 6th century AD. A copper -plate grant dated 531 AD, refers to a shipbuilding harbour. When the Palas became rulers of Bengal, they built a regular fleet for fighting purposes, with an admiral in command. The naval power of Bengal long outlived the collapse of the Pala dynasty. Bengal's reputation as a naval power continued even in the medieval period.

The Indus basin saw the state organize against piracy. Coastal pirates were known for heavy attacks of Persian forces, and trade; also inflicting heavy losses on Indian boats and coastal areas as well.

It was in the extreme south of the Deccan peninsula that naval power reached its climax. Literary evidence, both native and foreign, proves that from very early times they carried on overseas trade with Western Asia, Egypt and later with the Greek and Roman Empires. There were fewer naval operations in southern waters till later in our period of study. Tamil/Ceras were the first there to develop a naval power. The Colas seem to have begun their naval career later than the Ceras, but they attained to a much high point of achievement. Their age-long hostility with the kings of Ceylon necessitated the creation of a fleet of ships. They sailed and conquered extensive districts in the Far East.(Nakkavarum Islands, Isthmus of Kra, parts of the Malay Peninsula and Sumatra. The Bay of Bengal was converted into the"Lake of Cola." By the late Medieval period.

It will thus be evident that naval warfare was not unknown in ancient India. But it was certainly not as widely practiced as land warfare. Boats were indeed used in war, but probably more often as transports than as a fighting line of ships. Naval battles were fought, but only when the theater of hostilities made it impossible to fight on land.

Spies

Spies filled an important role in both the civil and military affairs of ancient India. They were employed as early as the Vedic age. Manu speaks of five classes of spies, and of their various disguises. They were to detect crime, keep watch on the conduct of officials in the districts, and constantly ascertain the king's and his enemy's strength.

Spies were an important feature of government. Cipher writing was used, carrier pigeons, infiltrating enemy camps to demoralize and spread misinformation.

Military Administration

In early Vedic times, the king probably maintained no standing army. His small retinue of personal attendants acted as his bodyguard served him in hall and bower, and went on his errands. When any expedition for offensive or defensive purposes was necessary, local levies were raised from the people. These brought their own arms and weapons, and probably were captained by their own chiefs.

It is certain that in the 4th century BC, when Alexander invaded India, standing armies had become a normal feature of Indian military life. The causes which led to this development seem to have been mainly the increasing unwillingness on the part of cultivators to leave their plow for an indefinite length of time and also the ambition of rulers to conquer more territories and absorb them in their growing empires. Classical authors offer us a glimpse of the sort of life led by the army of Candragupta Maurya. Megathenes says that when not engaged in active service, the soldiers passed their time in idleness and drinking. "They are maintained at the king's expense, and are always ready to take the field, for they carry nothing with them but their own bodies. They have only military duties to perform. Others make their arms, others supply them with horses, and they have others to attend them in the camp, who take care of their horses, clean their arms, drive their elephants, prepare their chariots and act as their charioteers. A long as they are required to fight, they fight; and when peace returns, they abandon themselves to enjoyment, the pay which they receive from the state being so liberal that they can with ease maintain themselves and others."

Inscriptions dated 738-739 AD. say that the rulers of the Maurya were "served by armies from afar." Indicating there were mercenaries, who were trained soldiers.

Brahmans according to law, "any priest might serve as a soldier if unable to support himself as a priest." Many celebrated warriors and leaders were born in the priestly class. The lower classes provided the rank and file of the army, while the warrior class provided trained troops. The army was divided into sections, platoons, brigades, etc. The army in ancient India usually received its wages and rations from the state, but of the rates and pay and rations, drawn by officers and privates, we hardly know anything. Besides the salaries and wages in cash, officers and privates in the army were sometimes rewarded with exemptions from land revenue, sometimes with assignments of land. In second century AD, and inscription shows military officers holding large fiefs of land. Land grants were usually made in favour of officers who had distinguished records of service to their credit.

Besides pay, either in the shape of salaries or land assignment., Officers and troops were occasionally give n special allowances on the eve of the expedition. It was considered a prime duty of the state to support the wife and dependents of soldiers dying while on duty. It was agreed that no foreign expedition should be taken when there were internal troubles, or an expectation of an attack from the rear.

It was a profitable policy in warfare to embarrass an enemy either by inciting other powers to attack it from the rear or by fomenting internal troubles within its territory. Certain seasons of the year were seen to be peculiarly well suited for military operations. Spring and Autumn provided cooler weather, plentiful water, foraging possibilities and animal feed were more readily available.

In spite of preferences, military actions were not restricted to these seasons. Different starting times were dependent on the composition of the invading army, internal strife, climate, water...

No expedition was undertaken without consulting astrologers. They decided the best starting time. It was a very important step but such blind faith in the occult must have hampered rational military operations. It also proved and obstacle to the Hindus' success in war, as it must have often prevented them from taking the most obvious advantages of the enemy. Religious rites and ceremonial duties were performed by the king before setting off.

In the forefront of the army were a group workmen who were to set up the destination camp. The army took a standard arrangement while traveling to its next destination. The king was in the centre with his harem! That's right he took almost the whole city with him! His treasure chests and weaker troops. The flanks were occupied by the horsemen, while the chariots would be placed beside them on both sides. The elephants should march beside the chariots, and beyond the elephants should be placed the forest men. Behind the traveling army was an entire host of rabble, retainers, servants, prostitutes, all led by the marching drum and the clamor of the masses.

A grand army could make an enormous traveling parade. A day's march was about 16 miles through the usual territory. They encamped in prepared quarters... The Royal Harem, the wives of the nobles, mistresses and and great retinue of courtesans. "According to texts, As soon as the army reached the encampment, the prostitutes pitched their tents, spread their beds, made themselves attractive and like old residents, began to receive strangers. The terrific noise and clouds of dust, produced by a marching host, became a busy, noisy encampment. Bullock trains, and bullock carts were used for transporting engines of war, food for the soldiers, and administered by a superintendent.

Sometimes forced labour was used in difficult terrain, or where preferred transports were not available. Bridges were crossed by elephants.. Planks spread over pillars erected, rafts, or boats.

Army in the Field

Great importance was given to positioning the army in the field according to the harmony of the ground. The two armies were drawn up in battle order facing each other. There are many descriptions of the numerous battle formations used in the era. War drums thundered, music was played (drum, tambourine, trumpet, conch shell, horn, and lyre)

Another useful custom was the provision of medical aid to the wounded officers and troops. The Mahabharata refers to surgeons and physicians marching with the Bandava army to battle. The king should have not merely a rich store of medicine, but also expert physicians equipped with surgical instruments. This was regarded as an important duty of state. It was also a great expense.

Fortification and Siegecraft

Prehistoric fortification consisted of sites located on hills and other easily defended locations... surrounded by a low rampart wall, a second wall much more substantial than the first, both built of stone boulders laid without mortar.

In the post Vedic period, as the country became more thickly settled, the tendency to surround towns and cities with defensive works for protection against enemies appears to have become more marked. An archaeological report says "The faces of the walls were build of massive undressed stones between 3 and 5 feet in length, carefully fitted and bonded together without mortar, while the core between them is composed of smaller blocks carefully cut and laid with chips or fragments of stone. The walls stood to an elevation of 11 to

12 feet. *4th century forts and strongholds*: The classical chronicles make it evident that when Alexander invaded India in the third century, forts and strongholds held by Hindu chiefs were scattered thickly over the country. The capitol of almost every state, however small, appears to have been fortified with defensive work of varying solidity. Natural water was important.

Gupta Forts

The chief note in the history of military architecture of this period was the increased tendency to construct hill forts. The typical site preferred for a hill fortress was a precipitous cliff sloping to a river on one, two or even three sides and with steel slopes falling away on the other side. At the highest point was build a fort serving as a citadel. Some of there were like eagles nests on lofty cliffs, places of last refuge rather than strategical positions, But others were of real strategical strength, commanding the countryside or the approaches to a state. Of the humourous hill fortresses established in our period, the most celebrated at the time of the Mohammedan invasions were Kalanjar, Gwalior, Mandor, Ghira and Kangra. It is noteworthy that Mohammedan historians have referred to some of these forts in terms of enthusiastic admiration.

Siegecraft

The military science of ancient India seems to have been more skillful at defence than in attack. The fortresses of the age could usually withstand the most powerful siege weapons know to the people. Of the tools of siegecraft, little is known. It is probable that the use of scaling ladders and battering rams was know, elephants were offasionally employed to batter in the games of a fort. (a major function of war elephants) In the Mahabharata elephants have been described as 'town breakers.' Tamil writer speaks of 'brigades of war elephants, with their tusks blunted by battering the enemy's forts.

Another device occasionally employed was mining, but due to the location of most forts this was not possible in the high rocky ground.

The use of fire, was used as well. But the most usual method employed to get over the resistance of a fortress by strict investment and starving out and cutting off its water supply. Sieges were often long and protracted.

Repelling a siege must have varied from age to age and locality to locality. In one instance it was mentioned that all thatch covered houses within the fort should be plastered with mud as a protection against fire, all possible impediments were to be placed before the enemy to prevent a close investment grass and firewood round the fortress were set on fire and destroyed as far as 5-6 miles; and a system of secret wells, hidden pits and barbed iron cords were to be devised round the fort. It appears in writings that heavy, immovable machines, worked by mechanical power (tech machinery) were placed over the gates and walls, kept in readiness for projecting large shafts at the foe or dumping rocks on them. (Sounds like catapults permanently installed) Hilltop forts employed rolling stones to stuck down the attackers.

Notes on bows...very early, early ones made of bamboo, cane or wood. Horn bows also, bowstrings made of silk thread,sinews of deer and buffalo, or one composed of bamboo twine with silk thread wrapped around it.

Hindu bows usually varied from 3.25 cubits to 4.5 cubits. Horn bows were a bit shorter. Arrows made of sara reed, sometimes of wood and bamboo, with feathers from heron, goose, brown hawk, osprey, peacock vulture and wild ****. The Mahabharata mentions all of these plus feathers of flamingos besides. Number of feathers preferred to be four, fastened by means of threads and sinews. Feathers trimmed to six inches long. If they were to be flamed, a burning agent was applied. Some arrows were built entirely of iron, which only the strongest archers could shoot... were a means against elephants. Some arrows were about three feet in length. A quiver held 20 arrows.

Yantras

(A contrivance of almost any kind) most any kind of addition, but seen for the most part as balistae and catas...

immobile "when rotated, throws stones in all directions... a tower situated on the top of a fort provided with a leather cover... as an archer's platform.. a crossbeam at the entrance of a city placed to fall on the arriving enemy, a water machine to put out fires, etc. These were also described in the Mahabharata

Swords

The sword appears to have come into use comparatively later than the bow. No sword has been discovered at Mohenjo-Daro and Harappa. And although it was known to the Vedic Aryans, it appears to have been seldom used in battles of the period.. But as centuries elapsed, it came more and more into prominence. The Bow was first, then came the sword.. In the later centuries of our period, the sword came to rival the bow as a weapon of offense.

Spears and Javelins

Developed from a sharp headed stake, the spear may be reckoned with the club as among the most ancient of weapons. The Mahabharata javelin/spear was seven cubits long, with a bamboo handle.

The Mace

the club or mace is one of the most primitive weapons of India. It was in use during the time of the Macedonian invasion. It varied in materials, design and size. A battle axe was mentioned in the Rig Veda, but seldom as an instrument of war. In the Mahabharata, it is mentioned under several names and is wielded as a weapon of the nobility.

Other parts of battle attire were shields of leather, metal, of body armour for early nobles, metal armour in Alexander's time. Armour of wadded quilts of cotton were for the rank and file.

Organized Religion

The many forms of Hinduism are henotheistic religions. They recognize a single deity, and view other Gods and

Goddesses as manifestations or aspects of that supreme God. Henotheistic and polytheistic religions have traditionally been among the world's most religiously tolerant faiths.

This religion is called:

- Sanatana Dharma, "eternal religion," and
- Vaidika Dharma, "religion of the Vedas,"

Hinduism: the most commonly used name in North America. Various origins for the word "Hinduism" have been suggested: It may be derived from an ancient inscription translated as: "The country lying between the Himalayan mountain and Bindu Sarovara is known as Hindusthan by combination of the first letter 'hi' of 'Himalaya' and the last compound letter 'ndu' of the word `Bindu.'" Bindu Sarovara is called the Cape Comorin sea in modern times. 1

- It may be derived from the Persian word for Indian.
- It may be a Persian corruption of the word Sindhu (the river Indus)
- It was a name invented by the British administration in India during colonial times.

Beliefs about the early development of Hinduism are currently in a state of flux:

The classical theory of the origins of Hinduism traces the religion's roots to the Indus valley civilization circa 4000 to 2200 BCE.

The development of Hinduism was influenced by many invasions over thousands of years. The major influences occurred when light-skinned, nomadic "Aryan" Indo-European tribes invaded Northern India (circa 1500 BCE) from the steppes of Russia and Central Asia.

They brought with them their religion of Vedism. These beliefs mingled with the more advanced, indigenous Indian native beliefs, often called the "Indus valley culture.".

This theory was initially proposed by Christian academics some 200 years ago. Their conclusions were biased by their pre-existing belief in the Hebrew Scriptures (Old Testament). The Book of Genesis, which they interpreted literally, appears to place the creation of the earth at circa 4,000 BCE, and the Noahic flood at circa 2,500 BCE. These dates put severe constraints on the date of the "Aryan invasion," and the development of the four Veda and Upanishad Hindu religious texts. A second factor supporting this theory was their lack of appreciation of the sophisticated nature of Vedic culture; they had discounted it as primitive.

The classical theory is now being rejected by increasing numbers of archeologists and religious historians.

Emerging theory: The Aryan Invasion view of ancient Indian history has been challenged in recent years by new conclusions based on more recent findings in archaeology, cultural analysis, astronomical references, and literary analysis. One scholar, David Frawley, has established a convincing argument for this new interpretation.

Archeological digs have revealed that the Indus Valley culture was not "destroyed by outside invasion, but...[by] internal causes and, most likely, floods." The "dark age" that was believed to have followed the Aryan invasion may never have happened. A series of cities in India have been studied by archeologists and shown to have a level of civilization between that of the Indus culture and later more highly developed Indian culture, as visited by the Greeks. Finally, Indus Valley excavations have uncovered many remains of fire altars, animal bones, potsherds, shell jewelry and other evidences of Vedic rituals. "In other words there is no racial evidence of any such Indo-Aryan invasion of India but only of a continuity of the same group of people who traditionally considered themselves to be Aryans...The Indo-Aryan invasion as an academic concept in 18th and 19th century Europe reflected the cultural milieu of the period. Linguistic data were used to validate the concept that in turn was used to interpret archeological and anthropological data."

During the first few centuries CE, many sects were created, each dedicated to a specific deity. Typical among these were the Goddesses Shakti and Lakshmi, and the Gods Skanda and Surya.

BUDDHISM

Soon after Buddha's death or parinirvana, five hundred

monks met at the first council at Rajagrha, under the leadership of Kashyapa. Upali recited the monastic code (Vinaya) as he remembered it. Ananda, Buddha's cousin, friend, and favourite disciple -- and a man of prodigious memory! -- recited Buddha's lessons (the Sutras). These were then committed to memory by other monks, to be translated into the many languages of the Indian plains. It should be noted that Buddhism remained an oral tradition for over 200 years.

In the next few centuries, the original unity of Buddhism began to fragment. The most significant split occurred after the second council, held at Vaishali 100 years after the first. After debates between a more liberal group and traditionalists, the liberal group left and labeled themselves the Mahasangha --"the great sangha." They would eventually evolve into the Mahayana tradition of northern Asia.

The traditionalists, now referred to as Sthaviravada or"way of the elders" (or, in Pali, Theravada), developed a complex set of philosophical ideas beyond those elucidated by Buddha. These were collected into the Abhidharma or"higher teachings." But they, too, encouraged disagreements, so that one splinter group after another left the fold. Ultimately, 18 schools developed, each with their own interpretations of various issues, and spread all over India and Southeast Asia. Today, only the school stemming from the Sri Lankan Theravadan survives.

ASHOKA

One of the most significant events in the history of Buddhism is the chance encounter of the monk Nigrodha and the emperor Ashoka Maurya. Ashoka, succeeding his father after a bloody power struggle in 268 bc, found himself deeply disturbed by the carnage he caused while suppressing a revolt in the land of the Kalingas.

Meeting Nigrodha convinced Emperor Ashoka to devote himself to peace. On his orders, thousands of rock pillars were erected, bearing the words of the Buddha, in the brahmi script -- the first written evidence of Buddhism. The third council of monks was held at Pataliputra, the capital of Ashoka's empire.

There is a story that tells about a poor young boy who, having nothing to give the Buddha as a gift, collected a handful of dust and innocently presented it. The Buddha smiled and accepted it with the same graciousness he accepted the gifts of wealthy admirers. That boy, it is said, was reborn as the Emperor Ashoka.

Ashoka sent missionaries all over India and beyond. Some went as far as Egypt, Palestine, and Greece. St. Origen even mentions them as having reached Britain. The Greeks of one of the Alexandrian kingdoms of northern India adopted Buddhism, after their King Menandros (Pali: Milinda) was convinced by a monk named Nagasena -- the conversation immortalized in the Milinda Pañha. A Kushan king of north India named Kanishka was also converted, and a council was held in Kashmir in about 100 ad. Greek Buddhists there recorded the Sutras on copper sheets which, unfortunately, were never recovered. It is interesting to note that there is a saint in Orthodox Christianity named Josaphat, an Indian king whose story is essentially that of the Buddha. Josaphat is thought to be a distortion of the word bodhisattva.

Sri Lanka and Theravada

Emperor Ashoka sent one of his sons, Mahinda, and one of his daughters, Sanghamitta, a monk and a nun, to Sri Lanka (Ceylon) around the year 240 bc. The king of Sri Lanka, King Devanampiyatissa, welcomed them and was converted. One of the gifts they brought with them was a branch of the bodhi tree, which was successfully transplanted. The descendants of this branch can still be found on the island.

The fourth council was held in Sri Lanka, in the Aloka Cave, in the first century bc. During this time as well, and for the first time, the entire set of Sutras were recorded in the Pali language on palm leaves. This became Theravada's Pali Canon, from which so much of our knowledge of Buddhism stems. It is also called the Tripitaka (Pali: Tipitaka), or three baskets: The three sections of the canon are the Vinaya Pitaka (the monastic law), the Sutta Pitaka (words of the Buddha), and the Abhidamma Pitaka (the philosophical commentaries).

In a very real sense, Sri Lanka's monks may be credited with saving the Theravada tradition: Although it had spread once from India all over southeast Asia, it had nearly died out due to competition from Hinduism and Islam, as well as war and colonialism. Theravada monks spread their tradition from Sri Lanka to Burma, Thailand, Malaysia, Cambodia, and Laos, and from these lands to Europe and the west generally.

Mahayana

Mahayana began in the first century bc, as a development of the Mahasangha rebellion. Their more liberal attitudes toward monastic tradition allowed the lay community to have a greater voice in the nature of Buddhism. For better or worse, the simpler needs of the common folk were easier for the Mahayanists to meet. For example, the people were used to gods and heroes.

So, the Trikaya (three bodies) doctrine came into being: Not only was Buddha a man who became enlightened, he was also represented by various god-like Buddhas in various appealing heavens, as well as by the Dharma itself, or Shunyata (emptiness), or Buddha-Mind, depending on which interpretation we look at — sort of a Buddhist Father, Son, and Holy Ghost!

More important, however, was the increased importance of the Bodhisattva. A Bodhisattva is someone who has attained enlightenment, but who chooses to remain in this world of Samsara in order to bring others to enlightenment. He is a lot like a saint, a spiritual hero, for the people to admire and appeal to.

Along with new ideas came new scriptures. Also called Sutras, they are often attributed to Buddha himself, sometimes as special transmissions that Buddha supposedly felt were too difficult for his original listeners and therefore were hidden until the times were ripe.

The most significant of these new Sutras are these:

- Prajñaparamita or Perfection of Wisdom, an enormous collection of often esoteric texts, including the famous Heart Sutra and Diamond Sutra. The earliest known piece of printing in the world is, in fact, a copy of the Diamond Sutra, printed in China in 868 ad.

- Suddharma-pundarika or White Lotus of the True Dharma, also often esoteric, includes the Avalokiteshwara Sutra, a prayer to that Bodhisattva.
- Vimalakirti-nirdesha or Vimalakirti's Exposition, is the teachings of and stories about the enlightened householder Vimalakirti.
- Shurangama-samadhi or Hero's Sutra, provides a guide to meditation, shunyata, and the bodhisattva. It is most popular among Zen Buddhists
- Sukhavati-vyuha or Pure Land Sutra, is the most important Sutra for the Pure Land Schools of Buddhism. The Buddha tells Ananda about Amitabha and his Pure Land or heaven, and how one can be reborn there.
- There are many, many others. Finally, Mahayana is founded on two new philosophical interpretations of Buddhism: Madhyamaka and Yogachara.

Madhyamaka

Madhyamaka means "the middle way." You may recall that Buddha himself called his way the middle way in his very first sermon. He meant, at that time, the middle way between the extremes of hedonistic pleasure and extreme asceticism. But he may also have referred to the middle way between the competing philosophies of eternalism and annihilationism — the belief that the soul exists forever and that the soul is annihilated at death. Or between materialism and nihilism... An Indian monk by the name of Nagarjuna took this idea and expanded on it to create the philosophy that would be known as Madhyamaka, in a book called the Mulamadhyamaka-karika, written about 150 ad.

Basically a treatise on logical argument, it concludes that nothing is absolute, everything is relative, nothing exists on its own, everything is interdependent. All systems, beginning with the idea that each thing is what it is and not something else (Aristotle's law of the excluded middle), wind up contradicting themselves. Rigorous logic, in other words, leads one away from all systems, and to the concept of shunyata.

Shunyata means emptiness. This doesn't mean that nothing exists. It means that nothing exists in and of itself, but only as a part of a universal web of being. This would become a central concept in all branches of Mahayana. Of course, it is actually a restatement of the central Buddhist concepts of anatman, anitya, and dukkha!

Yogachara

The second philosophical innovation, Yogachara, is credited to two brothers, Asanga and Vasubandhu, who lived in India in the 300's ad. They elabourated earlier movements in the direction of the philosophy of idealism or chitta-matra. Chitta-matra means literally mind only. Asanga and Vasubandhu believed that everything that exists is mind or consciousness. What we think of as physical things are just projections of our minds, delusions or hallucinations, if you like. To get rid of these delusions, we must meditate, which for the Yogachara school means the creation of pure consciousness, devoid of all content. In that way, we leave our deluded individual minds and join with the universal mind, or Buddha-mind.

Tantra

The last innovation was less philosophical and far more practical: Tantra. Tantra refers to certain writings which are concerned, not with philosophical niceties, but with the basic how-to of enlightenment, and not just with enlightenment in several rebirths, but enlightenment here-and-now!

In order to accomplish this feat, dramatic methods are needed, ones which, to the uninitiated, may seem rather bizarre. Tantra was the domain of the siddhu, the adept — someone who knows the secrets, a magician in the ways of enlightenment.

Tantra involves the use of various techniques, including the well-known mandalas, mantras, and mudras. mandalas are paintings or other representations of higher awareness, usually in the form of a circular pattern of images, which may provide the focus of one-pointed meditation.

Mantras are words or phrases that serve the same purpose, such as the famous "Om mani padme hum." Mudras are hand positions that symbolize certain qualities of enlightenment.

Less well known are the yidams. A yidam is the image of a god or goddess or other spiritual being, either physically represented or, more commonly, imagined clearly in the mind's eye. Again, these represent archetypal qualities of enlightenment, and one-pointed meditation on these complex images lead the adept to his or her goal.

These ideas would have enormous impact on Mahayana. They are not without critics, however: Madhyamaka is sometimes criticized as word-play, and Yogachara is criticized as reintroducing atman, eternal soul or essence, to Buddhism. Tantra has been most often criticized, especially for its emphasis on secret methods and strong devotion to a guru. Nevertheless, these innovations led to a renewed flurry of activity in the first half of the first millenium, and provided the foundation for the kinds of Buddhism we find in China, Tibet, Japan, Korea, Vietnam, and elsewhere in east Asia.

China

Legend has it that the Chinese Emperor Ming Ti had a dream which led him to send his agents down the Silk Road — the ancient trade route between China and the west — to discover its meaning. The agents returned with a picture of the Buddha and a copy of the Sutra in 42 Sections. This Sutra would, in 67 ad, be the first of many to be translated into Chinese. The first Buddhist community in China is thought to be one in Loyang, established by "foreigners" around 150 ad, in the Han dynasty. Only 100 years later, there emerges a native Chinese Sangha. And during the Period of Disunity (or Era of the Warring States, 220 to 589 ad), the number of Buddhist monks and nuns increase to as many as two million! Apparently, the uncertain times and the misery of the lower classes were fertile ground for the monastic traditions of Buddhism.

CHRISTIANITY

An early colony of Christians was started by the Apostle Thomas (the doubter) Kodungallur, known as Musiris in the whole ancient world, and where St. Thomas the Apostle first landed in our India, was till the 15th century the "Rome" of India both as the centre of the Indian Church and as its gateway to world-trade through its famous harbour at the mouth of the river Periyar.

ISLAM

More to come as this gets more organized.Non-Indian religion arrived in India as early as the Quick Facts about: 8th century Quick Summary not found for this subject8th century CE. During the following decades, significant numbers of Indians converted to Islam. A spotted record of kingship followed the influx of several Persian dynasties, some devastating the Hindu landscape and others encouraging halcyon days of coexistence between Muslims and Hindus. In the Quick Facts about: 1500s

Quick Summary not found for this subject1500s, the primary Mughal Empire was formed. Muslims contributed greatly to the cultural enhancement of an already rich Indian culture, shaping not only the shape of Northern Indian classical music (Hindustani, a melding of Indian and Middle Eastern elements) but encouraging a grand tradition of Urdu (a melding of Quick Facts about: Hindi The most widely spoken of modern Indic vernaculars; spoken mostly in the north of India; along with English it is the official language of India; usually written in Devanagari scriptHindi, Quick Facts about: Arabic The Semitic language of the Arabs; spoken in a variety of dialectsArabic and Persian languages) literature both religious and secular.

Among other monuments, the Quick Facts about: Taj Mahal Beautiful mausoleum at Agra built by the Mogul emperor Shah Jahan (completed in 1649) in memory of his favourite wifeTaj Mahal is a gift of the Mughals. As of 2001, there are about 130 million Muslims in India, most of whom live in the north and west of the country.

ZOROASTRIANISM

A form of the ancient Quick Facts about: Persia. An empire in southern Asia created by Cyrus the Great in the 6th century BC and destroyed by Alexander the Great in the 4th century BCPersian relgion Quick Facts about: Zoroastrianism.

System of religion founded in Persia in the 6th century BC by Zoroaster; set forth in the Zend-Avesta; based on concept of struggle between light (good) and dark (evil)Zoroastrianism continues to be practiced in India, where its followers are called Parsis.

A believer or follower of IslamMuslim rulers in what is now modern-day: A theocratic islamic republic in the Middle East in western Asia; Iran was the core of the ancient empire that was known as Persia until 1935; rich in oil; involved in state-sponsored terrorismIran, Zoroastrian immigrants were granted protection under a Hindu king in the Western section of India many centuries ago.

SIKHISMQUICK FACTS ABOUT: SIKHISM

The doctrines of a monotheistic religion founded in northern India in the 16th century by Guru Nanak and combining elements of Hinduism and IslamSikhism The only Indian originated monotheistic religion was founded in India's northwestern Quick Facts about: Punjab. A historical region on northwestern India and northern PakistanPunjab region about 400 years ago. As of 2001 there were 35 million Sikhs in India. Many of todays Sikhs are situated in Punjab,the Largest Quick Facts about: Sikh

An adherent of SikhismSikh Province in the world and the ancestral home of Sikhs. The most Famous Sikh Temple Is the Quick Facts about: Golden Temple Quick Summary not found for this subjectGolden Temple it is located in Amritsar. Many Sikhs serve in the Indina army. The current prime minister of India is a Sikh, (when I was taking notes on this country) Punjab is the spiritual home of Sikhs and is the only state in India where Sikhs form a Majority. In ancient India, the entire life of an individual was subordinated to religious concepts, to the customs imposed by there concepts and to the superstitions which insisted that each single act, however unimportant, must unavoidably entail a good or bad consequence. The religious mentality of the people was highly developed, and is this state of affairs was not only freely tolerated but even actively insisted upon.

From the moment that he was conceived, an Indian belonged to a caste corresponding to a religious social structure. Furthermore, he belonged not only to a caste, but also a clan (gotra), this tie of kindred being ratified by a sort of ritual communion. From birth to death he received a whole sequence of sacraments: those of infancy, brahmanic initiation, marriage or the eremitic state. Even after his death, ritual, which made him a father or ancestor, still bound him to his gotra and integrated him into the family's religious system. Apart from these fundamental modalities, each person's daily life was lived within a framework of countless religious and magical acts, while the annual cycle of festivals provided the rhythm of collective life.

HINDUISM

Hinduism differs from Christianity and other Western religions in that it does not have a single founder, a specific theological system, a single system of morality, or a central religious organization. It consists of "thousands of different religious groups that have evolved in India since 1500 BCE."

Hinduism is generally regarded as the world's oldest: The people of India have had a continuous civilization since 2500 B.C., when the inhabitants of the Indus River valley developed an urban culture based on commerce and sustained by agricultural trade. This civilization declined around 1500 B.C., probably due to ecological changes.

During the second millennium B.C., pastoral, Aryan-speaking tribes migrated from the northwest into the subcontinent. As they settled in the middle Ganges River valley, they adapted to antecedent cultures. The political map of ancient and medieval India was made up of myriad kingdoms with fluctuating boundaries. In the 4th and 5th centuries A.D., northern India was unified under the Gupta Dynasty. During this period, known as India's Golden Age, Hindu culture and political administration reached new heights.

Islam spread across the Indian subcontinent over a period of 500 years. In the 10th and 11th centuries, Turks and Afghans invaded India and established sultanates in Delhi. In the early 16th century, descendants of Genghis Khan swept across the Khyber Pass and established the Mughal (Mogul) Dynasty, which lasted for 200 years. From the 11th to the 15th centuries, southern India was dominated by Hindu Chola and Vijayanagar Dynasties. During this time, the two systems—the prevailing Hindu and Muslim—mingled, leaving lasting cultural influences on each other.

The first British outpost in South Asia was established in 1619 at Surat on the northwestern coast. Later in the century, the East India Company opened permanent trading stations at Madras, Bombay, and Calcutta, each under the protection of native rulers.

The British expanded their influence from these footholds until, by the 1850s, they controlled most of present-day India, Pakistan, and Bangladesh. In 1857, a rebellion in north India led by mutinous Indian soldiers caused the British Parliament to transfer all political power from the East India Company to the Crown. Great Britain began administering most of India directly while controlling the rest through treaties with local rulers.

In the late 1800s, the first steps were taken toward self-government in British India with the appointment of Indian councilors to advise the British viceroy and the establishment of provincial councils with Indian members; the British subsequently widened participation in legislative councils. Beginning in 1920, Indian leader Mohandas K. Gandhi transformed the Indian National Congress political party into a mass movement to campaign against British colonial rule.

The party used both parliamentary and nonviolent resistance and non-cooperation to achieve independence. On August 15, 1947, India became a dominion within the Commonwealth, with Jawaharlal Nehru as Prime Minister. Enmity between Hindus and Muslims led the British to partition British India, creating East and West Pakistan, where there were Muslim majorities. India became a republic within the Commonwealth after promulgating its constitution on January 26, 1950.

After independence, the Congress Party, the party of Mahatma Gandhi and Jawaharlal Nehru, ruled India under the influence first of Nehru and then his daughter and grandson, with the exception of two brief periods in the 1970s and 1980s. Prime Minister Nehru governed India until his death in 1964. He was succeeded by Lal Bahadur Shastri, who also died in office. In 1966, power passed to Nehru's daughter, Indira Gandhi, Prime Minister from 1966 to 1977.

In 1975, beset with deepening political and economic problems, Mrs. Gandhi declared a state of emergency and suspended many civil liberties. Seeking a mandate at the polls for her policies, she called for elections in 1977, only to be defeated by Moraji Desai, who headed the Janata Party, an amalgam of five opposition parties. In 1979, Desai's Government crumbled. Charan Singh formed an interim government, which was followed by Mrs. Gandhi's return to power in January 1980. On October 31, 1984, Mrs. Gandhi was assassinated, and her son, Rajiv, was chosen by the Congress(I)—for "Indira"—Party to take her place. His government was brought down in 1989 by allegations of corruption and was followed by V.P.

Singh and then Chandra Shekhar. In the 1989 elections, although Rajiv Gandhi and Congress won more seats in the 1989 elections than any other single party, he was unable to form a government with a clear majority. The Janata Dal, a union of opposition parties, was able to form a government with the help of the Hindu-nationalist Bharatiya Janata Party (BJP) on the right and the communists on the left. This loose coalition collapsed in November 1990, and the government was controlled for a short period by a breakaway Janata Dal group supported by Congress (I), with Chandra Shekhar as Prime Minister. That alliance also collapsed, resulting in national elections in June 1991. On May 27, 1991, while campaigning in Tamil Nadu on behalf of Congress (I), Rajiv Gandhi was assassinated, apparently by Tamil extremists from Sri Lanka. In the elections, Congress (I) won 213 parliamentary seats and put together a coalition, returning to power under the leadership of P.V. Narasimha Rao.

This Congress-led government, which served a full 5-year term, initiated a gradual process of economic liberalization and reform, which has opened the Indian economy to global trade and investment. India's domestic politics also took new shape, as traditional alignments by caste, creed, and ethnicity gave way to a plethora of small, regionally based political parties. The final months of the Rao-led government in the spring of 1996 were marred by several major political corruption scandals, which contributed to the worst electoral performance by the Congress Party in its history.

The Hindu-nationalist Bharatiya Janata Party (BJP) emerged from the May 1996 national elections as the single-largest party in the Lok Sabha but without enough strength to prove a majority on the floor of that Parliament. Under Prime Minister Atal Bihari Vajpayee, the BJP coalition lasted in power 13 days. With all political parties wishing to avoid another round of elections, a 14-party coalition led by the Janata Dal emerged to form a government known as the United Front, under the former Chief Minister of Karnataka, H.D. Deve Gowda.

His government lasted less than a year, as the leader of the Congress Party withdrew his support in March 1997. Inder Kumar Gujral replaced Deve Gowda as the consensus choice for Prime Minister of a 16-party United Front coalition. In November 1997, the Congress Party in India again withdrew support for the United Front. New elections in February 1998 brought the BJP the largest number of seats in Parliament—182—but fell far short of a majority. On March 20, 1998, the President inaugurated a BJP-led coalition government with Vajpayee again serving as Prime Minister. On May 11 and 13,

1998, this government conducted a series of underground nuclear tests forcing U.S. President Clinton to impose economic sanctions on India pursuant to the 1994 Nuclear Proliferation Prevention Act.

In April 1999, the BJP-led coalition government fell apart, leading to fresh elections in September. The National Democratic Alliance-a new coalition led by the BJP-gained a majority to form the government with Vajpayee as Prime Minister in October 1999.

INDIAN NATURAL HISTORY IN MAURYAN PERIOD

Indian natural history in Mauryan period saw protection measures to be taken, for the first time. The Maurya period is considered to be one of the most important periods in the Indian natural history. The Indian natural history in Mauryan period saw the protection of animals to become a serious issue, for the first time.

The Maurya dynasty ruled India during the fourth and third centuries B.C. and it was the first empire to provide a unified political entity in India. The Mauryan emperors had a positive and attitude towards the Indian forests, their denizens and the Indian fauna in general. Being the first dynasty to feel the need of protecting Indian wildlife, the Mauryan emperors for the first time looked at the Indian forests, as a resource.

The Indian natural history in Mauryan period witnessed significant changes in the way the people and the administration looked on Indian wildlife. The Mauryan emperors considered the elephants to be the most important forest product, as the military power during that period was dependent not only upon horses and men but also on battle-elephants.

The Mauryans successfully used the battle-elephants to beat Alexander's governor of Punjab, Seleucus. The main reason why they sought to preserve supplies of elephants was that it was more cost and time-effective to catch, tame and train wild elephants than to raise them. They appointed the officials like the Protector of the Elephant Forests and the world famous manuscript of that period, Kautilya's 'Arthashastra' unambiguously specifies the responsibilities of such officials. The main responsibility of the Protector of the Elephant Forests was to establish a forest for elephants on the border of forests, and it should be guarded by foresters. The Superintendent was required to protect the elephants whether along on the mountain, along a river, along lakes or in marshy tracts, with the help of guards.

They were also authorised to kill anyone slaying an elephant. With these measures taken, the Indian natural history in Mauryan period was heading towards proper preservation and protection of Indian wildlife.

· Apart from appointing the Protector of the Elephant Forests, the Mauryas also designated separate forests to protect supplies of timber, as well as lions and tigers, for skins. Apart from that, there were also the Protector of Animals, who worked for eliminating thieves, tigers and other predators to render the woods safe for grazing cattle.

In the Indian natural history in Mauryan period, certain forest tracts were valued in strategic or economic terms and the Mauryans instituted curbs and control measures over them. Though they regarded all the forest tribes with distrust, they employed some of them, mainly the food-gatherers or aranyaca to guard borders and trap animals. The eminent Mauryan emperor, Ashoka (304 - 232 BC) was one of the most notable preservers of Indian natural history in Mauryan period. He brought about significant changes in his style of governance to provide protection to fauna and he even relinquished the royal hunt.

He is thought to be the first ruler in India to advocate conservation measures for wildlife. Ashoka had rules inscribed in stone edicts, as well and the edicts proclaim that many people followed the king's example in giving up the slaughter of animals. The other rulers of that period also had rules like penalising the poachers of deer in royal hunting preserves, with 100 'Panas' fine. There were legal restrictions to restrict the freedoms exercised by the common people in hunting, felling, fishing and setting fires in forests, as well.

Chapter 2

The Nationalist View

HISTORY AFTER INDEPENDENCE

Indian natural history after Independence has seen contributions from many scientists from different fields. The Indian natural history after Independence has seen several naturalists with different specialisations, making their own contributions. The Ornithologists, the Entomologists, the Ichthyologists, the Herpetologists, etc have contributed vastly to the Indian natural history after Independence. They travelled throughout the country and collected valuable information about the Indian natural history and they also preserved their collections through various publications.

The most prominent Ornithologists in the Indian natural history after Independence were the famous naturalists, Salim Ali and his cousin Humayun Abdulali. Both of them used to work with the Bombay Natural History Society. Salim Ali also worked with the American collabourators like Sidney Dillon Ripley and Walter Norman Koelz and produced the most comprehensive handbook of Indian ornithology, till now. The introduction of field Ornithology was another major contribution during this period and the pioneers in this field included Horace Alexander.

Apart from those naturalists, the Zoological Survey of India also conducted its own collection surveys, led by Biswamoy Biswas. M. S. Mani and B. K. Tikader are counted among the most notable Entomologists in the Indian natural history after Independence. The tradition of entomology started in the colonial era and numerous Entomologists continued the tradition, after independence. Several Entomologists specialised especially on economically important insects (mostly pests) and they have made a huge contribution to the Indian natural history. Apart from the Entomologists, there were the famous Ichthyologists like Sunderlal Hora.

Hora was mainly famous for his Satpura hypothesis, which is actually a bio-geographical hypothesis based on his observations on the adaptations of hill stream fishes. Some of the other prominent Ichthyologists in the Indian natural history in after Independence include C. V. Kulkarni and S. B. Setna.

The Herpetologists also made their own contributions to the Indian natural history after Independence and C. R. Narayan Rao was one of the most notables, amongst them. He worked on the frogs of southern India and apart from him; Romulus Whitaker and J. C. Daniel also studied various aspects of the reptile fauna of India.

A large number of scientists from various other fields also contributed to the study of Indian natural history after Independence. Some of them worked in interdisciplinary areas and J. B. S. Haldane was foremost amongst them. Haldane was a British scientist who encouraged field biology in India on the basis that it was useful while at the same time requiring low investment unlike other branches of science. He was also among the first few people, who popularised quantitative approaches to biology in India.

The Indian natural history after Independence has contributions made by several popularisers. The mass media was definitely one of the most notable among them. The Indian natural history was made more popular through publications in the mass media.

The pioneering black-and-white wildlife photographer and artist, M. Krishnan wrote articles on various aspects of natural history in Tamil and English, and popularised study of natural history in southern India. His articles were also well illustrated with his photographs and artwork. Apart from him, Professor K. K. Neelakantan was another writer who popularized the study of birds in Kerala by writing books and articles in Malayalam. Some of the others prominent popularisers include Harry Miller, Ruskin Bond etc, who wrote about the wilderness, the hills and the wildlife in India, in English medium.

Apart from the popularisers, there were also the wildlife photographers who played an important role in popularising the study of Indian natural history after Independence. Numerous wildlife photographers like made their own contributions and the people like Loke Wan Tho, E. Hanumantha Rao, M. Krishnan and T. N. A. Perumal, are among the most popular amongst them.

They actually followed in the footsteps of the early pioneers of photography like E. H. N. Lowther, O. C. Edwards and F. W. Champion. There were also a large number of conservationists, who played a vital role in the Indian natural history after Independence. The urgent need to preserve the little remaining wildlife was realised by these conservationists and E. P. Gee (1904-1968), was one of the most eminent among them. Apart from him, a large number of people also got involved in conservation of Indian natural history, in later times.

INDIAN NATURAL HISTORY IN MUGHAL PERIOD

Babur and Jahangir were the biggest contributors to the Indian natural history in Mughal period. In the Mughal period, the Indian natural history saw the patronage of the emperors for gardening and art. The Indian natural history in Mughal period also saw the emperors going for excessive hunting of the animals in the forests.

Among all the Mughal emperors, Babur (1483 - 1530) and Jahangir (1569 - 1627) have to be mentioned specially, as they made huge contributions in the Indian natural history. The Mughal emperors used to lead a leisurely life and they used to decorate their gardens with their private zoos. They also hired artists to paint many subjects including plants and animals. They used to practice hunting and falconry, quite extensively and they also employed scribes. The most important thing in the Indian natural history in Mughal period was that, the Mughal emperors were the first one to document their observations of nature in India. Babur wrote some wonderful notes that indicate the former distribution of the Rhinoceros as far west as the Indus.

According to the notes of Babur, the Lesser Rhinoceros was found in the Bengal Sunderbuns, and a very few individuals were stated to occur in the forest tract along the Mahanuddy river, and extending northwards towards Midnapore. They were also found on the northern edge of the Rajmahal hills near the Ganges. Apart from that, the Lesser Rhinoceros used to occur more abundantly in Burmah and through the Malayan peninsula to Java and Borneo, as well. Apart from Babur, Jahangir also made some significant contributions in the Indian natural history in Mughal period, as well.

He used to keep detailed records of his hunts and it is found from the records that, he himself hunted about 17,167, from the age of twelve to forty-eight. The hunted animals include Tigers, Lions, Bears, Leopards, Foxes, Otters (ubdilao), Hyaenas, Blue bulls (Nilgai), and also Mhaka. Jahangir's records also have detailed description about some of his memorable hunts.

Jahangir appointed Ustad Mansur, as a court artist in the 17th century to make paintings of various animals. Hence, documentation of observations of nature in India is considered to be the most important contributions made by the Mughal emperors in the Indian natural history.

Chapter 3

The Marxist View

FRAMEWORK

Important reasons for India's distinctive path lie in geography and early historical experience. India's topography shaped a number of vital features of its civilization. The vast Indian subcontinent is partially separated from the rest of Asia (and particularly from east Asia) by northern mountain ranges.

Mountain passes linked India to civilizations in the Middle East. Though it was not as isolated as China, the subcontinent was nevertheless set apart within Asia. The most important agricultural regions are along the two great rivers, the Ganges and the Indus. During its formative period, called the Vedic and Epic ages, the Aryans (Indo-Europeans), originally from central Asia, impressed their own stamp on Indian culture. During these ages, the caste system, Sanskrit, and various belief systems were introduced.

PATTERNS IN CLASSICAL INDIA

By 600 B.C.E., India had passed through its formative stage. Indian development during its classical era did not take on the structure of rising and falling dynasties, as in China. Patterns in Indian history were irregular and often consisted of invasions through the subcontinent's northwestern mountain passes.

As a result, classical India alternated between widespread empires and a network of smaller kingdoms. Even during the rule of the smaller kingdoms, both economic and cultural life advanced. The Maurya and Gupta dynasties were the most successful in India, run entirely by Indians and not by outside rulers. The greatest of the Mauryan emperors was Ashoka (269-232 B.C.E.). The Guptas did not produce as dynamic a leader as Ashoka, but they did provide classical India with its greatest period of stability.

POLITICAL INSTITUTIONS

Classical India did not develop the solid political and cultural institutions the Chinese experienced, nor the high level of political interest of Greece and Rome. Its greatest features, still observable today, were political diversity and regionalism. The Guptas, for example, did not require a single language for all of their subjects. The development of a rigid caste system lies at the heart of this characteristic. In its own way, the caste system promoted tolerance, allowing widely different social classes to live next to each other, separated by social strictures. Loyalty to caste superseded loyalty to any overall ruler.

Religion, particularly Hinduism, was the only uniting influence in Indian culture. Religion and Culture. Two major religions, Hinduism and Buddhism, marked classical India. Hinduism, the religion of India's majority, is unique among world religions in that no central figure is credited for developing it. Hinduism encouraged both worldly and mystical pursuits and was highly adaptable to varying groups. Buddhism was founded on the teachings of an Indian prince, Gautama, later called Buddha, or "enlightened one." Buddha accepted many

Hindu beliefs but rejected its priests and the caste system it supported. Buddhism spread through missionaries into Sri Lanka, China, Korea, and Japan. Classical India also produced important work in science and mathematics. The Gupta-supported university at Nalanda taught religion, medicine, and architecture, as well as other disciplines. Indian scientists, borrowing ideas from

Greek learning provided by Alexander the Great, made important discoveries. Still more important were the mathematical advancements, including the concept of zero, "Arabic" numerals, and the decimal system. Indian artists created shrines to Buddha called stupas and painted in lively colours. Economy and Society. India developed extensive trade both within the subcontinent and on the ocean to its south. The caste system described many key features of Indian society and its economy.

The rights of women became increasingly limited as Indian civilization developed; however, male dominance over women was usually greater in theory than in practice. The economy in this era was extremely vigourous, especially in trade, surpassing that in China and the Mediterranean world. Merchants traded from the Roman Empire to Indonesia to China.

IN DEPTH

Inequality as the Social Norm. The Indian caste system, like the Egyptian division between noble and commoner and the Greco-Roman division between free and slave, rests on the assumption that humans are inherently unequal. All classical social systems (with the partial exception of Athens' democracy) played down the importance of the individual and emphasized obligations to family, group, and government. This runs counter to modern Western notions about equality. Classical China and Greece probably came closest to modern views about individuality, but in both civilizations, it was largely expected that rulers should come from society's elites. In nearly all societies throughout most of human history, few challenged the"natural order" of social hierarchy and fewer still proposed alternatives.

INDIAN INFLUENCE

Because of its extensive trading network, Indian cultural influence spread widely, especially in southeast Asia. Buddhism was a leading cultural export. Indian merchants often married into royal families in other areas. Political dominance of outside peoples was not a characteristic of Indian governments. China and India. China and India offer important contrasts in politics and society, yet they resembled each other in that both built stable structures over large areas and used culture to justify social inequality. The restraint of Chinese art contrasted with the more dynamic style of India. The latter developed a primary religion, Hinduism, while the former opted for separate religious and philosophical systems. Chinese technological advancements stressed practicality, while Indians ventured into mathematics for its own sake. Indian merchants played a greater societal role than their Chinese counterparts. Both, however, relied on large peasant classes in agrarian settings; both accepted political power based on land ownership. Global Connections: India and the Wider World. No classical civilization was more open to outside influences than India. None was more central to cross-cultural exchanges in the common era. Important innovations in mathematics and science came from classical India.

Buddhism is one of the few truly world religions. Indian influence was especially important in southeast Asia. Placed between the great empires and trading networks of the Mediterranean and of China, India was ideally situated for its culture to influence both East and West. Alexander the Great: Greek invader who provided important contacts between India and

HELLENISTIC CULTURE

Aryans: During the Vedic and Epic ages these Indo-European migrants developed the region's first epic stories, later written down in Sanskrit. Their rigid ideas about social order influenced India's caste system.

Maurya dynasty

First dynasty to unify much of the subcontinent. Borrowed political examples from Persia and Alexander.

- *Ashoka*: Greatest Mauryan ruler. Gained all but the southern tip of India through conquest. Converted to and greatly promoted Buddhism.
- *Gupta*: Empire began in 320 C.E. and provided two centuries of political stability. Overturned in 535 C.E. by invading Huns.
- *Caste system*: Social relationship developed on a large

scale uniquely in India. Five major castes regulated social status and work roles. Grew more complex over time into a multitude of subcastes. Governed society more than any political body.

- *Untouchables*: Lowest caste. It was widely held that any member of a higher caste who touched these people would be defiled. Held the most menial jobs but were not slaves.
- *Hinduism*: The religion of India's majority, developing at first in the Vedic and Epic ages. Hinduism has no single founder or central holy figure, unlike all other major religions.
- *Sanskrit*: The first literary language of India, introduced by the Aryans. Under the Guptas, it became the language of educated people but never became the universal language of India. was the language of the Vedas, the sacred books of early India.
- *Upanishads*: The Epic Age saw the creation of these poems with mystical themes. From these, the Hindu ideas of divine forces informing the universe developed.
- *Dharma*: A Hindu concept that was a guide to living in this world and at the same time pursuing spiritual goals. However, it was less prescriptive than other world religions' codes. Hindu avoidance of a fixed moral rule is why it allowed for more diversity than most religions.
- *Vishnu and Shiva*: Two important gods in the enormous Hindu pantheon. Vishnu was the preserver and Shiva, the destroyer.
- *Buddhism*: The Indian prince Gautama became the Buddha, or "enlightened one," when he questioned the poverty and misery he saw. Generally seen as a reform movement out of Hinduism. Buddhism had its greatest effect outside of India, especially in southeast Asia.
- *Panchatantra*: A collection of stories produced during the Gupta era, including "Sinbad the Sailor" and

"Jack the Giant Killer." Best-known Indian stories around the world.

- *Tamils*: Southern Indians who traded cotton, silks, and many other materials with the Middle East and with Rome. Reflected the strong merchant spirit in classical India.
- *Buddha*: (563 – 483 B.C.E.) Creator of a major Indian and Asian religion; born in the 6th century B.C.E. as son of a local ruler among Aryan tribes located near Himalayas; became an ascetic; found enlightenment could be achieved only by abandoning desires for all earthly things.
- *Himalayas*: Mountain system of south-central Asia which divides India from Asia, leaving India to develop in relative cultural isolation.
- *Vedas*: Meaning hymns to the gods; four ancient books of Aryan religious traditions in which can be found the origins of Hinduism.
- *Mahabharata* and *Ramayana*: Aryan epic poems composed in Sanskrit which include myths, legends, philosophy, and moral stories.
- *Varnas*: Aryan social classes.
- *Jati*: Subgroups of castes, each with distinctive occupations and tied to their social stations by birth.
- *Indra*: Aryan god of thunder and strength.
- *Chandragupta Maurya*: (322 – 298 B.C.E.) Ruler of a small Ganges Valley state who defeated the Greeks in the area and made himself king in 322 B.C.E. He then created and enlarged the Mauryan Empire.
- *Kushans*: Invaders of India c. 100 B.C.E. who were gradually absorbed into Indian culture and became the Kshatriya caste.
- *Kautilya*: Chief minister of Chandragupta Maurya who wrote the book *Arthashastra,* which gave advice on how to gain power and use it through whatever means as long as the ruler pleases his subjects.
- *Gurus*: Hindu mystics who gathered disciples around themselves.

- *Brahma*: Hindu idea that a basic holy essence formed part of everything in the world.
- *Reincarnation*: Hindu idea in which souls do not die when bodies do but pass into other beings, either human or animal. Where the soul goes depends on how good a life that person has led.
- *Yoga*: Hindu practice of mediation and self-discipline which has the goal to free the mind to concentrate on the divine spirit.
- *Bhagavad Gita*: Hindu sacred hymn which details the story of Arjuna, a warrior, who struggles with the decision of whether to go to battle against his own family.
- *Nirvana*: Buddist idea which literally means a world beyond existence itself. It is the ultimate goal of the reincarnation cycle.
- *Kamasutra*: A manual of the "laws of love" written in the 4th century C.E., which discusses relationships between men and women.
- *Stupas*: Spherical shrines to Buddha.

SOCIAL AND HISTORICAL BACKGROUND OF ISLAM

ISLAM-the Religion of Peace-was not the creation of Mohammad any more than other religions were of those to whom their origins are respectively attributed. No religion is the creation of any single individual, nor does it appear all of a sudden, revealed to this or that Seer as it is always claimed. Islam, like any other religion, was the product of the conditions of the time, and of the surroundings in which it flourished.

Though living on the side of the fateful road, on which the conquering armies of the Assyrians, Persians, Macedonians and Romans had marched back and forth, the inhabitants of the vast Arabian Peninsula maintained their freedom by virtue of the natural aspects of their country and the mode of life molded by those aspects. But the fierce love of freedom, together with the exigencies of a nomadic existence, had split the inhabitants of the Arabian Desert into a number of tribes perpetually engaged in feuds and warfare. Separated from the rest of mankind, the Arabs took the stranger for an enemy. The poverty of his country had added to the growth of that spirit. These two factors went into the making of the codes of law and morality of the Arabs.

They believed that, as descendants of the outlawed Ismael, they were doomed to live in a dreary desert while rich and fertile lands were assigned to the other branches of the human family. Consequently, they felt themselves justified in recovering by force a portion of the heritage, they believed, they had been deprived of.

The Roman historian Pliny, six hundred years before the appearance of Mohammad, found the Arabs occupied with two lucrative professions, robbery and trade, in addition to their native call of sheep-raising and horse-breeding. In the earlier stages of social evolution, these two professions of robbery and trade are usually distinguished by a thin and elastic line of demarcation.

"The trader makes his profit by purchasing things at the cheapest price, and selling them at the highest. The cheaper the price he pays, the greater is his profit. Robbery or theft places him in possession of things at the lowest price. Therefore, once the morality of the fundamental principle of trading is admitted, the right of the trader to act so as to make the greatest possible profit becomes legitimate. Then, competition keeps the price of his wares down. The most convenient way of eliminating competition is to rob the rival. By that stratagem, not only is the competitor kept away from the market, but his goods go there as the property of the more efficient party. Further, robbery is an effective weapon to establish monopoly on trade-routes and markets. In Its earlier stages of development, trade is everywhere conducted with these practical policies which must shock a modem merchant. Still, robbery was the weapon with which his less orthodox predecessors established the noble profession which he now carries on so righteously with the laudable maxim: Honesty Is the best policy.

Besides, robbery imperceptibly ripens into the manly political virtue of warlikeness, so much glorified in the savage adolescence of mankind. Given to robbery by the physical aspects of their homeland, the Arabs were naturally destined to develop unusual talent in trade as well as in war. Their bravery and warlikeness were almost legendary. The famous historical work. Ayam al Arab," composed in the most flourishing days of the Saracen Empire, records no less than seventeen hundred memorable battles fought by the Arabs before the rise of the Prophet. So, if the Saracens distinguish themselves as warriors, they did not derive that virtue from their Islamic faith. They had been warriors before they were called to wield the sword in the service of God. The military achievements of Islam should be credited not so much to the religious teachings of the Arabic Prophet as to the social conditions of the country in which it was born.

The wars conducted by the Arabs before the appearance of the Prophet were mostly internecine feuds, fought with savage fierceness, but strictly according to the quaint codes of honour, chivalry and nobility. The profuse spilling of blood did not fertilize the sands of Arabia, but it did, eventually, become prejudicial to the profitable economic consequences of robbery, the legitimate profession of trade conducted by the primitive Arabs. Economic necessity demanded termination of the proud but ruinous virtue of Internecine wars, and diversion of the traditional Saracen valour in more profitable channels. The ideas, born out of that necessity, eventually crystallized into the "Religion of Mohammad."

Itself a vast stretch of sandy wilderness, Arabia, however, is surrounded on three sides by fruitful, populous countries-homes of ancient civilizations, where industry and agriculture thrived from time immemorial. On the south is the ocean on which navigated vessels carrying the trade of India. Thanks to her geographical position, Arabia was interested by the routes of Caravan trade and maritime commerce, interchanged among India, Persia, Assyria, Syria, Palestine, Egypt and Abyssinia. In earlier days, the trade-routes connecting Africa and Asia lay through the south and north of the Peninsula, avoiding the unknown interior of the sandy wilderness. But the exorbitant taxation of Byzantine despotism, supplemented by the endless extortion of its local officials, drove the traders to hazard the encounter of the fierce, but hospitable Beduin in the heart of his home.

In the beginning, the Arab collected his tribute according to his peculiar code of law and morality. But in course of time, he discovered that trade would be more profitable than robbery. Of all the Arabian tribes, the Koreish were the first to exchange the turbulent for a peaceful, but more profitable profession. They inhabited the coast-line of the Red Sea, and had commanded the Abyssinian trade long before the Asiatic traffic also came their way. In the earlier centuries of the Christian era, the capital of the Koreish tribe, Mecca, had become the point where the important trade-routes from south to north and east to west intersected. At Yamen, on the Arabian Sea, the Koreish caravans took over the commodities from India; at a point near modern Aden, their precious burden was increased by the African riches from Abyssinia. The journey northwards terminated at the busy marts of Damascus, where corn and manufactured articles were bought at the exchange of aromatics, pearls, precious stones, tusks etc. The lucrative exchange diffused plenty and riches in the streets of Mecca. When, later, the east-west trade-route also passed through Mecca, the prosperity of the Koreish became unbounded, and their ambition proportionately grew.

But other Arabian tribes, jealous of their freedom, and envious of the prosperity of the Koreish, stood faithfully by their traditional codes of law and morality, whose profane origin was no longer admitted. They were raised to the nobility of offensive and defensive warfare, on the authority of tribal gods. The old national pastime of robbery which had previously been played at the expense of unwary strangers, turned out ruinous to the new national occupation of trade. Termination of the tribal feuds became an essential condition for further political task of establishing unity, by the logic of historical events, devolved upon those who controlled the economic forces making for the historically necessary goal. The

Koreish appeared as the chosen people of history. In the midst of their ceaseless feuds, all the Arabian tribes worshipped and sacrificed at the temple of Caabba near Mecca. The Koreish had seized the control of the seat of national worship, and the sacerdotal office of great power and extensive privilege had been captured by the Hashemites- the most important family of the tribe. The Hashemites, therefore, commanded national respect and veneration, in addition to the opulence derived from trade. Eventually, a scion of the Hashemite family issued the call for unity in the form of a new religion which denied all gods but one.

The severe Monotheism of Mohammad not only echoed the yarning for unity on the part of a people torn ass under by Internecine feuds; it was also destined to find a ready response from the neighbouring nations, tormented by the intolerance of the Catholic Church. The religious life of the people of Persia, Mesopotamia, Syria, Palestine and Egypt had been hopelessly confused by the conflicts of Magian Mysticism, Jewish conservatism and Christian bigotry. Rigid rites and rituals had taken the place of religion; hypocritical ceremonies had driven away devotion; dogmatic theology had prosecuted faith; and God had disappeared in a confusing crowd of angels, saints and apostles.

The stringent cry of the new religion.-"There is but One God"-softened by great toleration, subject to this fundamental creed, was enthusiastically hailed by the distressed multitudes searching for the secure anchor of a simple faith in the stormy sea of social disintegration, intellectual bankruptcy and spiritual chaos. The historic cry was raised by the caravan traders of Arabia who had stood outside the ruinous conflict of arms and beliefs, had prospered economically, and progressed in spirit, while their older and more civilized neighbours had stagnated, decayed and disintegrated. The propagation of the stern belief in the

Oneness of God prepared the ground for the rise of a military State which unified all the social functions-religious, civil, judicial and administrative. The Unitarianism of the Saracens laid the foundation of a new social order which rose magnificently out of the ruins of the antique civ11isation. Such a creed was sure to attract the attention of the multitudes barbarously persecuted for religious heterodoxy.The new faith allowed freedom of conscience to all who placed themselves under its protection. Islam rose as a protection against religious persecution and refuge for the oppressed.

The accommodating nature, cosmopolitan spirit, democratic policy and the monotheistic creed of Islam were the creation of the geographical position of the land of its birth. Surrounded with countries oppressed by native despotism or devastated by foreign invasions, Arabia maintained her freedom. The persecuted sects from Egypt and Persia as well as from the Christendom fled to the free and hospitable desert where they could profess what they thought, and practice what they professed.

When the Empire of the Assyrians was conquered by the Persians, and the altars of Babylon subverted by the Magis, the Sabian priests retired to the neighbouring desert with their ancient faith and the precious knowledge of astronomy. Previously, Assyrian invasion had driven many a devout son of Israel in the same hospitable wilderness. All the Hebrew prophets, down to John the Baptist, lived, meditated and preached in the depth of the Arabian Desert. The invasion of Alexander having avenged the wrong done to the Assyrians, the more orthodox disciples of Zoroaster, who did not wish to desecrate the purity of their faith by the toleration of Greek idolatry, migrated to the free atmosphere of the Arabian desert to join their hands with Babylonian adversaries.

Gnosticism and Manichaeism-those hybrids of oriental mystic cults-Greek metaphysics and Christian Gospel, all thrived luxuriantly on the sandy soil of free Arabia. Finally, Catholic orthodoxy drove to the same smelting pot of Arabian hospitality the Nestorian, Jacobite and Eutycian heretics who preferred the simplicity of the Gospel to the idolatry of the orthodox Church. The freedom of exile brought the representatives of those diverse faiths into closer contact enabling them to see what was common to them all. In the calm atmosphere of toleration, their heterodoxy disappeared, fire of proselytism died out and the common essence of the teachings the learned guests was imparted to the hospitable Beduin. In short, the Barbarians of the desert inherited the best the religion of antiquity had to offer, namely, the faith in the existence of one supreme God who is exalted above all the powers of heaven and earth, but who had revealed himself to the mankind from time to time through his Prophets. Here is the essence of Islam crystallized in the spiritual consciousness of the Arabian people before Mohammad appeared with the mission of building a new religion on its basis.

The spirit of Islam was not invented by the genius of Mohammad; nor was it revealed to him. It was a heritage of history conferred on the Arabian nation. The greatness of Mohammad was his ability to recognize the value of the heritage and make his countrymen conscious of it. The Arabs had acquired the notion of one supreme God; but out of habit and for tribal Interests, they still practiced their old polytheistic worship. To be benefited by the positive outcome of earlier religions, delivered to them as a heritage of history, they must change their traditional mode of worship. A supreme effort must be made with the purpose; and Mecca was the most strategic point to lead the attack from.

The particularist freedom and internecine feuds of the Arabian tribes were mutually compromised and composed at Mecca. All routes of trade led there. The unity of the economic interest of the decentralized nation had created at Mecca a symbol of precarious spiritual unity. All the tribes from distant parts of the vast desert, while visiting the market of Cecca, worshipped in the temple of Caabba. Each had introduced there its own emblem of devotion. The temple had been adorned with no less than three hundred and sixty idols of men, eagles, lions, etc., but the prosperous tribe of Koreish dominated the trade of Mecca, and the powerful family of Hashim had seized control of the temple. It was natural that the new spirit of a rising faith, which would further economic interest through national unity, should be first felt consciously at the heart of the nation. So, it happened that a member of the Hashemite family began to preach the new religion.

Once the family of Hashim and the tribe of Koreish were converted to the new faith, the whole nation would follow soon. All the tribes must visit Mecca for the purposes of trade. Those who controlled the trade of Mecca could easily dictate the faith and conscience of the entire nation. But prejudice and habit induced the Koreish to persecute ennovating zeal of their kinsman. They were afraid that trade would be driven away from Mecca, should the Pantheon of Caabba be disturbed. But there were others ready to assume the leadership of the revolution, when the most eligible candidate failed. Medina espoused the cause of the Prophet, and the call of unity found enthusiastic response in other quarters. The supremacy of Mecca was menaced. One family after another defected from the Koreish conservatism, and joined the revolutionary Hashemites. Before long, the Koreish capitulated before their exiled kinsmen, but only to capture the scepter of the"Commander of the Faithful." As soon as the followers of the Prophet captured Mecca, a perpetual law was passed that no unbeliever should be allowed to set foot on the territory of the Holy City. The new religion was imposed upon the entire nation with the potent weapon of economic boycott. Caabba was cleared of its idols, and became the shrine of"Mohammad's God." Once the standard of the new religion was raised, the whole nation flocked under it. The ground had been prepared. The faith had unconsciously taken hold of the mind of the nation before it was preached. Economic interest demanded its establishment.

THE CAUSES OF TRIUMPH

ITS historical background and the social conditions in which it was born put on Islam the stamp of toleration, which, to the undiscerning eye, may appear to be incongruous with the spirit of fanaticism traditionally associated with it. But there is no contradiction. The basic doctrine of Islam- There is but One God"-itself makes for toleration. If the whole world, with its defects and deformities, the entire mankind, with all its follies and frivolities, is admitted as the creation of the selfsame God, the believer in this elevating doctrine may" deplore the deformities and laugh at what appears to him to be absurdities and perverseness; but the very nature of his faith does not permit him to look upon them as the works or worships of some other God of Evil, and declare war upon them as such. Those, who worship dilf~rently, are for him mistaken and misled brethren, but none the less children of the selfsame Father, to be brought to the right road, or indulgently tolerated until they are ready for redemption.

The terrifying vision of the followers of the, Arabic Prophet offering to the world, Koran or the sword, cast such an ominous shadow over the history of the rise of Islam as concealed the third alternative so freely offered, and generally accepted. That was the main cause for the triumph of Islam. As a matter of fact, the alternatives were very differently offered. It was:"Accept the Koran or pay tribute to the Saracen conqueror!" The"Sword of God" was unsheathed only when neither of the alternatives was accepted. The economic interest of the Arab trader, which produced the monotheistic creed of Islam, was antagonistic to indiscriminate bloodshed.

The lands through which the trade routes lay must be conquered and brought under the domination of the unitary State. The object would be all the better realised should the conquered peoples accept the new religion; for, then the unitarian State would be established on a solid foundation. But production and consumption of commodities are the essential factors of trade. Therefore, it was not compatible with the historic role of Islam to massacre the artisan and peasant masses, or to destroy opulent cities for the impiety of rejecting the Koran. What was necessary was their subjugation to the believers of the new creed. Under the domination of the followers of the Prophet, unbelieving peoples were allowed to hold their imperfect faiths, and to continue their perverse worships.

When Jerusalem capitulated to Khalif Omar, the inhabitants of the vanquished city were left in possession of their worldly goods, and allowed the freedom of worship. A special quarter of the city was allotted for the residence of the Christian population with their Patriarch and his clergy. For the protection thus granted, a nominal tax of two pieces of gold was imposed upon the entire Christian community. The pilgrimage to the Holy City was stimulated rather than suppressed by the Muslim conquerors, on account of the commercial value of that devout traffic. Four hundred and sixty years later, when the Holy Land reverted to the Christian rule of the crusading knights of Europe,"the Oriental Christians regretted the tolerating Government of the Arabian Khalifs". (Gibbon,"Rise and Fall 0f the Roman Empire".)

In contrast to the toleration of the Muslims, the following account of the occupation of Jerusalem by the Crusaders is highly illuminating:"In the pillage of private and public wealth, the adventurers had agreed to respect the exclusive property of the first occupant. A bloody sacrifice was offered by mistaken votaries to the God of the Christians; resistance might provoke, but neither sage nor sex could mollify, their Implacable rage; they indulged themselves three days in a promiscuous massacre. After seventy thousand Muslims had been put to the sword, and the harmless Jews had been burned in their Synagogue, they could still reserve a multitude of captives whom interest or lassitude persuaded them to spare.

On the testimony of a whole series of authoritative historians, Christian as well as Muslim, contemporary as well as modern, the critical Gibbon conclusively proves that"to his Christian Subjects, Mohammad readily granted security of their persons, the freedom of their trade, the property of their goods and the toleration of their worship." This profitable principle of toleration was observed with more or less strictness, not only by all the immediate successors of the Prophet, but over the whole period of Arabic ascendancy. It was abandoned only after Islam had played out its historic role and its leadership has passed from the noble Saracens to the notorious barbarians of Tartary.

Even under the first Turkish Sultans. Islam was not completely divorced from its original spirit of toleration. In its days of glory, the native toleration of Islam not only developed into wide freedom of thought and rationalism, but, from the orthodox point of view, even degenerated into positively heretical and irreligious notions. Most of the earlier Abbassides Khalifs of Baghdad were not only devoted to the study of profane science, and free in their thought; some of them, Motassen for example, even did not believe in the divine origin of the Koran.

For centuries, the Saracen Empire offered hospitable asylum to the persecuted Jews as well as to the unorthodox Christians sects of the Nestorians, Jacobites, Eutychians and Paulicians. After the consolidation of the Saracen conquest, the toleration of Islam was extended even to the Catholic Church. Many Christian historians themselves bear testimony to this effect.

The Ecclesiastical historian Renaudot, for example, informs that"the rank, the immunities, and the domestic jurisdiction of Patriarchs, Bishops, and the clergy were protected by the (Muslim) civil magistrates (of Egypt); the leaning of Christian Individuals recommended them to the employment of secretaries and physicians; they were enriched by the lucrative collection of revenue; and their merit was sometimes raised to the command of clues and provinces." A Khalif of Baghdad declared that the Christians were most worthy of trust in the administration of Persia. The Paulicians, those valiant fore-runners of the Protestant Reformation, not only received freedom of worship in the Saracen Empire, but were actively supported by the Khalifs in their prolonged effort to subvert the degenerated Catholic Church, and reestablish Christianity In its original form.

The ancient religion of Zoroaster, with its pernicious doctrine of the dual principles of Good and Evil, both equally eternal, was particularly obnoxious to the stern worshipper of"One God". Yet, even the Magian creed did not altogether forfeit the toleration of the conquering Arab. As late as the third century of the Hegira, ancient temples of Fire stood splendourously overshadowing the modest Mosque by their side. Those proud monuments of an ancient faith crumbled not under the ruthless blow of the fanatical Sword of Islam; they were doomed to destruction, and fall to inevitable ruins in consequence of the general desertion of their votaries. No amount of coercion could possibly force a whole nation to abandon its traditional faith with so little resistance, and accept that of the conqueror with such surprising alacrity, as did the Persians over the vast territory from the Tigris to the Oxus. The ancient faith was decayed.

It no longer satisfied the spiritual requirements of a cultured people. The menacing shadow of Khariman had eclipsed the luster of the"Sun and Fire." The Persian masses embraced the simple Monotheism of Mohammad as the message of liberation from the dark despotism of the eternal principle of Evil. The north of Africa, from Alexandria to Carthage, was the only territory where the Christian faith was totally obliterated by the spread of Islam. There again, the cause of the sweeping religious revolution was not the Intolerance of the new creed, but the decay of the old faith, and the general chaos and despair caused by that decay. The faith of the gospel of Jesus, established by the talent, piety and power of Cyprian, Athanasius and Augustine, had been subverted by Arian and Donatist heresies, and the Catholic fury, with which the impoverished masses revolting under the banner of religious heresy were suppressed, had ruined the once prosperous provinces economically. Then, the Vandal and Moorish invader had devastated the ruins so mercilessly as to throw the people into a hopeless state of social chaos and spiritual morbidity which drove them to seek an 1llusive solace in the absurdities or Monasticism.

In that dense darkness of social dissolution and spiritual despair, the virile and optimistic message of the Prophet of Arabia flashed like an 1lluminatIng flame of hope. The mind of the multitude was lured by the temporal as well as the heavenly blessings offered by the new religion. The conquering trumpet of Islam awakened the despondent spirits who, defeated in the struggle of terrestrial life, had precariously entrenched themselves in the superstition of a divine existence. Healthy indulgence of nature, allowed, even encouraged, by the new faith, speedily overwhelmed the perverse notions of asceticism fomented by a degenerate version of the gospel of Christ. Islam opened up a new vision of hope before a people, sunk in the depth of despondency. The convulsion created by it ushered in a new society in which everyone had the opportunity of ascending the natural level of his courage and capacity.

With the exhilarating inspiration of Islam, and under the benevolent rule of the Saracen conquerors, the fertile soil and industrious peoples of North Africa soon recovered fruitfulness and prosperity.

It is altogether a misconception that the Arabian progress was due to the sword alone. The sword may change an acknowledged national creed, but it cannot affect the consciences of men. Profound though its argument is something far more profound was demanded before Mohammedanism pervading the domestic life of Asia and Africa.... The explanation of this political phenomenon is to be found in the social condition of the conquered countries. The influences of religion in them had long ago ceased; it had become supplanted by theology... How was it possible that unlettered men, who with difficulty can be made to apprehend obvious things, should understand such mysteries? Yet, they were taught that on those doctrines the salvation or damnation of the human race depended.

They saw...that personal virtue or vice were no longer considered; that sin was not measured by evil works but by the degrees of heresy... What an example when bishops are concerned in assassinations, poisonings, adulteries, blindings, riots, treasons, civil war; when Patriarchs and Primats were excommunicating and anathematising one another in their rivalries for earthly power, bribing Eunuchs with gold, and courtesans and royal females with concessions of episcopal love, and influencing the decisions of councils asserted to speak with the voice of God by those base intrigues and sharp practices resorted to by demagogues in their packed assemblies! Among legions of monks, who carried terror into the imperial armies and riot into the great cities, arose hideous clamours for theological dogmas, but never a voice for intellectual liberty or the outraged rights of man. In such a state of things, what else could be the result than disgust or indifference? Certainly men could not be expected to give help to a system that had lost all hold on their hearts.

"When, therefore, in the midst of the wrangling of sects... and anarchy of countless disputants, there sounded through the world... the dread battle cry,'There is but One God is it surprising that the hubbub was hushed? Is it surprising that all Asia and Africa fell away? In better times, patriotism is too often made subordinate to religion; in those times, it was altogether dead."

The principle of equality, preached by the followers of Mohammad, originated in the traditional freedom of the nomadic life of the Arabic tribes. They had all shown equal valour in the national profession of robbery. When that modest call of the olden times assumed the majestic proportion of conquest, the individual Arab did not forget that his horse could speed as fast and his scimitar was as sharp as those of any. He had taken an equal share in defending his desert home against the conquering armies of Sesostris and Gyrus, Alexander and Darius, Pompeii and Ashirwan, Ptolemy and Trajan.

He would not playa less noble part in the pastime of turning the table. But the principle of equality proclaimed by Islam proved to be a factor in its spectacular triumph no less potent than the scimitar of the Saracen hero. It contrasted sharply with the oppressive laws governing the class and caste-ridden societies of the Roman Byzantine, Persian and, later, of Indian Empires. Islam stood for freedom and equality which, as a matter of fact, had long been forgotten in all the lands of the degenerated ancient civilization.

The proud possession of the spiritual heritage of earlier civilizations having accrued to the Arabs, it became their mission to share it with the unfortunate multitudes groaning under the hideous rul1ls of those civilizations. The circumstances of the age were favourable to the dramatic expansion of Islam. It rose in the period of intellectual and spiritual decline of the ruling classes throughout the world of ancient civilizations. The dissatisfaction with the social conditions of decay, decomposition, and despotism had created in the masses of people the aspiration and striving for a better world. Christlan1ty had been the first child born of that revolutionary spirit. The unfortunate triumph of having enlisted the corrupting patronage of the old ruling class had transformed Christianity into an apologist of the established order of society. The Church Fathers had conveniently forgotten that their Prophet preached revolt against the Roman yoke, and had painted him as the meek sheep bleating the shameful Injunction:"Pay the Caesar his due"-an injunction which violated the whole tradition of Jewish history constituting the background of Christianity. Having compromised with the ruling class, Christianity could not but betray the mission of laying the foundation of a new social order commensurate with the objective striving of the age. It had refused to lead the destitute to the conquest of this world and had deceived them with the delusion of a world to come, flowing with milk and honey. The entrance to the Kingdom of Heaven was to be allowed only to the meek, that is, to those who would submit to the tyranny of the rulers of this world.

The debacle of Christianity made the appearance of a more vigourous religion an historical necessity. Islam not only promised its votaries the blessings of a brilliant paradise. It also inspired them to the conquest of this world. Indeed, the Paradise of the Arabian Prophet was nothing but an ideal of the life of happiness and enjoyment to be attained in this world. Mohammad not only provided his own people with a platform of national unity, but armed the united Arabian nation with a cry of revolt which found ready response from the oppressed and destitute masses in all the adjacent countries.

The cause of the dramatic success of Islam was spiritual as well as social and political. On this important point, Gibbon testifies:"More pure than the system of Zoroaster, more liberal than the laws of Moses, the religion of Mohammad might seem less inconsistent with reason than the creed of mystery and superstition which, in the seventh century, disgraced the simplicity of the Gospel." Still one more historian bears testimony to the fact that the spectacular triumph of Islam was rather due to its liberating and equalitarian principles than to the military valour of its early adherents. In almost every case in which the Saracens conquered a Christian nation, history unfortunately reveals that they owed their success chiefly to the favour with which this progress was regarded by the masses of the conquered people. To the disgrace of most Christian governments, it will be found that their administration was more oppressive than that of the Arab conquerors... The inhabitants of Syria welcomed the followers of Mahomet; the Copts of Egypt contributed to place their country under the domination of the Arabs; and the Christian Berbers aided the conquest of Africa. All these nations were induced, by the hatred for the government of Constantinople, to place themselves under the sway of the Mohammedans. The treachery of the nobles and the indifference of the people made Spain and the South of France easy prey to the Saracens."

MOHAMMAD AND HIS TEACHINGS

The founder of Islam has been characterized as"the man who, of all men, has exercised the greatest influence upon the human race." There was, however, nothing very extraordinary about the man until he claimed the credit of divine revelation. The foundation of that dubious claim was no more or no less fictitious than in the case of the prophets, apostles and saints of all other religions. Christian arrogance called the Arabian Prophet an"Imposter". But it has been forgotten that he was given that name together with Moses and Jesus. The authorship of the famous book, anonymously published,-"Three Imposters"-which created sensation in Europe towards the close of the middle-ages, was attributed to the Christian King Frederic Barbarossa as well as to the Muslim philosopher Averroes.

If Mohammad was an"imposter", he did not take up that role any more consciously than others who appeared as instruments through which the fiction of divine revelation became a reality and carried conviction with the ignorant and superstitious masses. Having conceived the ideal of national unity, Mohammad realised that it could not be made acceptable to the warring Arabian tribes unless it were backed up with a supernatural sanction. People enjoying the bliss of ignorance and thinking In terms of preconceived notions, could not be convinced with any other argument. The will of minor gods could be overwhelmed by the will of a greater and all-powerful God. The protection against the wrath of the former should be found in the mercy of the latter. The belief in the absolute sway of one supreme God can alone encourage people to revolt against the tyranny of a whole host of tribal deities. If the supreme God was not there he had to be invented. That was the chain of Mohammad's thoughts. There was no Imposture in it. Did not the rationalist Voltaire put forward the same argument more than a thousand years after it had found favour with the Arabian Prophet?

But in the latter case, the argument was put forward in defence of reaction; Voltaire advocated the necessity of inventing a God because that would be the only guarantee for the preservation of the decayed system of feudal monarchist society. At the time of Mohammad, and under the circumstances it was advanced, the argument served a positively revolutionary purpose. When man's mind is dominated by the belief in the supernatural, every progressive idea should be formulated in the terms of those beliefs if it were to secure popular support. Besides, the idea of One God was not the invention of Mohammad. Mohammad's mission was to discover evidence for the existence of the One God. And if you wish to convince people you must adduce only that kind of evidence which can carry conviction to them.

But Mohammad's search for God was not inspired by cynicism as in the case of Voltaire. It was an honest effort on the part of an ignorant man inspired by zeal. In quest of the God who alone could save the Arabian nation, he retired to the desert and gave himself up to meditation, fasting and prayer-those familiar practices adopted by the prejudiced seeking divine inspiration even in these days of the twentieth century. And the result was as usual in all such cases.

"He was visited by supernatural appearances, mysterious voices accosted him as the Prophet of God; even the stones and trees joined in the whispering." (Draper Ibid.) Such experiences always result from cerebral disorder which takes place whenever the prescribed practices are carried too far. Fixed ideas, however fantastic or imaginary, may appear to take concrete form if the mind is focused on them so as to exclude the consciousness of other sensations. A scientific study of the psychology of Seers reveals the fact that"inspiration" or any other"religious experience" is the result of a pathological state brought about either accidentally or purposely through prescribed practices.

Mohammad acted as all those of his kind had done before him, or did after him. But in his case, there was a fact which must go to his credit. He was too shrewd a man to be deluded by those psycho-pathological symptoms which are taken for the evidence of spiritual elevation. He was afraid that he was going mad; and might have abandoned his mission if his sagacious wife had not come to his aid in the nick of time. It was the rich merchant Khadija, mature with worldly wisdom, who was quick to appreciate the spiritual value of the mental aberrations of her husband. She persuaded him that his visions were not signs of insanity, but were messengers of God. Taking advantage of his psycho-pathological state of suggestibility, she could easily make him"see" an angel entering the room to deliver to him the Message of God.

Undoubtedly, the drama could be enacted only in the setting of ignorance, superstition and prejudice main characters being played under delusion. But that is how all religions are born. There is no reason to think that Islam was an exception. It was an exception in the sense that, except for the Invention of a divine sanction, it contained less of religious dogmas and metaphysical speculation than sound political sense, progressive social principles and admirable codes of personal behaviour.

"He did not engage in vain metaphysics, but applied himself to improving the social condition of his people by regulations respecting personal cleanliness, sobriety, fasting, prayer, above all other works he esteemed almsgiving and charity. With a liberality to which the world had of late become a stranger, he admitted the salvation of men of any form of faith provided they were virtuous." (Draper, ibid.)

Composed by man of practically no education, the Koran, naturally, is not a work of any intellectual standard. It is full of crude Ideas and fantastic speculations. These obvious defects of the Koran, easily over-shadow its great merit even as the source of Inspiration of a great religion. Mohammad's religion was rigorously monotheistic; and as a Monotheism It was uncompromising, which outstanding characteristic won for it the distinction of the highest form of religion. The idea of God is the foundation of religion in the ph1losophical sense.

That idea cannot be free of all fallacies unless it leads to the conception of creation out of nothing. The rationalism of ancient philosophers of Greece as well as of India-excluded the fantastic conception. Consequently, religions growing out of the background of that primitive rationalism could not conclusively establish the fundamental idea of God. The result was that all the great religions-Hinduism, Judaism and Christianity-eventually ended in some or other form of pantheism which logically liquidates religion as such. For pantheism identifying the phenomenal world with God puts the very Idea of God under doubt. It disposes of the Idea of creation and, consequently, the Idea of God must also go. If the world can exist, by itself, from eternity, it is not necessary to assume a creator. And, deprived of the function of creation, God becomes an unnecessary postulate.

Mohammad's religion cuts the Gordian knot. It frees the idea of God from the embarrassment of primitive rationalism by boldly asserting the highly irrational idea of creation out of nothing. The God stands out in all His glory. The ability to create not only the whole world but an endless series of worlds is the token of His all-powerfulness.

To have thus established the Idea of God, albeit in a dogmatic and primitive manner, was the credit of Mohammad. For that credit he has gone down in history as the founder of the purest form of religion. Because Islam as a religion is Irrationalism par excellence, it so easily triumphed over all other religions which, with all their metaphysical accomplishments, theological subtleties and philosophical pretensions, were defective as religion, being but pseudo-religions. Monotheism, however, is a highly subversive theory. While being itself the highest form of religion, it strikes at the root the religious mode of thought. Placing God above and beyond the world, it opens up the possibility of doing without him altogether. Islam as the most rigorous monotheistic religion closed the chapter of human history dominated by the religious mode of thought, and by its very nature was open to unorthodox interpretations which eventually liquidated the religious mode of thought and laid down the foundation of modern rationalism."We may compare the working of Monotheism to a mighty lake, which gathers the floods of science together, until they suddenly begin to break through the dam.

The third of the great monotheistic religions, Mohammedanism, is more favourable to Materialism. This, the youngest of them, was also the first to develop, in connection with the brilliant outburst of Arabian civilization, a free philosophical spirit, which exercised a powerful influence primarily upon the Jews in the Middle Ages, and so indirectly upon the Christians of the West.". Being the most perfected form of Monotheism, Islam played that role. The crudities of the Koran did not prevent its basic idea from flourishing into all its revolutionary consequences.

His severe Monotheism contradicted Mohammad's claim to the sole Prophecy of God. While the Koran recognized Moses, Jesus and other Hebrew Prophets as apostles of God, Mohammad's claim, if not openly disputed in the beginning, was secretly doubted even among his associates. Divinity of its founder is not the fundamental creed of Islam. And that distinction results from its strict Monotheism. Immediately upon the death of Mohammad, his followers were divided on that crucial question. When the news of the Prophet's death reached the camp of the army setting out for the conquest of Syria, the devout Omar refused to believe that the Prophet could die, and threatened to strike off the head of messenger whom he suspected to be an infidel. Upon that, the venerable Abu Bakr admonished the impetuous younger man with the following words:"Is it Mohammad or the God of Mohammad that you worship? The God of Mohammad liveth for ever; but the apostle was a mortal like ourselves, and according to his own prediction, he has experienced the common fate of mortality." It should be noted that the immediate successor of Mohammad, at the moment of his disappearance, called him an apostle, instead of the Prophet. With the less ambitious designation of an apostle, Mohammad was placed by his followers on the level of other religious teachers and law-givers. Denial of the divinity of the Prophet made Islam the purest doctrine of Monotheism. Once divinity is conceded to a Prophet, before long, he assumes the attributes supposed to belong only to the Supreme Being.

The unity of God or the absoluteness of the First Principle can no longer be maintained logically. Dubious theological devices endeavor to reconcile the contradiction. The original simplicity of faith is lost either in theological dogmatism or mystical self-deception. Without the severity of its theology, Islam could not claim the historic role as creditably as it did. When the Prophet is deprived of divinity, or his claim to it is not generally admitted, the scripture cannot command absolute and infallible authority. Consequently, a latitude is left for the mind of the faithful. The teaching of a mortal cannot have the majesty of eternal truth, and scriptural laws cannot claim immutability.

Until the twelfth century, Islam did not possess a homogenous body of dogmas. Subject to the belief in one God, the Mussulman had a practically unlimited latitude for his spiritual life. And history shows that the Arabian thinkers made free and full use of that flexibility of the new faith. In order to refute the Christian doctrines of Trinity, which they considered to be a vulgarization of the sublime idea of the Supreme God, Muslim theologists developed the fundamental idea of religion to the most abstract form ever conceived by human mind. They could perform that unparalleled feat of theological rasiocination because"the Monotheism of Mohammad was the most absolute, and comparatively the freest from mythical adulterations." The same authority testifies to the fact that the fundamental principles of religion laid down crudely by the founder of Islam were pregnant with the possibility of great development.

And because of their rigid monotheistic nature, the development inevitably transcended the narrow limits of religious thought and culminated into a spiritual aflorescence which closed the age of faith."Even before the communication of Greek philosophy to the Arabians, Islam had produced numerous sects and theological schools, some of which entertained so abstract a notion of God that no philosophical speculation could proceed farther in this direction, whilst others believed nothing but what could be understood and demonstrated... In the high school at Basra, there arose, under the protection of the Abbassides, a school of rationalists which sought to reconcile religion and faith."

During the first five or six hundred years of its history, Islam produced not only scholars who occupied themselves more with heavenly bodies than with heavenly beings, who quietly set aside the Koran and placed greater spiritual value on the study of profane books, but revolutionary thinkers who ruthless\y sacrificed faith on the altar of reason. Not a few"Commanders of the Faithful" themselves-those who reigned at Baghdad, Kairo or Cordova until the eleventh century-attached greater value to positive knowledge than to revealed wisdom. The independent Empire of Bokhara preferred poets to the priests, doctors of medicine to doctors of divinity, and encouraged scientific research rather than the propagation of faith. When we bear in mind that this line of intellectual development was opened up not only by the socio-political conditions created by the triumph of Islam, but originated in the central dogma of Mohammad's religion, neither the curiosities of the Koran nor the primitiveness of the Islamic faith should permit us to underestimate the historical role of Islam.

ISLAM AND INDIA

Although Islam came to India after it had played out its progressive role, and its leadership had been wrested from the learned and cultured Arabs, the revolutionary principles of the days of its origin and ascendancy were still inscribed on its flag; and a critical study of history might reveal that the Muslim conquest of India was facilitated by similar native factors as In the case of Persia and the Christian countries. No great people, with a long history and old cIv1lIsatIon, can ever succumb easily to a foreign invasion, unless the invaders command the sympathy and acquiescence, If not active support, of the masses of the conquered people. Brahmanical orthodoxy having overwhelmed the Buddhist revolution, India of the eleventh and twelfth centuries must have been infested with multitudes of persecuted heretics who would eagerly welcome the message of Islam.

Mohammad Ibn Kassim conquered Sindh with the active assistance of the Jats and other agricultural communities oppressed by the Brahman rulers. Having conquered the country, he followed the policy of the early Arab conquerors. "He employed the Brahmans in pacifying the country by taking them into confidence. He allowed them to repair their temples and to follow their own religion as before, placed the collection of revenue in their hands, and employed them in continuing the traditional system of local administration." (Elliot, "History of India) when even the Brahmans, some of them at any rate, were prepared to go over to the side of the mlechha conquerors, the social conditions of the country could not be very normal. Evidently, society was in such a disintegrated and chaotic state as to make the position even of the most privileged class insecure. That is usually the result of counter-revolution. A revolution may be defeated by a combination of forces; but that does not enable the triumphant forces of reaction to remove the causes of social disintegration which brought about the revolution.

In India, the Buddhist revolution was not defeated; it was miscarried owing to its internal weakness. Social forces were not sufficiently mature to carry the revolution to victory. Consequently, after the downfall of Buddhism, the country found itself in a worse state of economic ruin, political oppression, intellectual anarchy and spiritual chaos.

Practically, the entire society was involved in that tragic process of decay and decomposition. That is why not only the oppressed masses readily rallied under the banner of Islam which offered them social equality if not political liberty; even the upper classes offered their services to the foreign aggressor out of selfish motives. That shows that, while the masses were in a state of despair, the upper classes were thoroughly demoralized.

As regards the spread of Islam in India, an ardent admirer of ancient Hindu culture like Havell, who cannot be suspected of any sympathy or even fairness to the Muslims, gives the following highly interesting testimony: "Those who did so (embraced Islam) acquired all the rights of a Musalman citizen in the law courts, where the Quran and not Aryan law and custom decided dispute in all cases. This method of proselytism was very effective among the lower castes of Hindus, specifically among those who suffered from the severity of Brahmanical Jaw with regard to the 'impure' classes.

This is certainly not a very complimentary remark wrung from a firm believer in the perfection of Brahmanical law. In any ease, it is clear that In the time of Mohammedan conquest, there lived In India multitudes of people who had little reason to be faithful to Hindu laws and the traditions of Brahman orthodoxy, and were ready to forsake that heritage for the more equitable laws of Islam which offered them protection against the tyranny of triumphant Hindu reaction.

In another place, Havell chooses to deco precate the spiritual values of the teaching of the Arabian Prophet. But at the same time makes a very significant statement regarding the spread of those teachings in India. It was not the philosophy of Islam but its sociological programme, which won so many converts for It in India." Of course, for the masses philosophy has no appeal. They are always attracted by a œsociological programme" which offers them something better than the given conditions of their life. And a bad philosophy, that to say, a reactionary outlook of life, cannot be associated with a sociological programme which secures the support of the downtrodden masses. If the sociological programme of Islam found support of the Indian masses, it was because the philosophy behind that programme was better than the Hindu philosophy which had been responsible for the social chaos from which Islam showed a way out for the masses of the Indian people. By the above statement, Havell admits that even in the thirteenth and fourteenth centuries, when Islam was winning adherence in India, it had not altogether played out its social-revolutionary role, and that it was by virtue of its social revolutionary character that it struck So deep a root in India. That is to say even in its days of degeneration and decay, Islam represented spiritual, ideological and social progress in relation to Hindu conservatism.

Havell is a famous eulogist of Indo-European culture which he considers to be the noblest product of the creative genius of man. On the other hand, he has bitter antipathy for the Muslims. His opinion cannot be dismissed as biased against the Hindus. As a matter of fact, his bias is entirely on the Bide of the Hindus. So, if even a historian like him found distasteful things happening in India in the past, conditions were very deplorable indeed. He writes: "But the victorious progress of Islam in India Is not to be accounted for by external reasons. It was mainly due to the political degeneration of Aryavarta which set in after the death of Harsha... The social programme of the Prophet Gave every true believer an equal spiritual status made Islam a political and social synthesis and gave it an imperial mission Islam was a rule of life sufficient for the happiness of average humanity content to take the world as it is. Islam reached the zenith of its political strength at the critical period when the conflict between Buddhist philosophy and that of orthodox Brahaminism was a potent cause of political dissension in northern India." (Ibid).

King Harshavardhan died in the middle f the seventh century. Thus, the political disintegration of India was a process parallel o the rise of Islam. The death of a king, however great, does not mark the turning point of history. The process had been going on for many centuries. The Buddhist revolution arrested it for a time, only to be aggravated, accentuated and accelerated on its defeat. Indeed, the monastic degeneration of Buddhism and its disintegrating influence on the entire Indian society greatly helped the Muslim conquest just as Chr1stia~ monasticism had done elsewhere.

Commenting on Mahmud of Guzni's invasions, Havell further writes: "The almost invariable success of his arms added immensely to his prestige and brought Islam many adherents among the uncultured warrior classes of the North-Western Provinces to whom fighting was a religion and victory in the field the highest proof of inspiration." (Ibid). Mahmud's exploit could not but deal a staggering blow to the faith in the divinity of the shrines where the Indians had brought their offerings from times immemorial.

Consequently, the religious feeling which found expression in the worship at the shrines, and the faith in their presiding deities were rudely shocked and inevitably shaken. In such circumstances, "religious feelings' and spiritual instincts" induced the masses to transfer their devotion 1rom the gods of demonstrated impotence to the more mighty one, the belief in, and worship for whom, incidentally, was rewarded so magnificently.

For ages, millions had believed in the supernatural power of the gods worshipped at the famous temples of Thaneswar, Muttra, Somnath etc. The priests of those temples had amassed fabulous riches at the expense of the believing multitude by virtue of their pretensions to the ability of invoking the protection of the powerful divinities.

Suddenly, the whole venerable structure of belief and tradition collapsed like a house of cards under the cruel blow of the invading Infidel. When Mahmud's hosts approached, the priests told the people that the invaders would be devoured by the fiery wrath of the gods. The people confidently expected a miracle which failed to happen. Indeed, it was performed by the God of the Invader. Being based upon miracle, faith necessarily is transferred to the most miraculous. Judged by all the traditional standards of religion. Those who embraced Islam at that crisis were the most religious. A critical Investigation of the Internal as well as the external causes of the Muslim conquest of India is of practical value today. It will remove the prejudice that makes the orthodox Hindu look upon his Muslim neighbour as an Inferior being. Freed from preconceived ideas, the Hindus will be in a position to appreciate the constructive consequences of the Muslim conquest of India. That will enable them to live down the hatred of the conquered for the conquerors. Unless a radical change of attitude 18 brought about by a sobre sense of history, the communal question w1ll never be solved.

The Hindus w1ll never be able to look upon the Muslims as integral parts of the Indian nation until they come to appreciate the contribution they made towards the emergence of Indian society out of the chaos caused by the breakdown of the antique civ1l1sation.

Besides, a proper understanding of history derived from a correct understanding of the successful advent of the Muslims in India will enable us to ascertain and stamp out the deeper causes of our present misfortune.

On the other hand, few Muslims of our days may be conscious of the glorious role played on the stage of history by the faith they profess. Many may disown and repudiate the rationalism and skepticism of the Arabs as deviations from the teachings of the Koran. But Islam occupies a memorable place in history thanks rather to its original-unorthodoxy and irreligiosity made evident by the Arab philosophers, than to the later growth of a reactionary priesthood or to the barbarous fanaticism of the Tartar converts. Islam had played out its progressive role before it penetrated India.

Its nag was planted on the banks of the Indus and the Ganges not by revolutionary Saracen heroes, but by Persians demoralized by luxury and the barbarians of Central Asia who had embraced Islam, both had subverted the Arab Empire-that magnificent monument to the memory of Mohammad. Still, it was welcomed as a message of hope and freedom by the multitudinous victims of the Brahmanical reaction which had overthrown the Buddhist revolution and had consequently thrown the Indian society in a state of chaos. Neither the Persians nor the Mogul conquerors of India were entirely devoid of the traditional nobility, toleration and liberalism of the Saracen heroes. The very fact that comparatively small bands or predatory invaders from distant lands could make themselves the rulers of a vast country for such a long time, and their alien faith found millions of converts, proves that they did satisfy certain objective requirements of the Indian society. Even when much of its original revolutionary fervor had been overwhelmed by reaction. Islam still exercised certain revolutionary influence on the Hindu society. The Mohammedan power was consolidated in India not so much by the valour of the invaders' arms as owing to the propagation of the Islamic faith and the progressive significance of Islamic laws.

Even the fiercely fanatical anti-Muslim Havell grudgingly admits...The e1fect of the Mussalman political creed upon Hindu social life was twofold: It increased the rigor of the caste system and aroused a revolt against it. The alluring prospect which it held out to the lower strata of Hindu society was as tempting as it was to the Beduins of the desert "(It) made the Sudra a free man and potentially a lord of the Brahmans. Like the Renaissance of Europe, it stirred up the intellectual waters, produced many strong men, and some men of striking originality of genius. Like the Renaissance also, it was essentially a city cult; it made the nomads leave his tent and the Sudra abandon his village. It developed a type of humanity full of joie de vivre..." ('.Aryan Rule in India").

To the above highly illuminating statement, it may only be added that the rise of reformers like Kabir, Nanak, Tukaram, Chaitanya, etc. who evidenced a popular revolt against Brahmanical orthodoxy, was to a great extent promoted by the social ecects of Mohammedan conquest.

In view of this realistic reading of history, Hindu superciliousness towards the religion and culture of the Muslims is absurd. It insults history and injures the political future of our country. Learning from the Muslims, Europe became the leader of modem civilization. Even to-day, her best sons are not ashamed of the past indebtedness. Unfortunately, India could not be fully benefited by the heritage of Islamic culture, because she did not deserve the distinction. Now, in the throes of a belated Renaissance, Indians, both Hindus and Muslims, could profitably draw inspiration from that memorable chapter of human history. Knowledge of Islam's contribution to human cultured and proper appreciation of the historical value of that contribution would shock the Hindus out of their arrogant self-satisfaction, and cure the narrow-mindedness of the Muslims of our day by bringing them face to face with the true spirit of the faith they profess.

ISLAMIC PHILOSOPHY

The age of Arabian learning lasted about five hundred years, and coincided with the darkest period of European history. During the same period, India also was lying prostrate, under the triumphant Brahmanical reaction which had subverted or corrupted Buddhism. Eventually, it was, thanks to the inglorious success of having overcome the Buddhist revolution, that India fell such an easy prey to' Muslim invaders.

Under the enlightened reign of the Abbassides, the Fatemites and the Ommiades rulers, learning and culture prospered respectively In Asia, North-Africa and Spain. From Samarqand and Bokhara to Fez and Cordova, numerous scholars studied and taught astronomy, mathematics, physics, chemistry, medicine and music. The invaluable treasure of Greek philosophy and learning had been burled under the intolerance and superstition of the Christian Church. Had it not been for the Arabs, It would have been irretrievably lost, and the dire consequence of such a mishap can be easily imagined.

Vain piety and hypocritical holiness induced the Christians to spurn the science of antiquity as profane. In consequence of that vanity of Ignorance, the peoples of Europe were plunged into the medieval darkness which threatened to be bottomless and interminable. The happy resurrection of the divine light of knowledge, lit by the sages of ancient Greece, at long last dissipated the depressing darkness of Ignorance and superstition prejudice and intolerance, and snowed the

European peoples the way to material prosperity, intellectual progress and,spiritual liberation.

It was through the Arabian philosophers and scientists that the rich patrimony of Greek learning reached the fathers of modem rationalism and the pioneer of scientific research, Roger Bacon, was a disciple of the Arabs. In the opinion of Humboldt, the Arabians are to be considered "the proper founders of the physical sciences, in the signification of the term which we are now accustomed to give it." Experiment and measurement are the great instruments with the aid of which they made a path for progress, and raised themselves to a position of the connecting link between the scientific achievements of the Greek and those of the modern time.

AI Kandi, AI Hassan, AI Farabi, Avicena, Al Gazali, Abubakr, Avempace, Al Phetragius. (The Arabian names are so contracted in historical works written in European languages) -these are names memorable in the annals of human culture; and the fame of the great Averroes has been 1mmortalised as that of the man who made the forerunners of modern civilization acquainted with the genius of Aristotle, thereby giving an inestimable impetus to the struggle of the European humanity to liberate itself from the paralyzing influence of theological bigotry and sterile scholasticism. The epoch-making role of the great Arab rationalist, who flourished in the first half of the twelfth century under the enlightened patronage of the Sultan 0! Andalusia, is eloquently depicted by the well-known saying of Roger Bacon: "Nature was interpreted by Aristotle, and Aristotle interpreted by Averroes."

The standard of spiritual revolt against the authority of the Christian Church, and the domination of theology, was hoisted in the thirteenth and fourteenth centuries. The rationalist rebels drew their inspiration from the scientific teachings of the great philosophers of ancient Greece, and these they learned from the Arabian scholars, particularly Averroes.

The bigotry of the pious Justinian, in the beginning of the sixth century, finally purged the holy world of Christian superstition of the remaining vesiiges of pagan learning. The last Greek scholars were forced to leave the ancient seats of learning. They emigrated from the Roman Empire, and sought refuge in Persia; but there also sacerdotal intolerance proved equally hostile to profane learning.

Eventually, the derelict science of Athenian culture found a hospitable home in the court of the Abbassides Khalifs of Baghdad who were so impressed by the wisdom of those foreign infidels that neither Koran, nor sword was offered to them. On the contrary, all the remaining votaries of ancient learning, whose knowledge ridiculed faith, and indulgently smiled at all religion, were invited to accept the liberal hospitality of the Commander of the faithful.

The Khalifs not only took the exiled Greek scholars under their protection. They dispatched competent men to different parts of the Roman Empire with the instruction and the means to collect all the available works of the sages of ancient Greece. The precious works of Aristotle, Hipparchus, Hyppocrates, Galen and other scientists were translated into the Arabian language, and the Khalifs gave every encouragement to the propagation of those irreligious teachings throughout the Muslim world.

Schools established at State expense disseminated scientific knowledge to thousands of students belonging to all classes of society,-"from the son of the noble to that of the mechanic". Poor students received education free, and teachers were handsomely remunerated for their services which were held at the highest esteem. The Arab historian, Abul Faragius, records the following views of Khalif Al Mamon regarding the men of leaning: "They are the elect of God, his best and most useful servants, whose lives are devoted to the improvement of their rational faculties. The teachers of wisdom are the true luminaries and legislators of a world which without their aid would again sink into ignorance an barbarism.

The current notion of the bigotry and fanaticism of Islam loses all historical authenticity when it is known that the men of learning so highly appreciated by the successors of the Prophet, were mostly devoid of any religious fervour, not a few of them holding views frankly heretical; and the general burden of their teachings was the assertion of the reason of man as the only standard of truth. History does not provide the critical student with many instances of the head of a religious order encouraging the "improvement of rational faculties", as Khalif Al Mamon did. For, the cultivation of rational faculties is entirely incompatible with faith. Yet, Al Manon was but one of the illustrious lines of Abbassides Khalifs who not only encouraged the propagation of scientific knowledge, but themselves participated in it. Nor were the enlightened Abbassides an exception.

The Fatemites of Africa and the Omminades of Spain rivaled them in political power, material prosperity as well as in the patronage and propagation of knowledge. The library of Cairo contained over one hundred thousand volumes; whereas Cordova boasted of six times as many. This fact gives lie to another calumny which depicts the rise of Islam as an eruption of savage fanaticism, namely, the tale of the destruction of the famous library of Alexandria. One must have a pious mind or credulous disposition to believe that those who took delight in founding and supporting such noble seats of learning, would have callously set fire to the library of Alexandria; that, those who command the gratitude of mankind for having saved its most precious patrimony, could have possibly begun by contributing to the destruction of that treasure. When dispassionate and scientific study of history dissipates legends and discredits malicious tales, the rise of Islam stands out not as a scourge but a blessing for the mankind.

While books written in the eleventh and twelfth century indignantly detail the shocking tale of the burning of the library of Alexandria, the historians Eustichius and Elmacin, both Egyptian Christians, who wrote soon after the Saracen conquest of their country, are significantly silent about the savage act. The former, a patriarch of Alexandria, could be hardly suspected of partiality to the enemies of Christianity. An order of Khalif Omar has been usually cited as evidence of the barbarous act ascribed to his general. It would have been much easier not to record that order than to suppress any historical work composed by Christian prelates who had endless possibilities of concealing their composition. A diligent examination of all relevant evidence enabled Gibbon to arrive at the following opinion on the matter: "The rigid sentence of Omar is repugnant to the sound and orthodox precept of the Mohammedan Casuits; they expressly declare that the religious books of the Jews and Christians, which are acquired by the right of war, should never be committed to the flames, and that the works of profane scientists, historians or poets, physicians or philosophers, may be lawfully applied to the use of the faithful." ("Rise and Fall of the Roman Empire").

Since history began to be written with impartial criticism, the tale of the destruction of the Alexandrian library has either been discredited or subjected to grave doubt. In any case, at the time of the Saracen conquest, the library of Alexandria had ceased to be the repository of the valuable records of Greek learning. Long before that time, Alexandria had enshrined Christian bigotry in the place of scientific knowledge and philosophical wisdom. The character of the contents of the library must have changed accordingly.

The pagan scholars, driven by Christian intolerance away from the seat of ancient learning, must have carried away the treasures they valued more than all other things. If the flame was actually lit by the order of Omar, it consumed ponderous tomes of theological controversy which had done immensely more harm than good to mankind. The fire of Islam might have consumed the none too precious records of vain and futile theological disputations; but the admirable ardour the free-thinking Khalifs collected, preserved and improved the valuable records of ancient learning which had left the Alexandrian library before its useless and pernicious contents were put to the flames.

Byzantine barbarism had undone the meritorious work of the Ptolymies. The real destruction of the Alexandrian seat of learning had been the work of St. Cyril who defiled the Goddess of learning in the famous fair of Hyparia. That was already in the beginning of the fifth century. The Christian Saint would not tolerate that philosophical lectures and mathematical discourses held by a young pagan woman should be patronized by the elite of Alexandrian society, while the pious but incomprehensible sermons of the Archbishop were attended only by the rebels. If he was no match intellectually, he possessed the power to eliminate competition once for all Under his instigation, the rebels, led by a regiment of monks burning with religious frenzy, attacked the seat of Alexandrian learning and, in the name of religion, perpetrated crimes too painful to be recorded and too shameful to be remembered.

"Thus, in the four hundred and fourteenth year of our era, the position of philosophy in the intellectual metropolis of the world was determined; henceforth, science must sink into obscurity and subordination. Its public existence will no longer be tolerated. Indeed, it may be said that from this period for some centuries it altogether disappeared. The leaden mace of bigotry had struck and shivered the exquisitely tempered steel of Greek philosophy. Cyril's act passed unquestioned. It was now ascertained that throughout the Roman world, there must be no more liberty of thought...Such assertions might answer their purposes very well so long as the victors maintained their power in Alexandria, but they manifestly are of inconvenient application after the Saracens had captured the city.

For the next two dreary and weary centuries, things remained, until oppression and force were ended by foreign invaders. It was well for the world that the Arabian conquerors avowed their true argument, the scimitar, and made no pretensions to superhuman wisdom. They were thus left free to pursue knowledge without involving themselves in theological contradictions, and were able to make Egypt once more illustrious among the nations the earth,-to snatch it from the hideous fanaticism, ignorance and barbarism into which it had been plunged."

The works of the sages of ancient Greece were not only rescued, collected and preserved by the Arabs. They were profuse commented and improved upon. Complete works of Plato, Aristotle, Euclid, Appolonius, Ptolemy, Hyppocrates and Galen were available to the fathers of modern Europe at first only in Arabic versions, accompanied by erudite commentaries. Modern Europe learned from the Arabs not only medicine and mathematics. The science of astronomy, which widens the vision of man and reveals before him the mechanical laws of nature, was jealously cultivated by the Arabs. With the aid of new instruments of observation, Arab philosophers acquired exact knowledge about the circumference of the earth the position and number of planets. In their hand, astronomy began to outgrow its primitive form, (divinations of Astrology), cultivated more or less by the priests of all Oriental countries, and to develop into an exact science. Although algebra had been invented by Diophantus of Alexandria, it did not become an object of common study until the age of Arabic learning.

As a matter of fact, the name of the science has given currency to the theory of its Arabian origin. But the Arabs themselves modestly acknowledged their indebtness to the Greek master. Botany was studied for medical purposes; yet the discovery of two thousand varieties of plants by Dioscorides represented the birth of a new science. Alchemy was a secret, jealously guarded by the priests of ancient Egypt. It was also practiced at Babylon. In a much later period, rudiments of chemistry were also known to the physicians of India. But the science of chemistry owes its origin and initial developments to the industry of the Arabs. "They first invented and named the alembic for the purposes of distillation; analysed the substances of the three kingdoms of nature; tried the distinction and amenities of alkalis and acids; and converted the precious minerals into soft and salutary medicine."

It was in the science of medicine that the Arabs made the greatest progress. Masua and Geber were worthy disciples of Galen, and substantially added to what they had learned from the great master. Avicena, born in distant Bokhara, in the tenth century, reigned in Europe as the undisputed authority of the medical science for five hundred years. The school of Salermo, until the sixteenth century, was the centre of medical learning in Europe. It owed its origin to the Saracens and taught the lessons of Avicena. The distinctive merit of the Arab scholars was the zeal to acquire knowledge through observation. They discarded the vanity of airy speculation, and stood firmly on the ground known to them. That great merit of Arabian learning is decisively evidenced in the following view of its Doyen Averroes: "The religion peculiar to philosophers is the study of that which is; for no sublimer worship can be given to God than the knowledge of his works, which leads to the knowledge of him and his reality.

That is the noblest action in His eyes; the vilest is taxing, as error and vain presumption, the efforts of those who practice this worship, and who in this religion have the purest of religions." A religion which permitted the propagation of such irreligious views, though garbed in a pious phraseology, could not have its origin in intolerance and fanaticism. For this heterodox view, the philosopher, of course, incurred the wrath of the priesthood; but much more of the Christian than the Muslim.

After a short banishment, Averroes was restituted in his position in the court of the Sultan of Andalusia, and his books survived proscription in the Islamic world. But from their Latin version, the above and similar passages were expunged. Yet, the heretic movements of Europe, during the twelfth, thirteenth and fourteenth century, drew their inspiration from the suppressed teachings of the Arab philosopher; and it was the heretic movement that shook the foundation of the Catholic Church which had held Europe in spiritual subordination throughout the middle-ages.

From the twelfth century onwards, until the triumph of modern learning, Averroism was analogous to heresy in the horrified eye of Christian holiness. And it was for nothing that it was so. For, alone the passage quoted above indicated the surest point of departure for the quest of positive knowledge which eventually cleared away the debris of ignorance, sanctified as faith, and glorified as virtue on the authority of theological dogmas. In this passage, Averroes stated the basic principle of the inductive method-the surest way to true knowledge. On the preconceived notion of a creator is set aside, and of is made to know him (as distinct from the blind faith in his existence) in his reality through the empirical knowledge of his works, that is, nature, the divine object, recedes farther and farther, until it vanishes Into nothingness,- the only demonstrable reality about his existence; and a religion which promoted that singular quest for the knowledge of God certainly represented the greatest advance of human ideology under the garb of religion. The latest of Great Religions, Islam was the greatest; and as such destroyed the basis of all religions. That is the essence of its historical significance.

The centre of Islam and Arabic learning was in those very historical regions where the older civilizations of the Egyptians, Assyrians, Jews, Persians and Greeks had arisen, clashed and fallen. The positive outcome of those earlier civilizations went into the making of the Arabian culture, and the remarkable Monotheism of Mohammad made its own the cardinal principles of the religion of those ancient peoples. It stands to the credit of the Arabian philosophers that they, for the first time, conceived the sublime idea of a common origin of all religions. Not only did they hold the view, singularly broad for the epoch, that all religions were so many efforts of the human mind to solve the great mysteries of life and nature; they went so much farther as to make the bold suggestion that the effort more reconcilable with reason was the greater, nobler and sublimer. This rationalistic view of religion attained the highest clarity in the mind of Averroes.

Thus, together with the invaluable metaphysical and scientific teachings of the sages of Athens and Alexandria, the Arabs contributed something original to the foundation of modern civilization. It was skepticism-that powerful solvent of all faith. As soon as criticism challenges credulity, a new light dawns on the perspective of human progress. A curious book, anonymously published with the title "Three Imposters", occupies a prominent place in the early history of skepticism in Europe. The credit for that scandalous composition was attributed e1ther to the heretical Christian Emperor Frederic Barbarossa, or the Muslim philosopher

Averroes. The imposters were Moses, Christ and Mohammad. One of the suspected authors was a Christian and the other was a Mussulman. Religion certainly had fallen in bad days.

There had been skepticism before the thirteenth century, but no real incredulity. This doctrine and that had been disputed or rejected; but the foundation of Christian faith had never been touched. It was this foundation which was assailed when the idea was conceived that all religions have a common ground. If all religions are essentially the same, then the doctrine and dogmas peculiar to each other should be discarded as pernicious obstacles to the realization of the spiritual unity of mankind. But freed from doctrines and dogmas, religion has no leg to stand upon. Its rationalization amounts to its destruction. The revolutionary idea of the common origin of all religions was conceived for the first time by the Arab thinkers.

Although Arabian learning reached its climax in Averroes, he was but the greatest and the latest of a long succession of great thinkers and scholars who flourished from the ninth to the thirteenth century. A brief reference to the substance of the teachings of the more illustrious of them will give some idea of the revolutionary significance of the learning which owed its origin to the cardinal principle of the Mohammedan religion, and was promoted by the staggering achievements of the "Sword of God."

Having established unity, as the terrestrial reflection of their spiritual unitarianism, and promoted economic prosperity in consequence thereof, the new Islamic nation devoted itself to the culture of the mind. For a hundred years, it modestly learned from others, particularly the ancient Greeks. Thus equipped, it began to produce independent and original thought in every branch of learning.

Al Kandi was the earliest of the great Arabian philosophers. He flourished in the capital of the free-thinking Abbassides, and leaped into fame in the beginning of the ninth century. For teaching that philosophy must be based on mathematics; that is, it should cease to be idle speculation: abstract thought should be guided by precise reasoning, based on concrete facts and established laws, in order to produce positive results. The teacher of this doctrine deserves the great distinction of having anticipated Francis Bacon and Descartes by seven hundred years as a forerunner of modern philosophy. Even to-day there are many "philosophers" and scholars who' could be profited by the wisdom taught by the Saracen sage a thousand years ago.

Next to be mentioned is Al Farabi who lived in the following century, and taught at Damascus as well as Baghdad. His commentary on Aristotle was studied for centuries as an authoritative work on the subject. He also excelled in the medical science. Roger Bacon learned mathematics from him.

In the latter half of the tenth century appeared Avicena. He belonged to a rich landowning family of Bokhara engaged in prosperous trade. He wrote on mathematics and physics, but went down in history for his contributions to the medical science. The famous medical school of Salermo was a monument to his memory, and his work was the text book of medicine throughout Europe until the sixteenth century. The great physician's philosophical views were so unorthodox that even the free-thinking Emir of Bokhara could not resist the pressure of the Imams who were scandalized by the profanity of Avicena. He had to leave the court of his patron, and traveled all over the Arabic Empire teaching medicine and preaching his philosophy at different seats of learning.

In the eleventh century lived Al Hassan who deserves a place among the greatest scientists of all ages. Optics was his special subject. Having learned it from the Greeks, he went farther than they, who corrected their mistaken notion that the rays of light issue from the eye. By anatomical and geometrical reasoning, Al Hassan proved that the rays of light came from the object seen, and impinged on the retina. There is ground for belief, held by many historians of science, that Keppler borrowed his optical views from his Arab predecessor.

In the same century also lived AI Gazali, son of an Andalusian merchant. He anticipated Descartes in reducing the standard of truth to self-consciousness. He stands out as the connecting link between the antique and modern skepticism. His memorable contribution to philosophy is better stated in his own words: "Having failed to get satisfaction from religion, I finally resolved to discard all authority, and detach myself from opinions which have been instilled in me during the unsuspecting years of childhood. My aim is simply to know the truth of things; consequently it is indispensable for me to ascertain what is knowledge.

Now, it was evident to me that certain knowledge must be that which explains the object to be known in such a manner that no doubt can remain, so that in future all error and conjecture respecting it must be impossible. Thus, once I have acknowledged ten to be more than three, if anyone were to say: "On the contrary, three is more than ten; and to prove my, assertion I will change this stick into a serpent; and if he actually did the miracle, still my conviction of his error would remain unshaken. His maneuver would only produce in me admiration for his ability, but I should not doubt my own knowledge."

The principle of acquiring exact knowledge, stated nearly a thousand years ago, by the Muslim savant, still holds as good as then; and the scientific outlook which makes such knowledge possible, is still comparatively rare among the Indians, who even in these days of the twentieth century allow themselves to be imposed by feats of magic and "spiritual" charlatanism, and credit these as serious challenge to the reliability of scientific knowledge.

Al Gazali held that knowledge could not possess such mathematical exactness unless it were acquired empirically, and governed by irrefragable laws established by experience. He was of the opinion that incontestable conviction could be acquired only through sense perceptions, and necessary truth, that is, casualty. In reason (self-consciousness) he found the judge of the correctness of the perception of senses. One is amazed to find such unique boldness of thought in the atmosphere of a religion generally believed to be the most intolerant and fanatical. Yet, AI Gazali's skepticism was avidly studied throughout the Muslim world of his tine. His place in the history of philosophy can be judged from the opinion of the famous French Orientalist Renan, who thought that the father of modern skepticism, Hume, did not say anything more than what had been said by the Arab philosopher who preceded him by seven hundred years.

The immensity of the historical significance of Al Gazali's views is appreciated still more clearly when we remember that it was skepticism of Hume which gave impetus to Kant's "all shattering critical philosophy" that laid a cruel axe at the root of all speculative thought. But AI Gazali's views were a long way ahead of time.

Experimental science, as he visualized, was not yet possible. In the absence or infancy of technology, the nature of objects could not be as mathematically ascertained as the philosophers wished. Therefore, in his later years, AI Gazali fell into mysticism; but his fall was not more strikingly inglorious than of Kant. Objective drawbacks clipped the intrepid wings of the soaring spirit of the Arab thinker; whereas subjective predilection of class interest overwhelmed the critical genius of Kant.

Abubakr, who lived in the twelfth century, was the first astronomer to reject the Ptolemic notion regarding the position of heavenly bodies. He conceived of a planetary system, and celestial motion which tended towards the epoch-making discoveries of Giordano Bruno, Galileo and Copernicus. It is recorded that "in his systems all movements were verified, and therefore no error resulted." Abubakr dies before having set forth his theory in a complete treatise. His pupil, AI Phetragius, popularized his teaching that all planetary bodies moved regularly.

Throughout the middle-ages, the hypothesis was valued as a "great contribution to astronomical knowledge. The teachings of a Muslim philosopher, which upset the biblical view of the universe, penetrated the Christian monasteries. Not only Roger Bacon, but his illustrious opponent, Albertus Magnus, also acknowledged the indebtedness to the astronomical work of Al Phetragius in which Abubakr's views on planetary movement were expounded. The basic principle of the philosophy of Averroes, the greatest and the latest of the great Arabian thinkers, have already been outlined. He lived at the turning point of the history of the Islamic culture. By the twelfth century, the pinnacle had been reached, and the forces of reaction had gathered strength to overwhelm those of progress. Islamic culture was already on the decline.

The freedom of thought permitted by the simple faith of a nomadic people, had attained such soaring heights of boldness as eventually clashed with the temporal interests of the "Commanders of the Faithful." When the positive outcome of Islamic thought, developed so marvelously during five hundred years, was summarized in the highly revolutionary dictum of Averroes that reason is the only source of truth, Sultan Al Masur of Cordova, under the pressure of the priests, issued an edict condemning such heretical views to hell-fire, on the authority of religion.

The denunciation of the noblest product of Islam naturally marked the beginning of its degeneration from a powerful lever of human progress to an instrument of reaction, intolerance, ignorance and prejudice. Having played out its historic role-to rescue the precious patrimony of ancient culture out of the engulfing ruins of two Empires and the blinding darkness of two religions-Islam turned traitor to its original self, and became the black banner of Turkish barbarism and of the depredations of the Mongolian herds. Islam disowned its own.

Averroes was driven away from the court of Cordova-the home of free thought for centuries. His books were condemned to the flames, if not actually of fire, to those of the more merciless sacerdotal reaction. Rationalism came to be identified with heresy. The very names of Averroes and his master, Aristotle, became anathema. In course of time, reaction triumphed so completely that for an orthodox Mohammedan, philosophy stood for "infidelity, impiety, and immorality."

But the standard of spiritual progress, admirably held high, and boldly carried forward by the Arabs during five hundred years, could not be lowered and trampled under the fury of vain religiosity any more successfully by Islamic intolerance than previously by Christian piety and superstition. Averroes was disowned by his own people, only to be enthroned by those to whom belonged the future. The fierce contest between Faith and Reason, between despotic ignorance and freedom of thought, which rocked Europe and shook the foundation of the Catholic Church from the twelfth century onwards, drew inspiration from the teachings of the Arab philosophers. Averroes and Averroism dominated the scientific thought of Europe for four hundred years.

Chapter 4

Analysis and Formulations

Vedic civilization is the earliest civilization in Indian history of which we have written records that we understand. It is named after the Vedas, the early literature of the Hindu people. The Vedic Civilization flourished along the river Saraswati, in a region that now consists of the modern Indian states of Haryana and Punjab. The Vedic texts have astronomical dates, that some have claimed, go back to the 5th millennium BC. The use of Vedic Sanskrit continued up to the 6th century BC. Vedic is synonymous with Aryans and Hinduism, which is another name for religious and spiritual thought that has evolved from the Vedas.

The Early Aryans

Unfortunately, the origin of the Saraswati Valley civilization (Vedic culture) and its relation to the Indus Valley civilization remain hazy. The timeline of Vedic civilization is 4500 BC-1800 BC while that of Indus valley civilization is 3300 BC-1800 BC. The texts describe a geography that some believe to be north India.

The greatest river of the Rigveda was Saraswati, now dry and identified with Ghaggar, a seasonal river. It is believed that this river ceased to reach the Arabian Sea by about 1900 BC. Now, a dry river bed, that seems to fit the description of the Saraswati River, has been detected by satellite imagery. It begins in the modern Indian state of Uttaranchal and passing through Haryana,Punjab, and Rajasthan, reaches the Arabian Sea in Gujarat. Our knowledge of the early Aryans comes from the Rigveda, the earliest of theVedas.

Political Organization

The grama (village), vis and jana were political units of the early Aryans. A vis was probably a subdivision of a jana and a grama was probably a smaller unit than the other two. The leader of a grama was called gramani and that of a vis was called vispati. Another unit was the gana whose head was a jyeshta (elder). The rashtra (state) was governed by a rajan (king). The king is often referred to as gopa (protector) and samrat (supreme ruler). He governed the people with their consent and approval. It is possible that he was sometimes elected.

The sabha and samiti were popular councils. The main duty of the king was to protect the tribe. He was aided by two functionaries, the purohita (chaplain) and the senani (army chief; sena: army). The former not only gave advice to the ruler but also practiced spells and charms for success in war. Soldiers on foot (patti) and on chariots (rathins), armed with bow and arrow were common. The king employed spasa (spies) and dutas (messengers). He often got a ceremonial gift, bali, from the people.

Society and Economy

Rig Vedic society was characterized by a nomadic lifestyle with cattle rearing being the chief occupation. The Aryans kept hordes of cattle and cows were held in high esteem. Milk was an important part of the diet.

Agriculture was equally important and went hand in hand with cattle rearing. It grew more prominent with time as the community settled down. The cow was also the standard unit of barter; coins were not used in this period. Families were patrilineal, and people prayed for abundance of sons. Education of women was not neglected, and some even composed Rig Vedic hymns.

Marriage for love as well as for money was known. The concept of caste and hereditary nature of profession was unknown to the early Aryans. The food of the early Aryans consisted of parched grain and cakes, milk and milk products, and fruits and vegetables. Consumption of meat was common.

A passage in the Rig Veda describes how to apportion the meat of a sacrificed horse. It must be borne in mind that vegetarianism took firm root in India only after the rise of Buddhism in the sixth century BC.

Literature and Religion

Vedic or Hindu literature consists primarily of the Vedas; but also includes Shruti and various Smriti texts. The Vedic rites were meant to help the participant transform; this was primarily accomplished via sacrifices (such as the agnihotra).

Astronomical references in the Vedas help provide some broad approximations that help date the beginning of the tradition. Due to the precession of the equinoxes, the seasons shift with relation to the fixed zodiac at a rate of about a month every two thousand years. Some Vedic notices mark the beginning of the year at the vernal equinox in Orion; this was the case around 4500 BC.

The rishis saw the universe as going through unceasing change in a cycle of birth and death, free and yet, paradoxically, governed by order. This order was reflected in the bandhu (connections) between the planets, the elements of the body, and the mind. At the deepest level, the whole universe was bound to, and reflected in, the individual consciousness.

The place of sacrifice represents the cosmos. The three fires used stand for the three divisions of space. The course of the sacrifice represents the year, and all such ritual forms part of continuing annual performances. The rite culminates in the ritual rebirth of the yajamana (sacrificer), which signifies the regeneration of his universe. It is sacred theatre, built upon paradoxes of reality, where symbolic deaths of animals and humans, including the yajamana himself, may be enacted.

The Vedic gods represent the cognitive centres of the self. Vedic science is the science of consciousness. These have evolved into the Hindu paths of Yoga and Vedanta, which is a religious path that is the 'essence' of the Vedas.

The Vedic pantheon is considered to consist of thirty-three different gods, which are placed, in groups of eleven, into one of the three different categories: atmospheric, terrestrial, or celestial, each of which has its own area of responsibility. But just because a god is in one category does not mean that it is completely different from a god from another category; for sometimes a god from one category will have some of the same qualities of a god from another category.

This is because the Vedic system is recursive. It has developed into a broader group but it is also seen in Vedic philosophy that they are manifestations of one divine ground known as Brahman. This thought of unity is expressed severally in Vedic texts.

The categories of the gods are: 1) Agni, terrestrial; 2) Indra, atmospheric; and 3) Surya or Vishnu, celestial that mirrors the body, prana, and atman division of the individual. Since one aspires to reach the inner being through the prana (atmosphere), many Vedic hymns extol Indra.

The Vedic or Hindu religion presents a unitary view of the universe with God seen as immanent and transcendent in the forms of Ishvara and Brahman, respectively. Brahman is projected into various deities in the human mind. The main deities were Indra, Varuna, Surya (the Sun), Mitra, Vayu, Agni and Soma. Goddesses included Prithvi, Aditi, Ushas and Saraswati. Deities were not viewed as all-powerful. The relationship between the devotee and the deity was one of transaction. Each deity had a specific role; at any given point, a particular deity was considered superior to the others.

The mode of worship was performance of sacrifices and chanting of verses. The priests helped the common man in performing rituals. People prayed for abundance of children, cattle and wealth.

Later Vedic Period

The transition from the early to the later Vedic period was marked by the emergence of agriculture as the dominant economic activity and a corresponding decline in the significance of cattle rearing. Several changes went hand in hand with this. For instance, several large kingdoms arose because of the increasing importance of land and its protection.

Kingdoms

Several small kingdoms merged to form a few large ones which were often at war with each other. 16 mahajanapadas (great kingdoms) are referred to in some of the literature. By this time the Aryan tribes had spread from their original home in the west to much of the east and the south. The power of the king greatly increased. Rulers gave themselves titles like ekarat (the one ruler), sarvabhumi (ruler of all the earth) and chakravartin (protector of land). Note that in early Vedic times he was called gopa, protector of cows. The kings performed sacrifices like rajasuya, (royal consecration) vajapeya (drink of strength) and ashvamedha (horse sacrifice). The coronation ceremony was a major social occasion. Several functionaries came into being in addition to the purohita and the senani of earlier times. The participation of the people in the activities of the government decreased.

Society

The concept of varna and the rules of marriage became rigid, but not yet watertight. The status of the Brahmanas and Kshatriyas increased greatly. To legitimize their position and the increase their power, the Brahmanas proliferated a large number of sacrifices, developed extreme specialization, and also restricted social mobility. The proper enunciation of verses was considered essential for prosperity and success in war. Kshatriyas amassed wealth, and commissioned the performance of sacrifices. Many rituals emerged to strengthen the alliance between these two groups. But the varna system in India has remained fluid.

RIG VEDIC

The principal and, taken in its totality, the oldest of the four Vedic hymnbodies is the Rig-Veda. On this page I am primarily interested in the Reg-Veda of the early Vedic age. Although some later expository material seems to me to be consistent with the fundamental wisdom of the Vedas, I do not think that some other later material, such as, for example, the caste system of orders of human beings, is consistentwith the fundamental wisdom of the Vedas. The Sanskrit word ric, which for euphonic reasons is changed to rig, means literally"praise"... The Sanskrit word veda means literally"knowledge" or"wisdom"... The Rig-Veda is the oldest book in the Sanskrit language, indeed in any Indo-European language. More than that, if we are correct, it is the oldest book in the world... The fact that the Rig-Veda mentions a stellar configuration that corresponds to a date from 6000 B.C. to 7000 B.C. - the astronomical Ashvini era [according to Underworld, by Graham Hancock, quoting David Frawley:"... when the [winter] solstice first entered [the constellation of] Ashwini (i.e., when the winter solstice was at or very near the constellation of Aries)]... - must not be... denied... this date takes us back to the beginnings of the Indic civilization at the town of Mehgarh... in eastern Pakistan (Baluchistan)...[whre]... excavations have yielded the... date of around 6500 B.C... Writing about two thousand years ago, Greek historians Pliny and Arrian, who based themselveson reports from the ambassadors at the Maurya courts, mention that the native historical tradition of India knew of 154 kings, ruling over a period of 6,450 years.

When we reconstruct this tradition, it appears that during Mauryan times the calendar was taken to commence in 6676 B.C...". The 8 first generation fermion particles, the 8 first generation fermion antiparticles, and an 8-dimensional spacetime in the D4-D5-E6-E7-E8 VoDou Physics model, and all 24 form the vertices of a 24-cell.

According to The Constitution of the Universe by Maharishi Mahesh Yogi, printed in newspapers including The Sunday Times, The Sunday Telegraph Financial Times, The Guardian, The Wall Street Journal and The Washington Post a copy of which was sent to me in pamphlet form by John Small in August 2003:

"... modern science has systematically revealed deeper layers of order in nature, from the atomic to the nuclear and subnuclear levels of nature's functioning...

... the ancient Vedic wisdom... identifies a single, universal source of all orderliness in nature...

Both understandings, modern and ancient, locate the unfied source of nature's perfect order in a single, self-interacting field of intelligence at the foundation of all the laws of nature... The self-interacting dynamics of this unified field constitutes the most basic level of nature's dynamics.

The laws governing the self-interacting dynamics of the unified field can therefore be called the Constitution of the Universe... In Maharishi's Vedic Science... the Constitution of the Universe... is embodied in the very structure of the sounds of the Rik Ved, the most fundamental aspect of the Vedic literature.

According to Maharishi's Apaurusheya Bhashya, the structure of the Ved provides its own commentary - a commentary which is contained in the sequential unfoldment of the Ved itself in its various stages of expression. The knowledge of the total Ved... is contained in the first sukt of the Rik Ved, which is presented below and is also shown above, all on one line:

The precise sequence of sounds is highly significant; it is in the sequential progression of sound and silence thatthe true meaning and content of the Ved reside - not on the level of intellectual meanings ascribed to the Ved in the various translations.

The complete knowledge of the Ved contained in the first sukt (stanza) is also found in the first richa (verse) - the first twenty-four syllables of the first sukt (stanza 1). This complete knowledge is again contained in the first pad, or first eight syllables of the first richa, and is also found in the first syllable of the Ved, 'AK', which contains the total dynamics of consciousness knowing itself. [compare the 64 hexagrams of the I Ching which come from the 8 trigramswhich in turn come from Yin-Yang]

AK' describes the collapse of the fullness of consciousness (A) within itself to its own point value (K). [compare the quantum decoherence/collapse of superpositions of tubulin elecctron states in the formation of a thought in the human brain] This collapse, which represents the eternal dynamics of consciousness knowing itself, occurs in eight successive stages.

In the next stage of unfoldment of the Ved, these eight stages of collapse are separately elabourated in the eight syllables of the first pad, which emerges from, and provides a further commentary on, the first syllable of Rik Ved, 'AK'. These eight syllables correspond to the eight 'Prakritis' (Ahamkar, etc.) or eight fundamental qualities of intelligence...[compare the 8-dimensional real Clifford algebra of the D4-D5-E6-E7-E8 VoDou Physics modeland its 8-fold Periodicity leading to a Clifford Tensor Product Universe]...

The first line, or 'richa', of the first sukt, comprising 24 syllables, provides a further commentary on the first pad;

- The first pad expresses the eight Prakritis... with respect to the knower... observer... or 'Rishi' quality of pure consciousness.
- The second pad expresses the eight Prakritis with respect to the process of knowing... process of observation... of 'Devata' (dynamism) quality of pure consciousness.
- The third pad expresses the eight Prakritis with respect to the known... observed... or 'Chhandas' quality of pure consciousness... [compare the 3 pads with Triality]

The subsequent eight lines complete the remainder of the first sukt - the next stage of sequential unfoldment of knowledge in the Ved.

These eight lines consist of 24 padas (phrases), comprising 8 × 24 = 192 syllables. [compare the 192-element Weyl group of Spin(8), whose root vector polytope is the 24-cell, and whose Lie algebra comes from the bivectors of the Cl(8) Clifford Algebra]... these 24 padas of eight syllables elabourate the unmanifest, eight-fold structure o fhe 24 gaps between the syllables of the first richa (verse)... Ultimately, in the subsequent stages of unfoldment, these 192 syllables of ther first sukt (stanza) get elabourated in the 192 [?or is it 191?] suktas that comprise the first mandal (circular cyclical eternal structure) of the Rik Ved, which in turn gives rise to the rest of the Ved and the entire Vedic literature...".

Note that:

- the first richa of the first sukt has 24 syllables plus 24 gaps (if you include a silent gap at the beginning/ end to close the first sukt into a circle) and
- those 24 gaps are made relevant by being elabourated by the following 8 richas of the first sukt, which have 192 syllables so that the total number of relevant entities in the first sukt is 24+24+192 = 240, which is the number of vertices of the root vector polytope of the E8 Lie algebra.

Since the E8 Lie algebra has rank 8, it has dimension 240+8 = 248, and the 2^8 = 256-dimensional real Clifford algebra Cl(8) (or Cl(1,7) if you pay attention to signature) can be constructed as,

Cl(8) = E8 + 8-dimensional vector space.

Contains the structure of both: the D4-D5-E6-E7-E8 VoDou Physics model; and the 256-element structure of IFA = VoDou.

In my opinion, the Rig Veda may be the earliest reduction to writing of the original African-based orally transmitted early global wisdom of IFA = VoDou, and, as the earliest, it may be the most nearly complete written description of that wisdom.

The Rig Veda is the book of Mantra. It contains the oldest form of all the Sanskrit mantras. It is built around a science of sound which comprehends the meaning and power of each letter.

Most aspects of Vedic science like the practice of yoga, meditation, mantra and Ayurveda can be found in the Rig Veda and still use many terms that come from it... While originally several different versions or rescensions of the Rig Veda were said to exist, only one remains. Its form has been structured in several different ways to guarantee its authenticity and proper preservation through time.

The Rig Veda consists of the hymns to various aspects of the Divine as seen by various seers, called the "rishis". There are seven primary seers, identified not only in India but also in Persia and China with the seven stars of the Big Dipper. Their names are Atri, Kanwa, Vasishta, Vishwamitra, Jamadagni, Gotama and Bharadvaja, but they appear even in the hymns of these sages and may refer to an earlier group. They relate to the guiding lights of the seven chakras. The main family of the seers was called the Angirasas (a term related to the Greek Angelos and our English word angel)...

The Rig Veda is composed of ten books (called mandalas in Sanskrit). Seven of the books each relate primarily to one great seer and the family he belongs to;

- The first book is a collection of hymns from seers of different families, mainly earlier ones.
- The second book belongs to Gritsamada and his family, the Bhrigus;
- The third relates to Vishwamitra and his family;
- The fourth to Vamadeva and the Gotama family;
- The fifth to Atri and his family;
- The sixth to Bharadvaja and his family;
- The seventh to Vasishta and his family; and
- The eighth to the Kanwas.
- The ninth book is the collection of Soma hymns mainly from the Bhrigus and Angirasas. It is largely outside of and earlier than the family books.
- The tenth book is a collection of various earlier and later hymns.

As John Small said in e-mail: " The first encapsulates the whole thing, the Tenth complements the first and "fills in the gaps"... in the first, the remaining 8 form a sequence that is the expansion of the 8 fundamental forms displayed in the first sukta...". It is interesting that the central 8 correspond to the 7 seers plus 1 about Soma, similar to the 8 octonions corresponding to the 7 imaginary octonions plus 1 real octonion. The term "fills in the gaps" might mean that the tenth book explains the silent spaces between spoken/written syllables in the first book.

Each hymn is given to a certain deity (devata). The main deities are Indra, Agni, Soma and Surya... each of the Gods has his consort, like Indra and Indrani, Varuna and Varunani...

- Indra is the God of Prana or the awakened life-force...
- Agni is the God of consciousness, awareness and mindfulness. His symbol is the sacred fire...

- Soma is the mystic plant that yields the nectar of immortality. He is also the Moon and the lord of the waters. He symbolizes bliss, Ananda.
- Surya is the Sun which is the visible face and presence of the Deity. He symbolizes the enlightened mind and creative intelligence. He is the Divine creator and transformer.
- Varuna, the lord of the cosmic ocean and the Divine judge;
- Mitra the Divine friend and lord of compassion and
- Savitar, the Sun God of creative intelligence...
- Usha, the Goddess of the Dawn or spiritual aspiration;
- Saraswati, the Goddess of the Divine Word, of wisdom and inspiration;
- Aditi the Goddess of Infinite Oneness and Wholeness;...
- Apas, the Cosmic Waters...
- Brahma... the creator... is Brihaspati, also called Brahmanaspati, the priest of the Gods.
- Vishnu... the maintainer... is an important form of the Sun God and later all forms of the Sun God were merged into him. [Avatars of Vishnu include Rama and Krishna]
- Shiva... the destroyer... is present as Rudra, the seldom invoked but very much respected and feared father of all the Gods. Ganesha is a son of Shiva...

Collective deities exist like the Adityas, the solar deities, the Maruts or Rudras, Gods of the storm, the Ribhus or Divine craftsmen and the Vishvedevas, literally the universal Gods who symbolize the unity of all the Gods... Each God or Goddess can be any or all the Gods.

The concepts of monotheism, polytheism, pantheism and monism are all woven together in the Vedic vision of totality. The Divine is seen as both One and Many without contraction...".

Feuerstein, Kak, and Frawley, in their book In Search of the Cradle of Civilization (Quest 1995) also say:

Vedic cosmology evolved in conjunction with a complex system of sacrificial ritualism... the rituals are not to be done mechanically but with full attention and proper control of body, mind, speech, and breath. In other words, the constitute a form of yogic practice...

The Vedic rituals were generally performed at an altar... meant to symbolize the universe at large... the fire altars were surrounded by 360 enclosing stones; of these, 21... corresponded to... the earth..., 78...[to]... the atmosphere..., and 261...[to]... the sky... the two principal cosmological numbers were 21 and 339 (78+261)...

The Rig-Veda... was itself taken to represent a symbolic altar. Thus the number of syllables in the Rig-Veda is supposed to add up to the number of muhurtas (1 day = 30 muhurtas) in forty years, which is 432,000... In reality, however, the syllable count of the Rig-Veda is somewhat less... 397,265... compare the Torah because certain syllables are meant to be left unspoken...

Not counting the eleven supplemental hymns, the Rig-Veda consists of 1017 (or 3x339) hymns distributed over 10 books and gathered into 216 groups...

Books	Hymns	Groups
1	191	15
2	43	5
3	62	4
4	58	11
5	87	7
6	75	5
7	104	12
8	92	18
9	114	7
10	191	132

These groups are the natural divisions based on authorship, subject, or metre...

- The first four books contain 354 hymns, which correspond to the length of the lunar year...
- The total number of hymns in the middle four

books... is 324, which equals the nakshatra (constellation) year of 12x27 days. When this is multiplied by a close approximation of pi, we arrive at 1017, which corresponds to the number of hymns in the entire Rig-Vedic collection (excludng eleven supplemental hymns)...

- The number 108, which is one-half the number of hymn groups... is roughly the average distance between the Sun and the Earth in terms of solar diametres. It is also the average distance between the Moon and Earth in terms of lunar diametres... For example, if a pole of a certain height were to be separated from the observer by a distance that is 108 times this height, its angular size would be... equal to that of the Sun or the Moon... 108 beads are used in Hindu rosaries...
- 339... is simply the number of solar disks it takes to measure the Sun's path across the sky during equinox: pi × 108 = circa 339...
- The actual - rather than the idea - Vedic year was reckoned as consisting of 366 days... divided into two equal parts of 183 days... the ancients sought to reconcile the 339 steps of the Sun with th symbolic value of 183... by postulating a value of 78 for the atmosphere, since 339 - 183 + 2 × 78...
- The Rig-Veda speaks of the thirty-four"lights", which are the twenty-seven lunar constellations..., the five planets, and the Sun and the Moon...
- ... A tithi was reckoned as a 360th part of the lunar year... somewhat shorter than a day... There are 371 tithis in a year of 365 plus days, and when we multiply... by 9 we arrive at 3339... the total number of deities given in the Rig-Veda...

The sacred syllable om... is said to be the quintessence of the Vedas... The syllable om is not mentioned in the Rig-Veda, possibly because it was deemed too sacred to be spoken out loud [compare the Torah, in which the name of g-d is not to be written completely; and the Taoist Dao De Ching]... In one

Rig-Vedic hymn (I.164.39)... we may have an oblique reference to the sacred syllable om... also, no graphic representation of om has so far been found in the excavated Indus towns... om is first named or written out...in such Vedic scriptures as the Shukla-Yjur-Veda...".

Note that Maharishi says that the first Mandal of the Rig-Veda has 192 Suktas, while Feuerstein, Kak, and Frawley say that it (the first book) has 191 hymns (Suktas).

John Small told me by e-mail that: Maharishi considers the 192nd Sukta to be"... the"Avyukta Sukta", it means the"empty sukta" and it's just a complete absence of any sound at all. It complements the first sukta, and with it in place you can line up the first mandala in a circle with each sukta matching up to another diametrically opposite in the circle... The Avyukta Sukta... In Maharishi's scheme... there are two processes in operation, one the collapse from fullness to emptyness and then the expansion from emptyness back to fullness... in terms of Goedel's Theorems, any formal system that is complete must be inconsistent, that is it must contain a statement that negates the system itself...".

To see how the cycle of 192 Suktas in the first Mandal, start with a given system T. Then as you process that system you will find a Godelian undecidable thing A and then Maharishi's Avyukta (= avyakta = unmanifest) Sukta is used to make T"more complete" by adding A (true and false) as new propositions to make it a"pair" of possible systems like a quantum superposition of two possible worlds of the Many-Worlds:

S = T + Atrue combined with T + Afalse and then, you start again with the system S and process it again to find a new Godelian undecidable thing B - this is a second collapse"collapse" - and then expand again with Avyukta Sukta to get a"newer bigger"

R = S + Btrue combined with S + Bfalse giving you twice again as many possible quantum worlds, and you continue the process ad infinitum.

Each half-cycle T to A, S to B, etc..., corresponds to the first 191 Suktas of the first Mandal of the Rig Veda.

Each half-cycle A to S, B to R, etc..., corresponds to to the 192nd empty = soundless Avyukta Sukta, which constructs the helix covering the closed circle of the first Mandala.

Each cycle T to S, S to R, etc..., corresponds to introducing new branches: In the possible quantum worlds of the Many-Worlds Quantum Theory.

The"whole Veda" is therefore nothing that you can ever write down in any finite number of steps, but is an infinitely ranched Many-Worlds Tree of Helical Coils, with its Total Sound being OM, which is therefore, as John Small says,"... The OM sound is the sound of the whole of the Veda from a distance... like listening to a bee hive from a distance. Then as you get close you can distinguish the individual sounds themselves until finally you can experience each separate bit quite clearly...".

The process of a human trying to"tune in" to part of the"whole Veda" is a self-referential loop involving the Quantum Consciousness of the human brain.

In order to ensure that the Vedas can be repromulgated for future mankind after each pralaya... destruction and rebirth [as by floods at the end of an Ice Age about 11,600 years ago]... the gods have... designed an institution to preserve them... the Seven Sages... Sapta Rishis... a brotherhood of adepts... who reincarnate from age to age as the guides of civilization and the guardians of cosmic justice...[They] survive[d] the deluge in the Ark with Manu... According to Bal Ganghadar Tilak: The Vedas were destroyed in the deluge... the Sages... reproduced... the antediluvian Vedas...

Seven Sages in both the Sumerian and Vedic traditions...[have]... similarities...

- Both groups are associated with fish symbolism of some sort - the Seven Sages of Sumer are themselves half men, half fish, and the Vedic Seven Sages take refuge on Manu's survival ship, which is towed by a gigantic fish...
- Both groups of sages perform an identical function - which is to preserve the gifts of civilization and bring them to mankind in their respective areas...

The Rig Veda conjures up a compelling image of a demon in the form of a great dragon, or serpent, that has wrapped itself around the ice-covered mountain ranges... and strangled seven great rivers.

The name of the demon is sometimes Ahi but more often Vrta and the story of how he is slain by the god Indra and of how the seven rivers are freed, is repeated again and again in the hymns of the Rig Veda [compare the Chinese Jade Emperor Yu Di of about 4,200 years ago]...".

VEDIC MUSIC

According to the Hindu view of creation, it was sound and not light that appeared first. In Vedic parlance it is called Nada Brahma or the Sound Celestial. Vedic rishis believed that the evolution of the Brahmand or universe was caused as a result of Bindu Vsphot or an atomic explosion, that produced infinite waves of sound, which represent cosmic ascent and expansion.

The sound was a monosyllable: Om. Since Om is related to the beginning of the universe, Hindus consider it the most sacred syllable with which Vedic mantras commence. Om is the principal name of the Supreme Being. It refers to all that it manifest and beyond...

According to Vedic literature music originated from nada or sound, which is the product of akash or ether: There are two types of sound. The ahat or struck sound is audible whereas the anahata or unstruck sound is inaudible. Sound originates in living beings from the friction between air ñ pran vayu or vital breath and agni or heat energy (will power). It evolves first in a causal forms as anahata and then in the gross form of sound emanates from the vocal chord and is sweet and soothing, it is called snageetam or music. The anahata nada is most significant for yogis who have reached the highest level of consciousness. It is the internal sound they hear, after prolonged meditation and ardous yogic discipline. Ordinary human beings are engaged with the ahat nada.

Indian musical traditions trace the origin of music to the Sama Veda. It is a compendium of melodies, chants and rules required for the recitation of sacred hymns. It serves as a textbook for priests officiating at Soma sacrifices... Vedic chants are set in a musical pattern, collectively known as Samgan. To this day, the chants are in three accented musical patterns called swaras, precursor of the present seven-note musical system...".

According to an Indian Classical Vedas are considered the source of Indian Music, it should not be assumed that classical music in its present form was fully developed by then. Infact, concept of Raga, Tala, Shruti or even Nava Rasas come only later.

All except SamaVeda were sung using only three notes, Anudaatta (low), Udaatta(middle) and Svarita(high). As used today the Anudaatta, Udaatta and Svarita svaras of RigVeda, can be equated with Ni, Sa, and Ri of the North Indian Kafi scale (Kharaharapriya of the Carnatic). In early manuscrpts of RigVeda, the text was written along with accent notes. Anudaatta is marked with an underline and Svarita is marked with a small vertical line above the syllable. Udaatta is left unmarked.

Sama Veda consists of about 1900 verses, called samans. Ninety-five per cent of the verses of Sama Veda Samhita are in Rig Veda Samhita. One can see from the text of the Sama Veda mantra that the chanting notation in it is much more elabourate than that in the corresponding Rig Veda mantra. SamaVeda was chanted using all seven notes (prathama, dvitheeya, tritheeya, chathurtha, panchama, shashta and sapthama), in descending order, of the Vaidika scale (or of sama gana) which have been equated to (Ma,Ga,Ri,Sa, Dha,Ni,Pa) of the Laukika or Gandhara scale in later classical sanskrit texts like NaradiyaShiksha.

RigVedic hymns are directed at Gods, to be chanted during sacrifices to please them. It is possible Gods were thought to be fond of music and that it would be easier to please them if the hymns were sung rather than just chanted. Thus, many of the Rig Vedic hymns were set to music and sung and were known as samans, rather than just hymns (Rik). The chanted Sama-Veda hymns or Samans were believed to possess the supernatural qualities capable of petitioning and even supporting the deities that controlled the forces of the universe. Since Rig Vedic hymns are just metreed they could not be sung using all the seven notes. Thus started a tradition of insertion of a number of seemingly `meaningless' words or syllables(stobha) for musical and lyrical effect, such as o, hau, hoyi, va, etc. It was these stobha syllables which were extended vocally with long duration on various notes of the Sama-Veda scale by the priests who had the special function of summoning the gods to the celebration through the use of droning (monotone) on a number of these tones, believing them to hold magical properties. The wife of the chief sacrificer (i.e. chief priest, brahmana) would play the Vina, during sacrifices.

Precise methods of singing the Samans were established and preserved in three different schools, the Kauthumas, Ranayaniyas, and the Jaiminiyas, the oldest. Each has maintained a distinct style with regard to vowel prolongation, interpolation and repetition of stobha, metre, phonetics, and the number of notes in scales. Accordingly, there has been a fervent regard for maintaining continuity in Sama-Veda singing to avoid misuse or modification over many years. Since written texts were not in use, in fact prohibited, the priests memorized the chants with the aid of accents and melodies, and passed this tradition down orally from one generation to the next for over three thousand years...".

Indian Music is probably the most complex musical system in the world with a very highly developed melodic and rhythmic structure. This (structure) includes complicated poly-rhythms, delicate nuances, ornamentations and microtones which are essential characteristics of Indian music. This makes it very difficult to notate every detail in Indian music.

Originally Indian music was passed on by oral tradition... from one generation to another for centuries. The music was never written down until much later. The notation system was actually developed much later more as a memory-aid than something from which to learn or something from which to perform. This is why the tradition wherein the student learns from a Guru on a"one-on-one" basis is considered to be the only real way to learn music since there are so many aspects that cannot be learned from a book because the existing notations are only a skeletal representation of the music.

Indian Music had its origins in the Vedas... Four in number, the Vedas are the most sacred texts which contain about a thousand hymns. They were used to preserve a body of poetry, invocations and mythology in the form of sacrificial chants dedicated to the Gods. Great care was taken to preserve the text, which was passed down by oral tradition, so much so that both the text and the rituals remain unchanged to this day. The literature of the Vedas is divided into four parts: the Rig Veda, the Sama Veda, the Yajur Veda and the Atharva Veda.

- The oldest, the Rig... was recited, at first, in a monotone; it was later developed to three tones (one main tone, and two accents, one higher and the other lower called Udatta and Anudatta respectively.) This was done to accentuate the words since the text was of primary importance.
- The Yajur Veda which mainly consists of sacrificial formulas mentions the Veena as an accompaniment to vocal recitations during the sacrifices. By this time, the chants had evolved to two main notes with two accents forming the first concept of the tetrachord (four notes.)
- The Sama Veda laid the foundation for Indian Music. The origin of Indian Music can be traced back to this Veda. Three more notes were added to the original tetrachord resulting in the first full scale of seven notes; within this scale were all the important and known musical intervals. The concept of the octave is also mentioned here.
- The Atharva Veda was a collection of formulas that deal with... spells. The text of the Vedas is in Sanskrit, the classical language of India.

The period of the Epics, the Ramayana and the Mahabharata (500 B.C. - 200 A.D.) saw the development of the Jati system on which the modern Raga system is based. Also, various melodic and percussion instruments are mentioned during this time. Mention must be made of the Natyashastra, a treatise written by Bharata in 300 B.C. It is the most authoritative and ancient work on the classical science of music and dance...".

Love, humour, pathos, anger, heroism, terror, disgust, wonder and serenity are the nava rasas or nine basic emotions which are fundamental to all Indian aesthetics. Sage Bharata, the earliest Indian musicologist said to have lived in the 1st or 2nd century AD, enunciated these moods and believed that it was the musician's task to evoke a particular emotion or mood. The classical music tradition in India is based on the principles enunciated by sage Bharata and continues to be a form of meditation, concentration and worship.

The Raga, or musical mode, forms the basis of the entire musical event. The Raga is essentially an aesthetic rendering of the seven musical notes and each Raga is said to have a specific flavour and mood. Tala is what binds music together. It is essentially a fixed time cycle for each rendition and repeats itself after completion of each cycle. Tala makes possible a lot of improvisations between beats and allows complex variations between each cycle.

With the help of the Raga, Tala and the infinite shrutis or microtones, Indian musicians create a variety of feelings...".

Vedic Hymns are considered the foundation of later styles (like Gregorian chants)... Physical vibrations of musical sound (nada) is connected to spiritual world...

Raga and Tala form the basis of Indian music:

- Raga (rag in North, ragam in Tamil)... a scalar melody form including basic scale and basic melodic structure. Sanskrit ranj means to colour with emotion Scale of raga is shown in both ascending and descending form. Some raga include notes changing directions Some notes may have specific ornamentation (gamaka) Ground tone (beginning tone) is sa (like do in do re mi) Sa is most important note of the drone... Later... 72 possible combinations [compare 72 root vector elements of E6]...

- Tala = cyclic measure of time (rhythm) [compare toque of IFA] Laya = tempo (fast or slow) Druta = fast Madhya = medium Vilambita = slow Matra (Hindustani) or Akshara (Karnatak) = basic beat (like metronome) Tala cycle (Vibhaga or avarta) andendash; varies from 3 to 128 beats in length; 7-16 are common...". [compare 3 quaternion imaginaries and 3-sphere, 7 octonion imaginaries, 16 spinors of Cl(8) and 16 eyes of FA, and 128 elements of the even Clifford subalgebra Cl(8)e

SANSKRIT AND INFORMATION

According to Knowledge Representation in Sanskrit and Artificial Intelligence, by Rick Briggs: There is a widespread belief that natural languages arc unsuitable for th transmission of many ideas that artificial languages can render with great precision and mathematical rigor... But... There is at least one language, Sanskrit, which for the duration of almost 1000 years was a living spoken language with a considerable literature of its own Besides works of literary value, there was a long philosophical and grammatical tradition that has continued to exist with undiminished vigour until the present century. Among the accomplishments of the grammarians can be reckoned a method for paraphrasing Sanskrit in a manner that is identical not only in essence but in form with current work in Artificial Intelligence This article demonstrates that a natural language can serve as an artificial language also, and that much work in AI has been reinventing a wheel millenia old...

Hierarchical structure... and... explicit descriptions of set-relations are essential to really capture... meaning... and to facilitate inference. It is believed by most in the AI and general linguistic.community that natural languages do not make such seemingly trivial hierarchies explicit. Below is a description of a natural language, Shastric Sanskrit, where for the past millenia successful attempts have been made to encode such information.

The sentence:

- "Caitra goes to the village." (graamam gacchati caitra)

Receives in the analysis given by an eighteenth-century Sanskrit Grammarian from Maharashtra, India, the following paraphrase:

- "There is an activity which leads to a connection-activity which has as Agent no one other than Caitra, specified by singularity, [which] is taking place in the present and which has as Object something not different from 'village'."

The author, Nagesha, is one of a group of three or four prominent theoreticians who stand at the end of a long tradition of investigation. Its beginnings date to the middle of the first millennium B.C. when the morphology and phonological structure of the language, as well as the framework for its syntactic description were codified by Panini. His successors elucidated the brief, algebraic formulations that he had used as grammatical rules and where possible tried to improve upon them. A great deal of fervent grammatical research took place between the fourth century B.C and the fourth century A.D. and culminated in the seminal work, the Vakyapadiya by Bhartrhari.

Little was done subsequently to advance the study of syntax, until the so-called "New Grammarian" school appeared in the early part of the sixteenth century with the publication of Bhattoji Dikshita's Vaiyakarana-bhusanasara and its commentary by his relative Kaundabhatta, who worked from Benares. Nagesha (1730-1810) was responsible for a major work, the Vaiyakaranasiddhantamanjusa, or Treasury of definitive statements of grammarians, which was condensed later into the earlier described work. These books have not yet been translated. The reasoning of these authors is couched in a style of language that had been developed especially to formulate logical relations with scientific precision.

It is a terse, very condensed form of Sanskrit, which paradoxically at times becomes so abstruse that a commentary is necessary to clarify it. One of the main differences between the Indian approach to language analysis and that of most of the current linguistic theories is that the analysis of the sentence was not based on a noun-phrase model with its attending binary parsing technique but instead on a conception that viewed the sentence as springing from the semantic message that the speaker wished to convey. In its origins, sentence description was phrased in terms of a generative model: From a number of primitive syntactic categories (verbal action, agents, object, etc.) the structure of the sentence was derived so that every word of a sentence could be referred back to the syntactic input categories... It should be pointed out that these Sanskrit Grammatical Scientists actually wrote and talked this way.

The domain for this type of language was the equivalent of today's technical journals. In their ancient journals and in verbal communication with each other they used this specific, unambiguous form of Sanskrit in a remarkably concise way... it would seem that detailed analyses of sentences and discourse units had just received a great impetus from Nagesha, when history intervened: The British conquered India and brought with them new... means for studying and analyzing languages. The subsequent introduction of Western methods of language analysis... has for a long time acted as an impediment to further research along the traditional ways. Lately, however, serious and responsible research into Indian semantics has been resumed, especially at the University of Poona, India...

The main point in which the two lines of thought [AI computer language and Sanskrit] have converged is that the decomposition of each prose sentence into karaka-representations of action and focal verbal-action, yields the same set of triples as those which result from the decomposition of a semantic net into nodes, arcs, and labels.

It is interesting to speculate as to why the Indians found it worthwhile to pursue studies into unambiguous coding of natural language into semantic elements. It is tempting to think of them as computer scientists without the hardware, but a possible explanation is that a search for clear, unambiguous understanding is inherent in the human being. Let us not forget that among the great accomplishments of the Indian thinkers were the invention of zero, and of the binary number system a thousand years before the West re-invented them...".

Chapter 5

Indian Civilization

The apparently sudden rise and the dramatic expansion of Mohammedanism constitutes a most fascinating chapter in the history of mankind. A dispassionate study of great importance in the present fateful period of the history of India. The scientific value of the study by itself is great, and the meritorious quest for knowledge is sure to be handsomely rewarded. But with us, to-day in India, particularly with the Hindu, a proper understanding of the historical role of Islam and the contribution it has made to human culture has acquired a supreme political importance.

This country has become the home of a very considerable number of the followers of the Arabian Prophet. One seldom realises that many more Mohammedans live in India than in any single purely Islamic country. Still, after the lapse of many centuries, this numerous section of the Indian population is generally considered to be an extraneous element. This curious but extremely regrettable cleft in the loose national structure of India has its historical cause. The Mohammedans originally came to India as invaders. They conquered the country and became its rulers for several hundred years. That relation of the conqueror and the subjugated has left its mark on the history of our nation which to-day embraces the both. But the unpleasant memory of the past relation has been progressively eclipsed by the present companionship in slavery. The effect of British Imperialism is no less painful and ruinous for the bulk of the Muslim population than for the masses professing Hinduism. So completely have the Mohammedans become an integral part of the Indian nation that the annals of the Muslim rule are justly recorded as history of India. Indeed, Nationalism has gone farther in effacing the painful memory of the past.

The practice of seeking consolation for the shame of the present in the real or legendary glory of the past has dressed the Muslim rulers of India in brilliant national colours.

Yet, a Hindu, who prides in the prosperity of the reign of an Akbar, or boasts of the architectural accomplishments of a Shahjehan, is even to-day separated most curiously by an unbridgeable gulf from his next door neighbour belonging to the race, or professing the faith, of those illustrious monarchs who are believed to have glorified the history of India. For the orthodox Hindus who constitute the great majority of the Indian population, the Mussulman, even of a noble birth or high education or admirable cultural attainments, is a 'mlechha'-impure barbarian-who does not deserve a social treatment any better than accorded to the lowest of the Hindus.

The cause of this singular situation is to be traced in the prejudice born, in the past, of the hatred a conquered and oppressed people naturally entertained for the foreign invader. The political relation out of which it sprang is a thing of the past. But the prejudice still persists not only as an effective obstacle to national cohesion, but also as a hindrance for a dispassionate view of history. Indeed, there is no other example of two communities living together in the same country for so many hundred years, and yet having 50 little appreciation of each other's culture. No civilized people in the world is so ignorant of Islamic history and contemptuous of the Mohammedan religion as the Hindus. Spiritual imperialism is the outstanding feature of our nationalist ideology. But this nasty spirit is the most pronounced in relation to Mohammedanism. The current notion of the teachings of the Arabian Prophet is extremely ill-informed. The average educated Hindu has little knowledge of, and no appreciation for, the immense revolutionary significance of Islam, and the great cultural consequences of that revolution. The prevailing n0tions could be laughed at as ridiculous, were they not so pregnant with harmful consequences. These notions should be combated for the sake of the national cohesion of the Indian people as well as in the interest of science and historical truth. A proper appreciation of the cultural significance of Islam is of supreme importance in this crucial period of the history of India.

The great historian Gibbon describes the rise and expansion of Islam as "one of the most memorable revolutions which has impressed a new and lasting character on the nations of the globe." One is simply amazed to contemplate the incredible rapidity with which the two mightiest empires of the ancient time were subverted by the comparatively small bands of nomads issuing from the Arabian Desert, fired with the zeal of a new faith. Hardly fifty years had passed since Mohammad assumed the role of the singular Prophet spreading his Message of Peace at the point of the sword, his followers victoriously planted the banner of Islam on the confines of India, on the one side, and on the shore of the Atlantic, on the other. The first Khalifs of Damascus reigned over an Empire which could not be crossed in less than five months on the fleetest camel. At the end of the first century of the Hegira, the "'Commanders of the Faithful" were the most powerful rulers of the world.

Every prophet establishes his pretension by the performance of miracles. On that token, Mohammad must be recognized as by far the greatest of all prophets, before or after him. The expansion of Islam is the most miraculous of all miracles. The Roman Empire of Augustus, as later enlarged by the valiant Trajan, was the result of great and glorious victories, won over a period of seven hundred years. Still, it had not attained the proportions of the Arabian Empire established in less than a century. The Empire of Alexander represented but a fraction of the vast domain of the Khalifs. For nearly a thousand years, the Persian Empire resisted the arms of Rome, only to be subdued by the "Sword of God" in less than a decade. Let a modern historian describe the miracle of the rise of Islam.

The Arabs were poets, dreamers, fighters, traders; they were not politicians. Nor had they found in religion a stabilizing or unifying power. They practiced a low form of polytheism. A hundred years later, these obscure savages had achieved for themselves a great world power. They had conquered Syria and Egypt, they had overwhelmed and converted Persia, mastered Western Turkestan and part of the Punjab. They had wrested Africa from the Byzantines and the Berbers, Spain from the Visigoths.

In the West they threatened France, in the East Constantinople. Their fleets, built in Alexandria or the Syrian ports, rode the waters of the Mediterranean, pillaged the Greek islands and challenged the naval power of the Byzantine Empire. Their success had been won so easily, the Persians and Berbers of the Atlas Mountains alone offering a serious resistance, that at the beginning of the eighth century it must have seemed an open question whether any final obstacle could be opposed to their victorious course. The Mediterranean had ceased to be a Roman lake. From one end of Europe to the other, the Christian states found themselves confronted with the challenge of a new Oriental civilization founded on a new Oriental faith."

How did that stupendous miracle happen? That has been one of the baffling questions for historians. To-day the educated world has rejected the vulgar theory that the rise of Islam was a triumph of fanaticism over sobre and tolerant peoples. The phenomenal success of Islam was primarily due to its revolutionary significance and its ability to lead the masses out of the hopeless situation created by the decay of antique civilizations not only of Greece and Rome but of Persia and China-and of India.

THE MISSION OF ISLAM

Vulgar interpreters of the Islamic history lay stress upon its military achievements either to praise or to deprecate its far-reaching revolutionary significance. If the undoubtedly brilliant military con quests of the Saracens were the only measure of the historic role of Islam, then it would not be a unique historical phenomenon. The depredations of the barbarians of Tartary and Scythia (Goths, Huns, Vandals, Avars, Mongols etc.) approximated, if not equaled or excelled, their military accomplishments. But there is a vast difference between the tidal waves that occasionally rolled West, South and East, from the border land of Europe and Asia, and the Arabic eruption of religious frenzy.

Like tidal waves the former rolled on in their cataclysmic greatness, only to subside, sooner or later, having distributed death and destruction, far and wide. The latter, on the contrary, was an abiding historical phenomenon, which ushered in a brilliant chapter of the cultural annals of mankind. Destruction was only a subsidiary part of its mission. It pulled down the played-out old, to construct a necessary new. It demolished the holy edifices of the Cesars and the Chosroes, only to rescue from their Impending ruin the accumulated treasures of human knowledge, to preserve and multiply them for the benefit of the posterity.

The prodigious feats of the Saracen horsemen are not the only distinctive feature of Islam. They simply captivate our attention which must marvel at them, and impel us to search out and admire the causes of such a tremendously dynamic historical phenomenon. The miraculous performance of the"Army of God" usually dazzles the vision and the more magnificent achievements of the Islamic evolution are seldom known to the average student of history, even if he be a follower of Mohammad. Yet, the martial victories of the followers of the Arabian Prophet were but the prelude to a more magnificent and lasting performance in the social and cultural fte1ds. They only created the conditions for political unity which opened up an era of economic prosperity and spiritual progress.

The stupendous ruins of the Roman and Persian Empires had to be cleared away so that a new social order could rise with new ideas and new Ideals. The dark superstition of the Magian mysticism, and the corrupt atmosphere of the Greek Church vitiated the spiritual life of the subjects of the decrepit Persian and Byzantine Empires rendering all moral and intellectual progress impossible. The severe monotheism of Mohammad wielded the formidable scimiter of the Saracen not only to destroy the profane idolatry of the Arabian tribes;

it also proved to be the Invincible instrument of history for freeing a considerable section of mankind from the eternal evil spirit of Zoroaster as well as from degenerate Christianity given to the superstition of miracle-mongering, to the deadly disease of monasticism and to the Idolatrous worship of Saints. The amazing achievements of Saracen arms only prove that they were wielded at the service of history-for the progress of humanity.

The rich spiritual legacy of the glorious civilization of ancient Greece was almost burled under the dreary ruins of the Roman Empire, and lost in the darkness of Christian superstition. The grand mission of rescuing the invaluable patrimony, which eventually enabled the peoples of Europe to emerge from the depressing gloom of the holy middle-ages, and build the marvelous monument of modem civilization, belonged to the Saracen arms, and to the socio-political structure erected on the basis of Islamic Monotheism. The sword of Islam, wielded ostensibly at the service of God, actually contributed to the victory of a new social force-the blossoming of a new intellectual life-which eventually dug the grave of all religions and faiths.

Islam rose rather as a political movement than a religion in the strictest sense of the word. In the initial stages of its history, it was essentially a call for the unity of the nomadic tribes inhabiting the Arabian Desert. Upon its speedy realization, the politic-religious unitarian doctrine became the flag under which the Asiatic and African provinces of the Roman Empire survived the dissolution of the antique social order. The previous revolt had miscarried itself. Christianity had lost its original revolutionary fervor becoming, on the one hand, the ideology of social dissolution (Monasticism), and a prop for the decaying Empire, on the other. But the social crisis continued, aggravated by the degeneration of Christianity. The message of hope and salvation came from the Caravan traders of Arabia who had stood outside the corrupting atmosphere of the decomposed Roman world, and prospered by their advantageous position. The"Revolt of Islam" saved humanity.

A famous authority on Islamic history writes the following

about the mission of Mohammad:"He found a whole nation in the full tide of rapid improvement, eagerly In search of knowledge and power. The excitement in the public mind of Arabia, which produced the mission of Mahamet, induced many other prophets to make their appearance during his life time."

The people, for whom Islamic history is summarized in the exploits of fanatical hordes, dramatically offering the dismayed world the choice between the Koran and the sword, with the blood-curdling cry of"Allah Akhbar", do not know, or conveniently overlook, that only the immediate successors of Mohammad occupied themselves solely with temporal and religious conquests; and even they were distinguished from the barbarian ravishers of humanity like Alaric, Attila, Genseric, Chengis or Tamerlane, by the nobility of character, purity of purpose and piety of spirit. Their devoutness might have been fortified by superstition, but was not stained by hypocrisy. Their fanaticism was softened by generosity and sound common-sense. Their ambition was remarkably free from selfishness. Godliness, for them, was not a veil for greediness.

There are few figures in history more romantic, more devout, more sincere and more modest than the first"Commander of the Faithful"-Abu Bakr. His memorable injunction to the"Army of God" ran:"Be just; the unjust never prosper. Be valiant; die rather than yield. Be merciful; slay neither old men, nor women, nor children. Destroy neither fruit trees, nor grains, nor cattle. Keep your word even to your enemy. Molest not those men who live retired from the world." The irresistible march of the"Army of God" bears testimony to that this remarkable injunction was uttered sincerely by the venerable chief, and obeyed strictly by the devout followers.

Everywhere, the Saracen invaders were welcome as deliverers by peoples oppressed, tyrannized and tormented by Byzantine corruption, Persian despotism and Christian superstition. Fanatically faithful to the revolutionary teachings of the Prophet, and obediently acting according to the noble, wise and eminently practical injunctions of the Khalif, the

Saracen invaders easily enlisted the sympathy and support of the peoples they conquered. No invader can establish an abiding domination over conquered peoples, except with their active support or tacit toleration.

The second Khalif, Omar, whose impetuous horsemen had pushed their victorious march through the Persian Empire, to the distant banks of the Oxus, on the one side, and were masters of the second metropolis of the Roman world - Alexandria - on the other, made his triumphal entry into Jerusalem on a camel which also carried the entire royal provision and equipage-a small tent of coarse hair, a bag of corn, a bag of dates, a wooden bowl, and a leathern flask of water.

Gibbon offers the following account of the simplicity, devoutness, equity, and righteousness of the conquerors of Persia, Mesopotamia, Syria, Palestine and Egypt:"Wherever he halted, the company without distinction was invited to partake of his homely fare, and the repast was consecrated by the prayer and exhortation of the Commander of the Faithful. But in expedition or pilgrimage, his power was exercised in the administration of Justice; he reformed the licentious polygamy, the polygamy of the Arabs; relieved the tributaries from extortion and cruelty; and chastised the luxury of the Saracens by dispoiling them of their rich silk, and dragging them on their face in dirt."

Khaled, whom the Prophet called the"Sword of God," whose almost legendary valour had united Arabia, Mesopotamia and Syria under the banner of Islam, died in the possession only of his horse, his arms, and a single slave. The great hero is credited to have declared in his youth,"it is not the delicacies of Syria, or the fading delights of this world, that have prompted me to devote my life in the cause of religion, I only seek the favour of God, and his apostle". (Recorded by the historian Abul Feda.)

The valiant conqueror of Egypt, Omrou, was distinguished by a poetic genius in addition to martial valour. The following remarkable passage occurs in his report to Khalif Omar:"The crowds of husbandmen who blacken the land may be compared to a swarm of industrious ants; and their native indolence is quickened by the lash of the taskmaster. But the riches they extract are unequally shared between those who labour and those who possess." That was a view far in advance of time. The idea of social equity was unknown in all the lands of ancient civilization. The toilers, either as slaves or as Sudras, were the object of legitimate contempt and exploitation. They were hardly considered as human beings. The economic principle, primitively formulated in the memorable injunction of the first Khalif, evolved out of the interest of the Arab traders, revolutionized the old social idea. A part of the wealth produced by the toiling masses, when left with themselves, becomes a powerful impetus to trade. In his administration of the conquered kingdom of the Pharaohs and the Ptolemies, the Arab warrior sought with success to mend the glaring inequities that had offended his poetic vision. Egypt, robbed and despoiled for centuries by the Greeks and the Romans, prospered under the Saracens.

There is no end of testimonies to prove that even in the predominantly martial period of their history, the Saracens were far from being barbaric bands of fanatical marauders, spreading pillage and rapine, death and destruction in the name of religion. Then, the period of conquest was short, as compared to the long era of learning and culture that flourished subsequently under the patronage of the Khalifs as well as of the tributary and independent Empire.

The military period terminated with the establishment of the Abbassides at Baghdad- the"City of Peace"-just about a hundred years after the ascendancy of the Prophet at Medina. Since then, the military activities of the Arabs were essentially of the nature of current defensive and offensive operations of a far-flung Empire.

The stern enthusiasm of the Saracen warriors was softened by time and prosperity. They began to seek riches no longer in war, but in trade and industry; fame, not on the field of battle, but in the pursuit of science and literature; and happiness, no longer in the fanatical worship of one God and his only Prophet, but in the harmless enjoyment of social and domestic life. War was no longer the passion and proud profession of the Saracens, because they had found interest and delight in a peaceful world created by the prowess of their forefathers. The progeny of the intrepid heroes, who had flocked to the belligerent standard of Abu Bakr and Omar, with the hope of paradise and incidentally earthly spoils, found the modest occupation of trade and industry more profitable, and science and philosophy more gratifying.

Three hundred years of peace, prosperity and progress elapsed before the martial valour of the Saracens was rekindled by Christian aggression in the deceptive form of the crusades. Pillage and plunder, tyranny and oppression came to be associated with Muslim conquests only after the power of the Saracens had been overwhelmed by the. Mongol barbarians from Central Asia; Arab learning and culture had been corrupted by the degenerating luxury of the court; and the proud standard of Islam, havl11g lost its original revolutionary luster, had been prostituted in the rapacious hands of the Turks and the Tartars.

It is a gross misreading of history to confound Islam with militarism. Mohammad was the Prophet not of the Saracen warriors, but of the Arab merchants. The very name with which he baptized his creed contradicts the current notion about its aim. Etymologically, Islam means to make peace, or the making of peace: to make peace with God by doing homage to his Oneness, repudiating the fraudulent divinity of idols which had usurped His sole claim to the devotion of man; and to make peace on earth through the union of the Arabian tribes. The peace on earth was of immediate importance, and greater consequence. The temporal interest of the Arabian merchants required it; for, trade thrives better under peaceful conditions. Since decayed states and degenerated religions bred the germs of continued wars and perennial revolts, their destruction was a condition for peace. The creed of Mohammad: made peace at home, and the martial valour of the Saracans conferred the same blessing on the peoples inhabiting the vast territories from Samarqand to Spain. As soon as a country came under the domination of the Arabs, Its economic life was quickened by the encouragement of industry and agriculture. The spirit and Interest of the Arab traders determined and directed the policy of the Islamic State. In the Roman world as well as in all the other lands of antique civilization, the ruling classes detested all productive labour,-looked down upon trade and Industry. War and worship were their noble professions. With the Arabs, It was different. Nomadic life in a desert had taught them to appreciate labour as the source of freedom. With them, trade was an honourable as well as a lucrative occupation of the free man. Thus, the Islamic State was based upon social relations entirely different from those of the old. Religion extolled industry, and encouraged a normal indulgence of nature. Trade was free, and as noble a profession as state craft war, letter and science. The Khalifs of Baghdad were not only great traders; the earlier ones learned, and actually practiced some craft to purchase their personal necessities with the proceeds of manual labour. Most of the great Arab philosophers and scholars came from opulent trading families. The culture and refinement of the courts of Bokhara and Samarqand, the munificence of the Fatemite rulers of Africa and the splendor of the Sultans of Andalusia were equally produced rather by the profits of prosperous trade than by taxes extorted by despotic measures.

Under certain conditions, trade is a potent instrument of spiritual revolution. The aspiration of the Arab merchant produced the Monotheism of Mohammad. This, in its turn, inspired the nomads of a desert to establish one of the vastest and most flourishing empires of history.The laws of Koran revolutionized social relations. Increased production, the result of this revolution, quickened trade which ushered in an era of cosmopolitanism and spiritual uplift. Trade broadens the vision of man.

Visiting distant lands, getting used to the sight of strange customs.mixing with peoples of diverse races, the trader frees himself from the prejudices and limitations born of the local conditions of his native land. He develops the capacities of toleration, sympathy and understanding for the habits, views and faiths of others. Observation and inquisitiveness, which guide his voyage on the unknown sea, or direct his steps in lands, k1ll in him the comfort of credulity. The growth of critical faculty places him at the gate of knowledge. he essence of his occupation teaches the trader to think in abstraction.

He is not interested in his merchandise as such. His mind is occupied with the idea of profit. It is all the same to him whether his camels or ships are laden with wool or corn or spices. He is concerned with something which is neither these nor other concrete things he handles. These are simply the means to attain his end-to make profit which is a category abstracted from the concrete commodity he buys or sells. He appreciates things, not in their intrinsic value, but according to their capacity to produce profit.

Toleration for strange things, the attempt to understand them, freedom from prejudice, faculty of observation, ability to think In abstract-all these qualities acquired by the trader, thanks to the nature of his occupation, go into the making of a ph1losophical outlook. Having seen different peoples cherish diverse forms of superstitions as divine wisdom, practice equally absurd rites and rituals or expressing devotion, extol prejudices to the dignity of eternal truth, the cosmopolitan mind of the traveled trader indulgently smiles upon the credulity of all, deplores their depravity equally, and respects the common element of faith beneath the superficial diversities of theological dogmas and forms of worship.

The main arteries of international trade of the medieval world ran through the countries which embraced Islam and were united in the Saracen Empire. The northern routes of trade with China, which passed through Constantinople to Italy and other countries of Western Europe, had become extremely risky owing to the Scythian Inroads and the ruinous fiscal policy of the Byzantine Empire. After their conquest of Syria, Mesopotamia, Persia and the territories across the Oxus, the Arabs captured the Chinese trade and diverted it to pass through their domain of North-Africa and Spain, ultimately to reach the markets of Western Europe.

During the eighth to the eleventh centuries, practically the entire trade between India and China, on the one hand, and

Europe, on the other, was done by the Arabs. Thousands of traders traveled with their Caravans, loaded with precious cargoes, from the remote frontiers of China and India all the way to Morocco and Spain. They were not persecuted or detested as their kind had been in all the countries of antique civilization with the honourable exception of Greece. In the Empire of the Saracens, they belonged to the ruling class.

Consequently, the learning and culture, that thrived so luxuriantly owing to the prosperity of the Saracen Empire, bore the stamp of their native broad-mindedness, cosmopolitanism and Incredulity. Under the leadership of a martial aristocracy and jealous priesthood, human Ideology takes the form of dogmatic faith for misty mysticism. Philosophy-the search for a rational explanation of the Universe originates in a society ruled by an aristocracy engaged in trade. The city states of the Ionian Greeks were therefore the birth-places of philosophy.

Islam was a necessary product of history,-an instrument of human progress. It rose as the ideology of a new social relation which, in its turn, revolutionized the mind of man. But just as it had subverted and replaced older cultures, decayed In course of time, Islam, in its turn, was also overstepped by further social developments, and consequently had to hand over its spiritual leadership to other agencies born out of newer conditions. But it contributed to the forging of new ideological instruments which brought about the subsequent social revolution. The instruments were experimental science and rationalist philosophy. It stands to the credit of Islamic culture to have been instrumental in the promotion of the ideology of a new social revolution.

Capitalist mode of production rescued Europe from the chaos of medieval barbarism. It fought and in the long run vanquished Christian theology and the spiritual monopoly of the Catholic Church with the potent weapon of rationalist phılosophy. This weapon, invented by the ancient sages of Greece came to the possession of the founders of modem civilization through the Arab scholars who had not only preserved the precious patrimony, but added to it handsomely.

The historic battle, begun by the nomads of the Arabian Desert, under the religious flag of Islam, was fought step by step through a thousand years on fields scattered over the three continents, to be won finally in Europe under the profane standard of the eighteenth century Enlightenment and Bourgeois Revolution.

Chapter 6

Vedic Culture

The period between B.C. 1000 and B.C. 600 is generally known as Later Vedic period. This age is also called as the Epic Age because the two great epics Ramayana and Mahabharata were written during this period. The Aryans during this period moved to the Gangetic Valley.

SOURCES

The Sama, Yajur, Atharva Vedas, Brahmanas, Upanishads, Aranyakas and the two epics are the sources of information for this period.

POLITICAL LIFE

The Gangetic Valley or Aryavartha became the centre of political activity. Kingdoms like Kosala, Videha, Kuru,Magadha, Kasi, Avanti and Panchala came into existence. The position of the king was considerably high. Sabha and Samiti did not stand in his way. Kingship became hereditary. The kings were in charge of defence and maintaining law and order of their kingdoms. They built vast empires. They tried to extend their territories. Therefore frequent wars were fought. Rituals and sacrifices such as Rajasuya Ashvamedha, Vajapeya and Yagas were performed by the kings.

Kings assumed titles like Ekrat Samrat and Sariahaurna, Village administration was looked after by the village councils. Taxes like Pall, Sulk and Bhaga were collected from the people. The revenue was spent for the benefit of the subjects.

SOCIAL LIFE

Family conhnued to be the basic unit of the society. The

father was the head of the family. Joint family system was quite common. Varna or Caste system developed during the later' Vedic period. To start with the fourfold caste came into existences, namely, the Brahmins Kshatriyas, Vaishyas and Sudras. The Brabmins were priests and teachers.'The Kshatriyas were rulers and soldiers. They enjoyed high position in the society. The Vaishyas were traders, artisans and farmers. The Sudras were the uneducated workers who served for the other three castes. According to the religious texts, the life of an individual was divided into four stages or Ashramas They were Brahmacharya or student life, Graihasta or life of a father and husband. Vanaprasta or life as a hermit and finally Sanyasa or total renunciation of the world.

POSITION OF WOMEN

There was a decline in the status and dignity of women during the Later Vedic period. Women were subordinated. Submissiveness was considered as an ideal virtue of a wife. Women were not allowed to participate in public affairs. They could not own property. Child marriage was not prevented. Widow Remarriage was not allowed. Though monogamy was the rule, polygamy was practised Women degradation started from the later Vedic period.

EDUCATION

Education was limited to the three upper castes. Pupils stayed with their teachers at the Gurukula. Women were not sent to the Gurukula. However, women like Gargi and Maitreyi were educated. Students were taught philosophy logic, religion, grammar, astronomy, medicine, ethics and arithmetic. Dhanur Veda or war tactics was taught to princes. Pupils observed strict discipline, obedience and respect for the teachers.

ECONOMIC LIFE

Farming was the chief occupation. Iron was used extensively in this period. Iron ploughs substituted the wooden ploughs. Another improvement of this period was maturing the field. It increased the yield Barley. Wheat, rice and dhal were produced. Cattle rearing continued. Wealth was calculated in terms of cows. Nishka, Swarna and Sathamana were the names of gold coins in circulation. Copper produced war weapons and ornaments. They obtained copper from the Khetri mines of Rajastan. Ironsmiths produced arrowheads and spearheads. They also crafted agricultural tools. Weavers, leather workers, carpenters, chariot - makers and jewel makers also lived in the villages. People in the Later Vedic period used painted grey mud vessels. The Gray wares were painted. Such vessels have been found in many places in North India, Archaeologists call these sites as"Painted Gray ware sites".

Both internal and foreign trade flourished. Medicinal plants, medicine, clothing's and leather products were exported to countries like Babylonia.

FOOD AND ENTERTAINMENTS

Rice, wheat, barley, milk and milk products, vegetables and fruits were their diet. Fish was also eaten. The flesh of oxen, sheep and goats were eaten Soma and Sura were their common drinks. Indoor and outdoor games were played during this period. Gambling, dicing, chariot racing and horse racing were some of their pastimes. The people were fond of music and dance.

DRESS AND ORNAMENTS

Woolen and Cotton dresses were used by the people. Ornaments made of gold and silver were worn. The other metals used by the Later Vedic period were iron, copper and tin.

RELIGION

Many changes occurred in the field of religion. The Gods of early Vedic age lost their significance. In the Later Vedic period, people worshipped new Gods like Prajapathi, Pasupathi, Vishnu and Krishna. Prayers and scarifies became important ways of worshipping God. Animals were killed during sacrifice. The religion became complex affair. The theory of Karma and the theory of incarnation were accepted. People believed that the God is the supreme head and he was not only a creator but also a destroyer. They believed in the concept of Moksha.

VEDIC AGE

Duration: 1500 BC to 500 BC

The Vedic Period or the Vedic Age refers to that time period when the Vedic Sanskrit texts were composed in India. The society that emerged during that time is known as the Vedic Period, or the Vedic Age, Civilization. The Vedic Civilization flourished between the 1500 BC and 500 BC on the Indo-Gangetic Plains of the Indian subcontinent. This civilization laid down the foundation of Hinduism as well as the associated Indian culture. The Vedic Age was followed by the golden age of Hinduism and classical Sanskrit literature, the Maurya Empire and the Middle Kingdoms of India.

Vedic Texts

Linguistically, the texts belonging to the Hindu Vedic Civilisation can be classified into the following five chronological branches:

Rigvedic

The oldest text of the Vedic Period, Rig Veda has many elements that are common with the Indo-Iranian texts, both in language and in content. One cannot find such similarity in any other Vedic text. It is believed that the compilation of the Rig Veda had stretched over a number of centuries. However, there is a conflict as to the completion date of the Rig Veda. Some historians believe it to be 1500 BC, while the others believe it to be 3000 BC. This time period coincided with the Indus Valley Civilization.

Mantra Language

The period of the Mantra Language includes the time of the compilation of the mantra and prose language of the Atharvaveda (Paippalada and Shaunakiya), the Rigveda

Khilani, the Samaveda Samhita and the mantras of the Yajurveda. Though derived from the Rig Veda, all these texts experienced wide scale changes, in terms of language as well as at the time of reinterpretation. This time period coincided with the early Iron Age in northwestern India and the Black and Red Ware culture.

Samhita Prose

The period of Samhita Prose represents the compilation and codification of a Vedic canon. The linguistic changes of this time include the complete loss of the injunctive, the subjunctive and the aorist. The commentary part of the Yajurveda belongs to the Samhita Prose period. During this time, the Painted Grey Ware culture was evident.

Brahmana Prose

This period signifies Brahmanas proper of the four Vedas, along with the oldest Upanishads.

Sutra Language

The last division of the Vedic Sanskrit can be traced upto 500 BC. During this time, a major portion of the Srauta Sutras, the Grihya Sutras and some Upanishads were composed.

Epic and Paninian Sanskrit (Post Vedic)

In the post-Vedic Period, the compilation of Mahabharata and Ramayana epics took place. The Classical Sanskrit described by Panini also emerged after the Vedic Age. The Vedanta and the Pali Prakrit dialect of Buddhist scripture belong to this period. During this time, the Northern Black Polished Ware culture started spreading over the northern parts of India. The end of the Vedic Period Civilization in India was marked by significant changes in the field of linguistics, culture and politics. With the invasion of the Indus valley by Darius I, in the 6th century, outside influences started creeping in.

Early Vedic Period (Rigvedic Period)

The Rigvedic Period represents the time period when the

Rig Veda was composed. The Rig Veda comprises of religious hymns, and allusions to various myths and stories. Some of the books even contain elements from the pre-Vedic, common Indo-Iranian society. Some similarities are also found with the Andronovo culture and the Mittanni kingdoms. Thus, it is difficult to define the exact beginning of the Rigvedic period.

Political Organization

The political units during the Rigvedic or the early Vedic period comprised of Grama (village), Vish and Jana. The biggest political unit was that of Jana, after which came Vish and then, Grama. The leader of a Grama was called Gramani, of a Vish was called Vishpati and that of Jana was known as Jyeshta. The rashtra (state) was governed by a Rajan (King) and he was known as Gopa (protector) and Samrat (supreme ruler). The king ruled with the consent and approval of the people. There were four councils, namely Sabha, Samiti, Vidhata and Gana, of which women were allowed to attend only two, Sabha and Vidhata. The duty of the king was to protect the tribe, in which he was assisted by the Purohita (chaplain) and the Senani (army chief).

Society and Economy

Numerous social changes took place during the early Vedic period. The concept of Varna, along with the rules of marriage, was made quite stiff. Social stratification took place, with the Brahmins and the Kshatriyas being considered higher than the Shudras and the Vaisyas. Cows and bulls were accorded religious significance. The importance of agriculture started growing. The families became patriarchal and people began praying for the birth of a son.

Vedic Religious Practices

Rishis, composers of the hymns of the Rig Veda, were considered to be divine. Sacrifices and chanting of verses started gaining significance as the principal mode of worship. The main deities were Indra, Agni (the sacrificial fire), and Soma. People also worshipped Mitra-Varuna, Surya (Sun),

Vayu (wind), Usha (dawn), Prithvi (Earth) and Aditi (the mother of gods). Yoga and Vedanta became the basic elements of the religion.

Later Vedic Period

The later Vedic Period commenced with the emergence of agriculture as the principal economic activity. Along with that, a declining trend was experienced as far as the importance of cattle rearing was concerned. Land and its protection started gaining significance and as a result, several large kingdoms arose.

Political Organization

The rise of sixteen Mahajanapadas, along with the increasing powers of the King, comprise of the other characteristics of this period. Rituals like rajasuya, (royal consecration), vajapeya (chariot race) and ashvamedha (horse sacrifice) became widespread. At the same time, the say of the people in the administration diminished.

Society

As far as the society is concerned, the concept of Varna and the rules of marriage became much more rigid than before. The status of the Brahmanas and Kshatriyas increased greatly and social mobility was totally restricted. The proper pronunciation of verses became to be considered as essential for prosperity and success in war. Kshatriyas started amassing wealth and started utilizing the services of the Brahmins. The other castes were slowly degraded. Around 500 BC, the later Vedic Period started giving rise to the period of the Middle kingdoms of India.

n India, around 1500 BC to 600 BC, a completely new civilization and culture has developed. The country had seen various cultures and civilization since the Bronze Age. The most popular Indus Valley civilization had declined by around 1500 BC due to several unknown factors including invasion of Aryans and deforestation. Most of the archaeologists considered the invasion of Aryans the main reason of collapsing the Harappa civilization. The Aryans came from the Central Asia and entered India through Khyber Pass around 2000 BC-1500 BC. They forcefully introduced their own culture and civilization to the Indus people.

Thus, the Indus people began to follow Aryans culture and civilization. However, the social status of Aryans was the rural one as compare to the urban civilized Indus people. This age of Aryans in India is termed as the period of Vedas. In this epoch, four Vedas–Rig Veda, Sam Veda, Yajur Veda, and the last Atharva Veda–came into existence.

The Aryans daily life and beliefs are described in four Vedas. These Vedas are the main literary sources of this Vedic era. The whole Vedic period is divided into two: early Vedic period (2000 BC-1000 BC) and the Later Vedic period (1000 BC to 600 BC).

Chapter 7

Tribal and Flok Culture

EARLY VEDIC PERIOD

In the early Vedic period, religious practice was in the form of nature worship. In this period, sun, fire, wind, trees and sky were worshipped. The worship of early Vedic period incorporated chanting of Rig Vedic verses and singing of mantras (yajus). In this early Vedic period, people migrated from one place to another in search of fertile land for agriculture.

The caste system was not very rigid. Although, people made differences between white skinned peoples (Aryans) and dark skinned peoples (actually the non Aryans). They lived on agricultural products and other dairy products obtained from their cattle. Almost all the religious performances were to get the victory in battles and to ensure the good productivity from their crops.

Later Vedic period was more synchronized than the early Vedic period. During the later Vedic period, the people started worshipping Gods like Krishna, Vishnu, Prajapati, and Pasupathi Nath. In addition to that, in the later Vedic period, the theory of incarnation and the theory of Karma were broadly accepted and these theories actually became the philosophical truth in the Vedic civilization. In this later Vedic period, animals were sacrificed during worship of God.

Ashram system came into existence in the Vedic period. These ashrams of Vedic period are: Bramacharya ashram, Grihashta ashram, Vannaprashta ashram and the last, Sannyasa ashram. The ashram system was introduced in order to make understand the individual the idea of both karma and dharma in his life. The patriarchal family system was broadly accepted in this era. Marriage was considered as one of the main rituals in an individual's life. Cattle carving and agriculture were the two main occupations of the people. People began to live in permanent settlements, which were protected and fortified by warriors. It was mentioned in the Ramayana that the increase in the population led the people of late Vedic period move to the southern part of India.

EPIC AGE

The later Vedic period is also known as Epic age. In this epoch, great epics, Ramayana and Mahabharata, and Upanishads were written. Vedic civilization is the forerunner of modern Hinduism. These epics contain broad principles of Hinduism within them. This period is largely characterized by the hereditary form of kingship. The society was divided into four main casts based on their work: Brahmins, Kshatriyas, Vaishya, and Shudra.

The Brahmins are for conducting the religious duties and Kashtriyas are for protecting the kinship groups. The Vashiyas are merchants and Shudras are for serving the other upper castes. Since the caste system was based on the work performed by the individuals, it was very flexible in the Vedic period. People were allowed to change their occupation and hence their class as per their needs and interests. However, the scope of rising in the society was quite less.

The late Vedic period was noted by the introduction of sixteen Mahajnapadas, marked in some of the literature. Vedic period actually formed the basics for the modern Hinduism. This epoch has contributed immensely for the development of Vedas and other Indian literatures.

- The first and also the last empire whose borders extended from Hindukush in the north-west to modern Karnataka in the south and from Makran in the west to modern Bangladesh in the east. "Chandragupta Maurya had reached those scientific borders of India for which the Great Mughals yearned and the British sighed for their life." – Vincent Smith in his "Oxford History of India"

- Chandragupta Maurya is the first truly historical emperor of India for the amount of information that is available for him in Indian and foreign sources alike, is unmatched by any other that is available for other great ancient emperors such as Sudas, Bimbisara, Ajatashtru, etc.
- The Mauryan Empire is important also because with their advent the chronology of Indian history becomes clear.
- There have been many instances of invasion of India by foreigners and subsequent loss of independence in the long history of India. But Chandragupta Maurya was the first to defeat a foreign power and that too a powerful king like Seleucus and also forced him to cede his territories for Chandragupta Maurya.
- Mauryas were also the first to form diplomatic alliances or relations with foreign powers. Megasthenes, Deimachus and Dionysius who were representatives of Selecus, Antiochus I and Philadelphus Ptolemy I respectively attended the Mauryan Court.
- For the first time an efficient administration was set up which guided many such future arrangements.
- The tradition of inscriptions, development of arts and also the spread of Buddhism outside India were some of the landmarks associated with this period.

SOURCES OF MAURYAN HISTORY

- Arthashastra of Kautilya
- Puranas – Despite their exaggerated description and factual errors, they give much information regarding the overthrow of Nandas, the establishment of Mauryan Empire, the contribution of Kautilya, the Mauryan dynastic order and also some chronological details.
- Mudrarakshasa of Vishakhadatta describes how Chanakya won the diplomatic battle against the

Nanda minister Rakshasa, how Rakshasa was compelled to work for Chandragupta and also how the Nandas were finally over thrown.

- The Commentary on Vishnu Purana by Ratnagarbha
- Mudrarakshasa Vyakhya, a commentary on Mudrarakshasa by Dhundiraj.

  The account of Dhundiraj is corroborated by:
  - Mudrarakshasa Katha by Mahadeva
  - Chanakya Katha by Ravi Nartak (Irwi Chakyar)
  - Rashasa Purva Katha and Purvapithika by Ananta Kavi
- Katha-Sarit-Sagar by Somadeva is based on Brihat-Katha of Gunadhya.
- Brihat-Katha-Manjari of Kshemendra
- Sinhalese Buddhist texts Dipavamsha and Mahavamsha are based on Ath-Katha and Uttar-Vihar-Ath-Katha. These texts give information about Ashoka.
- Mahavamsha Tika also known as Vamshattha Pakasini
- Mahabodhivamsha (9/10 centuries A.D.) written by Upatisshya narrates the story of the planting of the Bodhi tree at Anuradhapur in Ceylon by Mahendra.
- Milinda-Panho written by Nagasena gives a few facts about the defeat of Nandas and the establishment of the Mauryan Empire.
- The Mahavamsha of Molglan, also known as Combodian Mahavamsha gives some information about Chanakya and Chandragupta.
- Aryamanjushri Mulakalpa, historical account upto 8th century A.D., gives information regarding Nandas, Chandragupta Maurya, Chanakya, Bindusara and Ashoka.
- Among the Jain texts, Uttaradhyana Sutra, Avashyaka Sutra, Das-Vaikalpik-Sutra, Nishitha Sutra and Brihat-Kalpa-Sutra are important for Mauryan history.

- The most important Jain text for Mauryan history is Parishista Parvan, a part of Tri-Shashthi-Shalaka Purusha-Charita.
- Pataliputra-Nagar-Kalpa, a part of Vividha-Tirth-Kalpa written by Jinprabha Suri, a courtier of Mohd. BinTughlaq.
- Vichar-Shreni written by Melutunga. A very important text which gives the description of the seers and kings that followed after Mahavira.
- Brihat-Katha-Kosha, belonging to Digambara tradition, which is written by Harisena. It narrates the southward journey of Chandragupta Maurya in the event of the terrible drought which took place in north India during his reign and says that he alongwith Bhadrabahu led the life of a Jaina monk and finally starved himself to death in true Jaina tradition.
- Ramachandra Mumukshu's Punyashrava-Katha-Kosha which deals with the origin of Mauryas, the alliance of Chandragupta and Chanakya.

FOREIGN HISTORIANS AND THEIR WORKS

- The Indica of Megasthenes
- Bibliotheca Historica of Diodorus gives some information regarding conditions in the north-west at the time of Alexander's invasion.
- The 17th Chapter of Geography of Strabo deals with Persia and India.
- Curtius, who was a contemporary of Roman emperor Claudius (1st century A.D.), wrote History of Alexander. It talks about the origin of Nandas and also the conditions in the north-west India.
- Pliny's Natural History gives some information regarding Chandragupta Maurya which is based on the 'Indica' of Megasthenes.
- Arrian's Annabasis of Alexander gives the life-history of Alexander. It contains some information regarding

the Mauryan India based on the 'Indica' of Megasthenes.

- Ptolemy's Geography contains the earliest, though incorrect, map of India.
- Clemen's Alexandrinus' Stromatis, which is based on the work of Megasthenes, gives a description of Indian Brahmans.

THE ORIGIN OF MAURYAS

On the one hand, Brahmanical texts assign a low origin to Mauryas; on the other hand, Buddhist texts claim that they were Kshatriya. Some other associate them with peacocks on the basis of their name.

- Puranas equate Nandas with Shudragarbhodbhava. They speak about the low origin of Nandas but claim no knowledge about the low origin or otherwise regarding Mauryas.
- Mudrarakshasa equates Chandragupta Maurya with Apratith-kula, Vrishal i.e. of low origin.
- Ratnagarbha in Vishnu Purana Tika equates Chandragupta as a son of King Nanda from his Shudra wife Mura i.e. of low (Shudra) origin.
- Dhundiraj in Mudrarakshasa Vyakhya equates Chandragupta Maurya as the son of Mauyra who was the son of the king Sarvartha-Siddhi from his wife Vrishalatmaja i.e. low origin.
- Markandeya Purana equates Mauryas with Asura.
- Several Buddhist texts such as Mahavamsha, Mahavamsha Tika, Mahabodhivamsha, Divyavadan, Mahaparinibbana sutta etc. equate Mauryas with Kshatriyas.
- Mahabodhivamsha – The Piplivan Mauryas who vied for Buddha's ashes equates them with Kshatriyas.
- Divyavadan equates Bindusara and Ashoka with Kshatriyas.
- Buddhaghosha in the commentary on Mahaparinibban Sutta says that Mayuras (peacocks) were many in their kingdom, hence Mauryas. Indian

tradition of dynastic names derived from nature – Pallavas, Kadamb, Ashwayana etc.

- Parishishta Parvan says that Chandragupta Maurya was the son of the daughter of the chief of peacock-rearers.

  Peacock (Mayura) connection was clear from the following:
  - Peacock on punch-marked coins
  - Peacock on the pillar at Lauriya-Nandangarh
  - Peacocks along with Ashoka's pilgrimage of Gaya-engraved at Sanchi
  - Peacocks in Mauryan palace – Arrian
- D.B. Spooner says that Mauryans were of "Persian origin". Justin as "Sandrokottus of humble origin".
- Plutarch – "Androkottus calls Nandas low" therefore Mauryans could themselves not be low ("met Alexander"). Diodorus – "Nandas of low origin but not Chandragupta".

MAURYAN ADMINISTRATION

The Mauryan period marked the culmination of historical process into the formation of a state which was characterized by a centralized system with a developed taxation system, a professional army and a cadre of officials.

Two factors contributed to the rise of Mauryan Empire. Firstly, the development of a money economy which was aided by the use of iron and the subsequent spurt in agriculture and crafts on one hand and the use of punch marked coins on the other causing the kinship ties to decline and the rise of a private spirit. This made possible centralized fiscal collection and integrated authority. The increasing supply of various taxes facilitated the growth of a state apparatus.

Secondly, in the social sphere, the forces of urbanism and a strong agriculture base intensified the process social differentiation as the varna system filled the void created by the decline of kinship ties. This social differentiated and the strengthening of varna system facilitated state formation; the elected chief became hereditary as that genealogical right became entrenched in India because of the varna system. It further strengthened the position of the chief. His right to rule derived the secular and religious sanction; former through contract theory of state which speaks of taxation in lieu of protection and latter by religious validation. Thus the main reason for the exaltation of royal power lay in the growing importance of warrior class from the Mauryan times. The coexistent policy of aggrandizement followed by Magadha steeled the warriors and brought them to the fore.

Two strands are evident on the question of the origin of monarchy in ancient Indian thought – the mystical and the contractual. The mystical was woven around the divine appointment of king strengthened around ceremonies like rajsuya, vajpeya and asvamedha. The contractual theory spoke of taxation in lieu for protection. The Mauryan state essentially rested on the latter thought. Arthashastra doesn't deny the propaganda value of the former.

The king was the supreme authority of the state and the nucleus of the administrative system. In the Kautilyan scheme, royal order supersedes all other sources of authority including Dharma. The all embracing power of king is furnished by Ashokan edicts which talk of paternal despotism and seek to regulate even social and religious lives of the people. Legislation was largely a matter of confirming social usage and king had a fairly free hand but was expected to consult with his ministers. However the final decision laid with the monarch. Though the king was an autocrat, not limited by constitutional controls, there were many checks on his sovereignty which included dharma, council of ministers and most significantly, the public opinion. The king's duties included appointment and removal of the ministers, defence of treasury and the people, work for progress and welfare of the people, punish evil and influence the praja through his morality.

The large empire necessitated the presence of a strong and elabourate bureaucracy which was essentially supported by the economy. This bureaucracy supported not only the administration of political and civil affairs but also the economic affairs where the state was directly engaged in commercial activities. The council of ministers was an advisory body with no fixed number of ministers. Arthashastra stresses that councilors should speak freely and openly and work should be carried out according to majority verdict though the king could turn down their decision. It also lays down qualifications for the appointment of ministers, like the person should not be lured by wealth, not succumb to pressure etc. i.e. he should be'sarvopadashudha' (purest of all).

The state tried to control all the spheres of life through its vast bureaucracy. Kautilya mentions 18 Tirthas who were probably called mahamatras or high functionaries. He also provides for 27 superintendents concerned mostly with economic functions. Some of them also performed military duties. He also refers to duties of Gopa, sthenika, dharmastha, nagaraka etc. These were employed in urban, rural and border administration. Also a new class of mahamatras worked as dharmamahamatras, enforcing the social and political order ushered in by Ashoka.

Various lists indicate a tendency to increase the no. of officials. The bureaucracy was paid mainly in cash and was highly hierarchical. It is suggested by the pay scales for different categories of employees, the highest like mantrin, purohita, senapati and yuvaraj receiving 48,000 panas and lowest being paid only 60 pannas.

Bureaucracy formed the arm of the royal power, but the crucial factor that contributed to it was the development of the coercive power of the state on an unprecedented scale. According to Justin, Chandragupta Maurya possessed 600,000 troops which was thrice the no. of infantry possessed by Nandas. The usual limbs, the infantry, the cavalry, the chariots, the elephants were strengthened by the addition of 2 wings-the navy and transport and commissariat - a development suggested by both Megasthenes and Kautilya. The power of Sword was strengthened by the royal monopoly of arms and the control over the artisans who produced arms.

The Mauryan Kingdom was divided into four provinces which were further divided into districts and villages. The provincial governor was directly appointed by the king and was usually a member of the royal family. District governors were usually appointed by the provincial governors. The provincial governors were powerful and could act as a check on the viceroy and on occasions acted as effective rulers. Ashoka sent inspectors for tours every five years for an additional audit and check on provincial administration. The district was divided into a group of villages and the final unit of administration was the village. The group of villages was staffed with an accountant who maintained registered land and the tax collector who was concerned with various kinds of revenues. Each village had its own official such as the headman who was responsible to the accountant and the tax collector. The Mauryan rural administration as can be inferred from above was mainly designed to meet the needs of revenue administration though enforcement of law and order also remained an important task.

Thc growing economic activities of the state and the needs of urban settlements led to the creation of a machinery for town administration. The municipal administration of Patliputra described by Megasthenes does show the concern of the government for certain basic urban problems, such as sanitation, care of foreigners, registration of births and deaths etc. Kautilya does not give any indication of the association of local elements with town administration which is imposed from above. He lays down in detail the duties of the Nagaraka which included maintenance of law and order, supervision of sanitation arrangement and to take measures against outbreaks of fire. The Nagaraka has under him subordinate officials called sthanika and gopa who were placed in charge of the wards into which the town was divided.

Border administration was also an important element of administration. Ashoka introduced an element of moderation in his border administration and his dealings with the tribal people. The dharmamahamataras were asked to persuade the border people to confirm to dharma, rules to peaceful social conduct such as obeying the king and desisting from violence. But if they did not obey these rules, they were threatened with punishments.

The governance of the vast territory with the help of an expanding bureaucracy and a huge standing army involved expenditure. This seems to have been the guiding principle of the Mauryan state in undertaking and regulating numerous economic activities which brought it profit. It founded new settlements and sought to rehabilitate the decaying ones. The shudras for the first time were aided by the state to settle as farmers in these settlements. Kautilya deliberately fostered the rusticity of villages to augment agricultural output so as to achieve the maximum levels of surplus. The other source of taxation included the water tax (on land using the irrigation facilities of the state), tax on trade of cattle, livestock and dairy produce etc. Vishti (forced labour) was practiced. All this required strong and efficient machinery for assessment, collection and storage. However Kautilya considers assessment more important than storage and depositing.

The list of taxes is impressive and must have proved oppressive. But even all these were not considered adequate to meet the needs of exchequer, which had to finance the vast military and bureaucratic establishments. These, therefore had to be supplemented by the reclamation of virgin lands, exploitation of mines and the running of goldsmiths' shops, liquor shops and weaving concerns, all done under the aegis of the state.

The first efficient system of police and criminal administration buttressed by an elabourate system of espionage was developed during the Mauryan period. The kantakasodhana was organised to deal with a large number of eco crimes. The organisation of criminal administration was evidently an indigenous phenomenon. Similar is the case with various categories of spies who were employed to keep an eye and report on the criminal and anti-government activities of the people. The Dharmasthiyas were courts which decided personal disputes.

The nearest approach to a modern police-cum-magisterial officer was the Pradista, but he had some revenue functions also. On the other hand the samaharta, the sthanika and the gopa who had mainly judicial functions were also assigned some police and magisterial duties. Fines served as punishments in most cases. But certain crimes were considered too serious to be punished by fines alone and capital punishment was inflicted even by Ashoka, although he was a supporter of non-violence. Penalties, however, were based on varna hierarchies i.e. for the same kind of offence, brahmanas were punished far less severely than a shudra.

The Mauryan maintained friendly relations with several contemporary powers. Chandragupta received the Greek ambassador Megasthenes, Bindusara had cordial relations with Antiochus and Ashoka's edicts mention Antiochus Theos of Syria, Ptolemy III Philadelphus of Egypt, Antigonus Gonatus of Macedonia and Alexander etc. Ashoka also exchanged missions with Ceylon and gave his daughter in marriage to a Nepalese nobleman. Friendly political relationship with foreign rulers promoted commerce and communications with the outside world as well as exchange of ideas.

The Mauryan state took a keen interest in public works. These included:

- Interest in irrigation as it could be a major source of revenue e.g. Sudarshan lake
- Provision of medical treatment and medicines to both men and animals.
- State also helped citizens during natural calamities
- The Arthashastra mentions that king should look after orphans, old, unattended women etc.
- Laying down and repairing of roads etc.

  Thus, though essentially a police state, the Mauryan Empire also worked for the welfare of the people.

CONQUESTS OF CHANDRAGUPTA MAURYA

Conquest of Punjab

From the time of Alexander's departure from India to his death in 323 B.C. (June) in Babylonia, there were chaos, instability and infighting among the Greeks in N.W. India. Chandragupta took advantage of these conditions and gained control of this area. It must be noted that the Treaty of

Triparadisus does not mention those areas in Punjab and Sindh which were conquered by Alexander. It proves that Chandragupta had wrested these before the conclusion of this treaty. Treaty of Triparadisus was concluded in 321 B.C., according to which the territories conquered by Alexander were divided among his Generals.

Defeat of Nandas and Gaining the Control of Magadha

Puranas, Mudrarakshasa, Milindpanho, Parishishta Parvan and Mahavamsha Tika tell us that with the help of the cunning of Chanakya, Chandragupta overthrew Nanda king and Chandragupta wrested the control of Magadha.

War with Seleucus (306-305 B.C.)

After consolidating his position in Babylonia and Bactria upto 312 B.C., Selecus decided to fulfill the wish of Alexander of conquering India. He invaded India and faced Chandragupta Maurya. Surprisingly, the classical writers (Justin, Strabo, Plutarch, Arrian) don't mention this war explicitly.

Plutarch says that Chandragupta gave 500 elephants to Seleucus and Strabo says that Seleucus gave Asiana and took 500 elephants from Chandragupta in return for a matrimonial alliance. Generally, it is agreed that Seleucus was defeated in this war and had to cede 4 important territories to Chandragupta Mauyra. These were – Asiana (Herat), Arachosia (Kandhar), Gedsosia (Baluchistan) and Paropanisadar (Kabul Valley). This victory gained for Mauryas the scientific border.

Conquest of Saurashtra (West India)

The Girnar (Junagarh) inscription of Rudradaman states that during the rule of Chandragupta Maurya, Pushyagupta was the provincial governor of Saurashtra. He constructed the Lake Sudarshan by constructing dams across the rivers Suvarnasikta and Palasani. This shows that Chandragupta's sway was extended to this area also.

South India

Jain texts, early medieval inscriptions and evidence from Tamil sources indicate that Chandragupta had South India under his control as well.

Kalinga

On the basis of Megasthenes' account, Pliny says that Kalinga was an independent province during Chandragupta's reign.

But the evidence for Nanda's control of Kalinga, their subsequent overthrow by Chandragupta, and also Chandragupta's influence further south point towards Chandragupta's control over Kalinga also.

Bangladesh

The Mahasthan inscription (from Bogara, BD) which is an early Mauryan script mentions the image of Kakini. On this basis, Chandragupta's rule on this area is accepted. Jain texts like Kalpa Sutra and Parishishta Parvan call Chandragupta as ruler of Avanti.

BINDUSARA (298-273 B.C.)

- Puranas mention him as Nandasara, Bhadrasara and also as Varisara. One Chinese text Fa-Iu-An-Chu-Lin mentions him as Bindupala. Rajavali Katha, a Jain text calls him Singhasena. Jain texts call him as the Cesarean emperor of India.
- Athenius calls him Amitrochates, and Strabo calls him Alitrochates (Alitrochadis). These are thought to mean Amitraghat or Amitrakhad ('Slayer of Foes').
- Tibetan historian Taranath tells that on the advice of Chanakya, Bindusara had defeated sixteen kings whose kingdoms lay in the land between the two seas.
- According to the Divyavadan, during Bindusara's reign, the people of Taxila had revolted owing to the exploitative policies of the amatyas. This unrest was quelled by Ashoka who was the governor of Ujjain at that time.

- Athenius tells us that Bindusara had diplomatic relations with the Seleucid King of Syria, Antiochus-I, whom he requested to send him sweet wine, dried figs and a sophist. The last was refused as going against the tradition law by Antiochus-I.
- Bindusara has also been called as Nemit, the ruler of Champaran by Taranath.
- Since Ashoka is credited to have conquered only Kalinga, the extention of the Mauryan Empire beyond the Tungabhadra must have been the work of his predecessors. It was probably in the reign of Bindusara that the Mauryan control of Deccan and the Mysore plateau was firmly entrenched.

ASHOKA

- Ascended the throne in 273 B.C. Crowned himself as King in 269 B.C. Died in 232 B.C.
- For Ashoka's administration, religion, policies and achievements, his own inscriptions are a very important source material. Their importance is also due to the fact that Buddhist texts, which otherwise form an important source, have created such an aura around Ashoka's name that his true character and achievements could seldom be gleaned from them.

CLASSIFICATION OF ASHOKA'S EDICTS

Major Rock Edicts

Manshera	-	Hazara, Pakistan
Shahbazgarhi	-	Peshawar, Pakistan
Girnar (Junagarh)	-	Gujarat
Sopara	-	Thana, Maharashtra
Yerragudi	-	Kurnool, A.P
Jaugarh or Jaugada	-	Ganjam, Orissa
Dhauli	-	Puri, Orissa
Kalsi	-	Dehradun, Uttrakhand

- Due to deterioration by erosion, only 1/3rd remains of the Eighth Rock Edict at Sopara were found.
- At Dhauli and Jaugada, in place of No. XI, XII and XIII, two different Edicts have been engraved, which are known as Separate Kalinga Edicts No. I and II
- At Dhauli, a statue of elephant was found along with the inscriptions.
- The Major Rock Edicts were found mostly in the areas bordering the empire. At Yerragudi, two Minor Rock Edicts have also been found.

Major Rock Edict-I:	Condemnation of Killing of animals, restrictions on various festivities, gatherings, scaling down of animal killing in royal kitchen and the proposal to stop them altogether are the things mentioned here.
Major Rock Edict-II:	Provision for the treatment of human beings as well as animals in all parts of the empire as well as the bordering kingdoms like Cholas, Pandyas, Sattiyaputtas, Keralaputtas, Tanuraparni (Ceylon), the kingdom of King Antioka and his neighbour mentioned.
Major Rock Edict-III : (257 B.C.)	After he had been consecrated 12 years, Ashoka asked the Rajukas, Yuktas and Pradeshikas to tour the land every 5 years apart from following their routine duties. They were to look it to that the people followed the path of dharma (dhamma). The same Edict also talks about "expending a little and saving a little."
Major Rock Edict-IV:	Lays down various principles to be followed in the path of dhamma and asks children, grandchildren and

	great grandchildren to further these.
Major Rock Edict-V:	The appointment of Dhammamahamatras. Their main duty was to protect the dhamma and development of dhamma. They were to look after the religious welfare and well-being of people.
Major Rock Edict-VI:	Appointment of Prativedakas. They acquainted the Emperor with the problems of people. Ashoka says in this Edict that "there is no greater deed than the welfare of others".
Major Rock Edict-VII:	The importance of self-control and self-purification.
Major Rock Edict-VIII:	Pilgrimage of Bodh Gaya (Sambodhi) by Ashoka 10 years after he had been consecrated. Also the meeting and giving away of gold to brahmanas and shramanas
Major Rock Edict-IX:	The greatness of dhammadana over the charities performed during household ceremonies etc.
Major Rock Edict-X:	Ashoka would rather his people listen to dhamma and dharmopadeshakas than seek material pleasure and fame.
Major Rock Edict-XI:	Dhammadana, friendship and relationship according to dhamma; looking after the well-being of one's parents – all aspects of Dhamma.
Major Rock Edict-XII:	Expresses the desire of encouraging in people the growth of religious tolerance and in the sphere of religion the growth of essence (Dharmavridhi and Sarvridhi). For the growth of essence is essential – control of speech

	and somavaya. Samavaya – gathering to hear to one another's dhamma/ dharma.
Major Rock Edict-XIII:	Kalinga War after 8 years of consecration, its impact on Ashoka, his repentance. Several foreign kings, borderline kingdoms, semi-independent tribes are mentioned where Ashoka gained victory by Dhamma. It also contains the warning to some forest tribes.
Major Rock Edict-XIV:	It attempts to emphasize the relevance of the sentiments, repeated elsewhere again and again.
Separate Kalinga Edict I:	It is addressed to the Mahamatras of Toshali (or Samapa), who are also the judicial officers of the city. Here the emperor tells them that just as every individual prays for the well-being of his children in this and the other world, the emperor too wishes the same for his subjects whom he considers his children. The Mahamatras are asked to make efforts in achieving this. It also mentions that Mahamatras were being sent from Ujjain and Taxila to hear to imbibe the habits of right behaviour and following of Dhamma in the administrators of Kalinga's cities. They are asked to follow the 'middle path'.
Separate Kalinga Edict II:	It explicitly says that the emperor considers as his children all his subjects and an attempt to win over the confidence of the inhabitants at Kalinga is evident here

Minor Rock Edicts

Ahraura	-	U.P.
Sahasram	-	Bihar
Rupnath	-	M.P.
Gujjarra	-	M.P.
Panguraria (Budhni)	-	M.P.
Bhabru	-	Rajasthan
Bairat	-	Rajasthan
Yerragudi	-	Andhra Pradesh
Maski	-	Andhra Pradesh
Rajul-Mandagiri	-	Andhra Pradesh
Govimath	-	Karnataka
Palkigundu	-	Karnataka
Siddhapur	-	Karnataka
Jatinga-Rameshwar	-	Karnataka
Brahmagiri	-	Karnataka
Udayagolam	-	Karnataka
Mittur	-	Karnataka
Sannatai	-	Karnataka
New Delhi	-	Amarpuri colony of Lajpat Nagar
Bahapur	-	New Delhi.

- These are two edicts in this category, either or both of them occur at all these places with minor variations and their subject matter is always same. Except for Bhabru, the subject matter of which is very different from the rest

Minor Rock Edict I: It says that $2^{1/2}$ years before it was engraved, Ashoka had become an Upasaka, and 1 year before he had entered the Sangha and made efforts for the propagation of Dhamma. Ashoka also declares that owing to his efforts, many people in Jambudvipa had come under the fold of Dharma. According to Senart, this inscription

	was caused to be engraved 12 years after coronation.
Minor Rock Edict II:	It discusses the different principles and views regarding following of Dharmma.
Bhabru Edict:	"Priyadarshi, the king of Magadha, salutes to the Sangha and prays for its well- being. Buddham Sharanam Gachchhami, Dhamman Sharanam Gachchhami, Sangham Sharanam Gachchhami". Further Ashoka says that apart from what Buddha has said, which is all very well, he himself thought it fit/ apt to declare certain things for the furtherance of this great religion. He goes on to prescribe certain Buddhist texts which were to be read by the Bhikkhus, which are: Vinay Samukase, Aliyavasani, Anagatabhayani, Munigatha, Mauneya Sutta, Upatispasin and Chula-Rahulodeva Sutta.1

Pillar Edicts

Delhi	–	Topara		
Delhi	–	Meerut		
Lauriya	–	Araraj	–	Bihar
Lauriya	–	Nandangarh	–	Bihar
Rampurva:				
Prayag	–	Kaushmbi	–	U.P.

- The Pillar Edicts are seven in number, but all seven are to be found only in Delhi – Topra. All others have only six Edicts on them. The subject matter of all is the same.
- *Delhi-Topra:* It was found at Topra in Haryana from where it was brought to Delhi by Firuz Shah Tughlaq. Shams-i-Shiraj Afif has described it in his work. This pillar also bears the inscription of one Beesaldev

Chahman or Vigraharaj IV.

- *Delhi-Merrut*: According to Shams-i-Shiraj, Firuz Tughlaq brought it from Merrut and installed in the hills of Kashmiri Gate. Shiraj calls it Kushka-i-Shikar.
- *Lauriya-Nandangarh*: It also bears an inscription of Aurangzeb.
- *Prayag-Kaushambi*: Originally it was at Kaushambi. Akbar shifted it to Prayag. It bears Ashoka's instructions to the Mahamatras of Kaushambi and hence believed to have been at Kaushambi. Apart from Ashoka's Six Edicts, it also bears the inscription where Ashoka warns the wayward Buddhist monks, Queen's Edict, Harishen-Prashsti and also an inscription of Jahangir.

Minor Pillar Edicts		
Rummindei	-	Nepal border
Nigliva-Sagar	-	Nepal, near Rummindei
Sanchi	-	M.P.
Sarnath	-	U.P.
Prayag	-	U.P. (Warning to monks)
Queen's Edict	-	Prayag

Total Pillar Edicts = 12
Total Pillars = 10 with Edicts.

Minor Rock Edict I:	It says that $2^{1/2}$ years before it was
Pillar Edict I:	As a result of Ashoka's efforts, the people as well as the different officials were inspired to follow the dharma.
Pillar Edict II:	Ashoka defines the dharma and expounds on it.
Pillar Edict III:	The vices which are obstacles in the path of dharma and cause the downfall of an individual – Kodhe, Mane, Ishya, NIthuliya, Chande.
Pillar Edict IV:	The appointment of Rajukas to secure

	the welfare and happiness of subjects; to enable people perform their duties.
Pillar Edict V:	After 26 years of coronation, the ban on the killing of various animals was placed. Goes on to name some more which it expresses a desire should also be brought under the ban.
Pillar Edict VI:	Mentions that these religious writings are for the welfare of the people.
Pillar Edict VII:	Mentions the public works undertaken by Ashoka like planting of trees, digging of wells, building of rest-houses etc. The appointment of Dhammamahamatras and various principles of dharma, like service to/looking after one's parents are also mentioned
Rummindei Pillar Edict:	Visit by Ashoka 20 years after his coronation. Waiver of religious tax and reduction of land tax to 1/8th
Niglivasagar Pillar Edict:	It says that after 14 years of his coronation, Ashoka enlarged the stupa of Konakamuni Buddha, and 20 years after coronation he came here and offered prayers. It also mentions erection of a stone pillar.
Schism Edict (Sarnath):	An inscription on the Sarnath Pillar warns those Buddhist monks who were trying to break the Sangha with their behaviour.
Sanchi Pillar Edict:	It expresses the desire that till there are Sun and Moon, the dynasty of Emperor flourishes and his successors are expected to guard against any attempts at splitting the sangha.

Prayag Pillar Edict:	Also enjoins upon the Mahamatras of Kaushambi that they stop those who are trying to bring about a schism in the sangha.
Queen's Edict on:	Accepts the right of Kaurvaki, the
Prayag Pillar	mother of Tivar on the grants made to her.

CAVE EDICTS

- Ashoka's Edicts have been located in the caves in the Barabar Hills (old name Khallitak and Pravaragizi), which were donated to Ajivikas. These caves are called – Sudama, Karnachopar and Vishwajhonpadi.
- A cave of Lomash Rishi was also found here but with no inscriptions.
- *Dusharatha's Cave Edicts*: In the Ajivika caves in the Nagarjuni Hills which were called – Gopi, Vapi and Vadathik.

Cave Edicts I and II: Donation of the caves to Ajivikas after 12 years of Ashoka's coronation.

Cave Edict III: Donation after 19 years on coronation.

EDICTS IN FOREIGN LANGUAGES

- Two Aramaic Edicts and one stone tablet from Laghman (Lampaka) and Pul-i-Darunta respectively.
- A Greek and an Aramaic edict from Kandahar and a Graeco-Aramaic bilingual record from Shaz-i-Kuna (Kandahar).
- Aramaic inscription from Taxila.

PERSONAL INFORMATION ABOUT ASHOKA

- Inscriptions don't tell much about his early life. Buddhist literature, accounts of Chinese travellers, Kalhana's Rajatarangini do. Important in this regard are Samanta Paradika, the commentary on Vinay

Pitaka by Buddhaghosha, Divyavadan, Ashoka-vadan-mala, Asyamanjushrimulkalipa, Mahavamsha and Mahavamsha Tika etc.

- *Rajatarangini*: 'Creation of Shrinagar on the banks of Vitarta by Ashoka'.
- *Fa-Hsien, Hsuan Tsang*: Ashoka built thousands of viharas and stupas.
- *I-tsing*: saw Ashoka as an image of Bhikkhu at Pataliputra.
- *Dipavamsha and Mahavamsha*: Bindusara had 16 Queens and 101 Sons.
- *Mahavamsha*: The eldest son of Bindusara was Suman, in Divyavadan – he is called Sushim.
- *Fa-yu-an-chlin*: Chinese text calls him Sushim but calls Bindusara as Bindupala.
- *Divyavadan*: Vigatashoka was Ashoka's real brother, in Mahavamsha and Dipavamsha – he is called – Tissa, who was the youngest son of Bindusara. Vigatashoka and Tissa are one and the same person.
- *Hsuan-Tsamg calls Mahendra as Ashoka's brother, but in many Pali texts*: he is the famous Bhikshu.
- *Ashoka's son in inscription*: Tivar and his wife – Kaurvaki.
- *Ashoka's sons in literature*: Mahendra, Jalok, Kunal and wives - Asandhimitra, Tissazakshita, Padmavati and Devi. His daughters in Literature – Charumati, Sangamitra. Sangamitra was married to Kumaragnibrahma, son of Ashoka's sister. Charumati was married to Khattiya Devapala of Nepal.
- Initially Ashoka was known only as Priyadarshi, it was Turner who equated Ashoka with Priyadarshi on the basis of Dipavamsha. Afterwards the edicts at Maski, Udegolam and Mittur were found which give Ashoka's name.
- Buddhist texts tell exaggerated accounts of Ashoka's cruelty before he embraced Buddhism. Divyavadan tells that Ashoka had burnt alive 500 women and 500 amatyas. Both Divyavadan and Hsuan-Tsang's

account tell the story of the Hellhouse created by Ashoka and the torture carried out there.

- According to the Mahavamsha, Ashoka was called Chandashoka because he had ordered his ministers to kill bhikshus.
- According to Ashokavadan mala, Ashoka had ordered the killing at brahmans since they had insulted the image of Buddha.
- Samantapasadika, Dipavamsha, Mahavamsha, say that Ashoka embraced Buddhism under the influence of Nigrodh. It was Balapandit according to Divyavadan. Hsuan-Tsang says it was Upagupta.
- On the basis of Kharvela's Hathigumpha inscription, the ruler of Kalinga at the time of the famous Kalinga war was Mahameghavarman. Romila Thapar says that Kalinga War was for commercial purpose.
- Rajatarnagini calls Ashoka as the ruler of Kashmir but not Chandragupta or Bindusara, therefore Ashoka must have won it. Ashoka's sway over Khas or Swas and also Nepal is corroborated by Rajatarangini and Taranath.
- The Inscriptions which testify to Ashoka's being a Buddhist –
  - *Minor Rock Edict I*: mentions Ashoka's embracing of Buddhism
  - *Rock Edict VIII*: Sambodhi Yatra after 10 years of coronation
  - Bhabru Edict
  - Edicts at Sanchi, Sarnath, and Prayag
  - *Maski Edict*: Ashoka calls himself 'Buddha Shakya'
  - *Minor Rock Edict (Ahraura)*: 'Enthroning of Buddha's ahses'
  - Rummindei Pillar Edict
  - Niglirasagar Pillar Edict
- The obstacles in the path of Dhamma mentioned in Pillar Edict – III as Kodhe (Anger), Mane (Pride), Ishya (Jealousy), Nithuliya (Cruelty) and Chande.

- The Dharma as expounded by Ashoka is taken from Chula-Rahulodeva Sutta. Preaches of Dhamma from Mahavamsha and Dipavamsha (After IIIrd Buddhist Council) are–

Madhyantik	-	Kashmir, Gandhar
Mahadeva	-	Mashishamandala
Rakshit	-	Vanavasi
Dharmarakshit	-	Aparantaka.
Mahadharmarakshit	-	Maharashtra
Maharakshit	-	Yonaloka
Majjhim	-	Himavant Pradesh
Soma and Vitara	-	Suvarnbhumi (Burma)
Mahendra, Sanghamitra, Bhadrashala, Samlal	-	Tamraparni (Ceylon)

FACTS ABOUT MAURYAN ADMINISTRATION

- *Sources*: Arthashastra, Indica, Inscriptions of Ashoka
- *Remarkable features*: Centralizing tendency and enormous powers of the ruler. According to Kautilya, King's order overrides religious injunctions, historical traditions and prevalent customs.

Four branches of knowledge (Kautilya):

Trayi	-	Religious and moral aspect
Varta	-	Agriculture, animal husbandry and commerce, i.e. commercial aspect
Anvekshiki	-	Logical aspect (derived by common sense)
Dandaniti	-	State power

According to Kautilya, first three are possible through fourth:

- According to him, the Saptangas of State are: Raja, Amatya, Janapad, Durga, Mitra, Danda (sena) and Kosa (Kosha). Enemy – eighth added by Kautilya.
- Hellenistic influence – centralizing tendency. But even then, according to Kautilya the aim of all such power is welfare of the people.
- Rock Edict VI – "There is no greater deed than service to others". – Ashoka.
- Controls on the power of the king are Niti and

Dharm, education and training of the king, consulting institutions like cabinet of ministers, and people and their opinion.

- There were 18 high officials namely, Mantri, Sannidhata, Purohit, Pradeshtha, Senapati, Vyavaharika, Yuvaraj, Nayak, Mantriparishada-dhyaksha, Danapala, Dauvarik, Antarveshik, Prashastri, Samaharta, Karmantika, Durgapala, Antapala and Paur. Purohit, Senapati and Yuvaraj were the most important. They received 48000 panas per anum. Dauvarika, Antarveshika, Samaharta, and Sannidhata next. They received 24,000 panas per anum.
- *Officers mentioned in Adhyaksha Prachara Chapter of Arthashastra*:

Shulkadhyaksha	-	Chief Controller of Customs and Octroi
Pautavadhyaksha	-	Chief Controller of Weights and Measures
Manadhyaksha	-	Chief Surveyor and Timekeeper
Sutradhyaksha	-	Chief Textile Commissioner
Sitadhyaksha	-	Chief Superintendent of Crown Lands
Suradhyaksha	-	Chief Controller of alcoholic beverages
Sunadhyaksha	-	Chief Superintendent of Slaughter-houses
Ganikadhyaksha	-	Chief Controller of Entertainers
Mudradhyaksha	-	Chief Passport Officer
Vivitadhyksha	-	Chief Controller of Pasture Lands
Navadhyaksha	-	Chief Controller of Shipping
Kupyodhyaksha	-	Chief Superintendent of Forest Produce
Panyadhyaksha	-	Chief Controller of State Trading
Lakshanadhyaksha	-	Chief Master of the Mint
Sauvarnik	-	Chief Master of the Mint
Nivigrahaka	-	Lower level treasurer

- *The State was divided into following parts*:

Uttarapath	-	Takshila
Dakshinapath	-	Suvarnagiri
Kalinga	-	Toshali (Samapa)
Avanti	-	Ujjain
Prachya	-	Pataliputra

- There were 6 Committees of 5 each for town administration – Taxation (revenue), Commerce, arts and crafts, registration of births and deaths, and industries and foreigners as mentioned in Indica. Kautilya mentions only Nagaraka for this purpose or Nagaradhyakshas.
- *Other political units were like*:

Janpad	-	a district-like entity under Samaharta
Sthaniya	-	800 towns/ villages
Dronamukha	-	400 towns/ villages
Kharvatika	-	200 towns/ villages
Sangrahan	-	100 towns/ villages
Gram		
A group of about 20 villages had their chief	-	Gopa

- Army according to Megathenes had 6 wings – Horse, Elephant, Chariot, Cavalry, Navy and Military transport. According to Kautilya, there were only 4 wings (the first four), therefore called 'chatturangini sena'. According to him, Brahmans should not be admitted into army.
- According to Kautilya, there were two Courts namely, Kantakashodhana (Criminal) and Dharmasthiya (Civil). There were two types of spies (Gudhapurushas): Sanstha and Sanchara.
- *Sources of income*:

Durg	-	Income from cities and townships through various taxes, customs etc
Rashtra	-	Income from various Janpadas e.g. Bhag (land tax), Sita (income from Crown land), and Bali (from pilgrimage places and other religious places)
Nadipalastar	-	Toll for the transport on bridges on rivers
Vartani	-	Road tax
Vivitap	-	Tax from pasture lands
Khani	-	Income from mines

Satu	-	Income from fruits, vegetables etc.
Vraj	-	Income from animals
Vana	-	Forest produce

- Seven "Castes" as mentioned by Megasthenes were Philosophers or brahmanas/ darshanik, Cultivators or farmers, Soldiers, Herdsmen, Artisans, Magistrates and Councilors.
- Officers appointed by Ashoka

Rajuka: Officers in control of land and justice who were authorized to award honours and penalties. Their duty was to promote the welfare of people. Strabo calls them Officers of bandobast.

Yuktas: Subordinate officers entrusted with secretarial work and accounting

Pradeshika: Administration of law and order, revenue. Administration of large land tracts, etc

Prativedak: Special reporters of king and they had direct access to him

Dhammamahamatra: The most important official entrusted with establishing and promoting Dhamma. Authorized to tour and alleviate the woes of people.

China, the cradle of civilization of amazing continuity was controlled by imperialistic interest of many countries in 19th and early 20th century. 1911 revolution under Kuomintang and Sun Yat Sen hijacked by Yuan Shikai failed to realise its objective although middle kingdom was abolished. After Shikai's death, China entered into an era of warlords of anarchy. 1919 revolution, a result of global ramification of October Revolution, failed to find any permanent footing.

In 1921, Chinese Communist Party was formed by some professors and interested people in Peluing University with Russian help. Russian commission wanted to expand in a global manner and China was one of their targets. Many Russian communists like Borodin tried to organize the Chinese Communist Party and helped it in initial stages. Russia wanted Kuomintang and CCP to work together. They even started a university with the name of Sun Yat Sen in Moscow to train Chinese in military and revolutionary ideas.

Kuomintang and CCP worked together till their break in 1927. Sun Yat Sen died in 1925 and Chiang Kai Shek, his co-brother came to power. Kuomintang was slowly establishing power in south China in and around Canton and spreading to the north.

Slowly but surely, Kuomintang spread to the north, and captured Peluing and other urban areas. Chiang, whose policies were becoming increasingly right wing, lacked Sun Yat Sen's vision and abilities even though he was initially able. But he viewed communists with suspicion and started vigourous campaign against them with intentions of purging China of the communist menace.

Meanwhile Chinese communists who had been trying to build mass base in peasantry established Soviet in Lelaugsi province in south China. Mao Tse Dung, founder member of CCP, was the organizer of Lelaugsi Soviet and they did commendable job there. They started organizing Red Army under Bia and Chu Teh. Red Army, later Peoples' Army, organized with the help of Russians was the main prop and trump card of Chinese in later struggle.

Meanwhile Chiang Kai Shek increased the intensity of purges. Soviet was not able to withstand continuous pressure. So Mao made the historic decision to take up long march covering 6000 km across land terrain, mountains, rivers, jungles covering 24 miles a day. Out of motley crowd of 90000 people who started the journey, only 20000 survived.

But long march, one of the worlds' most enduring sagas of human endurance established Mao as a leader and helped spread of Communism. The marching communist spread the message throughout peasantry and helped to get a foothold in interior China.

They established Shensi Soviet in northern China, and started their work in earnest. The areas under Communist came to be known as liberated areas. They did many reforms and aimed at emancipation of peasantry and won their hearts. Meanwhile Chu Teh did a commendable job of recruiting and disciplining Red Army which went on increasing. Its size made it a formidable fighting machine with zeal in its ideologies.

Japanese aggression on Chinese mainland from 1932 pushed back both Kuomintang and nationalist towards the interior. All the coastal urban areas were taken over by the Japanese. Chiang Kai Shek was forced by the nationalists to have an understanding with the Chinese. So CCP and Kuomintang came to reluctant agreement against common enemy - Japanese.

At the Start of World War-II, allies started helping nationalists against Japanese. But Chiang was half hearted in his attempt to push back Japanese. The guerilla army of CCP was more successful in harassing the Japanese. Chiang was more interested in preventing Chinese communists' spread.

After Japanese withdrawal, there was scramble for territories and the Red Army was ordered to take as much as they can. The retreating Russian armies from Manchuria had left behind enough ammunition for the communist who with their revolutionary zeal were able to fight their way into the Chinese heartland. Kuomintang was hopelessly divided and had to beat retreat. Meanwhile U.S.A. which wanted to prevent spread of communism started supporting Chiang and send Marshal to have dialogue and to bring both parties into an understanding. But Chiang's insistence that Red Army should be placed under his command broke off the negotiations and civil war started.

Once civil war started, Chiang's weakness came to the fore. He like Hitler hailed to order retreat and his armies were hopelessly surrounded in Peluing and Nanhing. Red Army with peasant support and discipline was able to easily route the Kuomintang, and Chiang's nationalist forces were pushed to Formosa (Taiwan), and Mao proclaimed Republic of China as October 1, 1949.

Reason for CCP's success was that they had support of peasantry whose lot they tried to improve. In territories under their control, they established rule of law, decreased rent and revenue, distribution of land, and emancipation of serfs. Meanwhile Kuomintang was trying hard to curtail inflation and tottering economy. His policies were becoming increasingly right wing and upper class oriented. CCP got"mandate of heaven" which gave them legitimacy in the eye of ordinary Chinese peasant.

China was an industrially backward agrarian economy. Marxian communism deals with proletariat and their revolution which brings the social revolution. In China, there was no proletariat (working class - Industrial worker) worth their name. And Chinese communism had support among peasants who were not able to understand intricacies of the theoretical dogma.

Mao, the great visionary leader gave a new look to communism. He says that party workers are like fish among water (peasants). He built up a strong worker base. With his dedicated band of workers he tried to spread his ideas among the ordinary peasantry.

Maoist communism has an earthly appeal. He did not give much importance to the theoretical intricacies. He was much more a practical man. His communism was suited for the ground realities of the Chinese society. It was elite band of communist workers of party controlling the peasant and guiding the country to prosperity. Since peasants are not able to rule or take part effectively in the ruling of the country, he argued that the party elite should be able to judge what is good and bad for them. Chinese revolution added a new chapter to world history of communism. 40 years after October 1917 revolution, 1/3rd of the world's population was under communism. No ideology after the Islam is 1st century of its existence was able to exert such influence in the world. Later on Mao tried to change the Chinese society with policies like great leap forward, Cultural Revolution. He was only partially successful. Chinese communism still survives albeit in different forms. It had suited to the changing world while its mentor USSR has collapsed a decade ago.

CHANDRAGUPTA -- EMPEROR AND MARTYR

Hortly after the passing of Alexander, India's first great empire arose, ruled by Chandragupta Maurya. According to legend, Chandragupta Maurya was the son of a herdsman. When he was a young man he met Alexander the Great, and days later he was awakened by a lion gently licking his body -- an omen that he would become royalty.

Chandragupta's counselor and advisor was his adoptive father, Chanakya, who is said to have kept Chandragupta's youthful impulses in check and to have been learned in medicine, Hellenism and Zoroastrianism. And it is said that he guided Chandragupta in a bloody war that began two years after Alexander left India, a war that ended with Chandragupta overthrowing the Nanda dynasty that had been ruling the state of Magadha.

Chanakya became Chandragupta's Prime Minister, and legend describes Chanakya (Kautilya) as the author of a book entitled Arthasastra, which appears to have been written during the time of Chandragupta but with writings added centuries later. Arthasastra means science of property and material success, and in the book this success includes political and diplomatic strategy aimed at uniting India. It has a flavour to it similar to the Legalism that rivaled Confucianism and Taoism in China. The book advises a king to control his subjects, especially his ministers, and the Brahmins, wealthy merchants and his beautiful women. To help in this, according to the author, the king should employ an army of various artful persons as spies who keep watch at all levels of society. Arthasastraadvises a king to be energetic, ever wakeful, to make himself accessible to his subjects and to guard against six enemies: anger, greed, lust, exuberance, hauteur and vanity.

Foremost is the book's advocacy of military expansion. In Arthasastra it is claimed that aggrandizement is human nature, that a power superior in strength to another power should launch a war against that power, and that war keeps a nation's blood circulation regular. Chanakya was aware that toward the northwest, in the Indus Valley, were tribal republics and monarchies that had been weakened by war against Alexander. Moreover, Alexander had demonstrated that a disciplined and strong force could conquer the region. And it appeared that an India united by a great conqueror was the best defence against a recurring foreign intrusion. Chandragupta, in accordance with the views of Chanakya, sent an army of infantry, cavalry, many chariots and elephants to the Indus Valley, extending his rule there and beyond, into the Hindu Kush. The first Seleucid king, Seleucus I, attempted to recover lands taken by Chandragupta. But in the year 305 BCE, Chandragupta turned back Seleucus' drive. Seleucus was forced to settle with Chandragupta. Chandragupta then conquered northward from Magadha, into the Himalayas, and he conquered the rest of northern India.

CHANDRAGUPTA AS AUTOCRAT, SENSUALIST AND MARTYR

The agricultural lands around the capital belonged to Chandragupta, which he "rented" for a quarter or sometimes a half of what was produced on them. And Chandragupta made those peasants working his fields exempt from service in his military or other obligations to the state.

Chandragupta divided his empire into districts, which were administered by his closest relatives and most trusted generals. Civil servants ruled various departments such as trade, taxation, mining, roads, and irrigation canals. His government held trade monopolies and owned slaughter-houses, gambling halls, mines, shipbuilding operations, armament factories and spinning and weaving operations. His government oversaw the standardization of weights, measures and coinage. It controlled prices and trade, including trade in liquor and prostitution. It obliged drinking places to have couches, scents, water and other amenities, and drinking places and "public houses" were not to be near each other.

Chandragupta feared revenge and assassins. Against these possibilities he had a network of spies. He expected authorities in various districts to know all comings and goings. People who were considered dangerous to his rule might disappear without a trace. He had food tasters to avoid being poisoned. And, like Shih Huang-ti, he never slept in the same bed two nights in succession.

Eliciting confessions by torture remained a normal method in police work. Punishment depended on class: Brahmin's were not tortured, but upon conviction of a crime they could be branded, exiled or sent to work in the mines.

The low incidence of thievery described by Megasthenes might have been a result of the punishment for such a crime. Common people were executed for theft, for damaging property of the king, breaking into someone's home, evading taxes, injuring an artisan working for the state and many other crimes. Failure to meet a contract could lead to a fine if not a harsher penalty, as could incompetence in various forms of work, from washing clothes to treating the ill.

Toward the end of his more than twenty years of rule, Chandragupta surrounded himself with dancing girls and courtesans — women who also worked as housemaids, cooks, garland makers, shampooers and who fanned Chandragupta or held an umbrella for him. He seldom left his palace, except for an occasional festival. But he remained a man of religion and concerned about his subjects. According to legend he was converted to Jainism by a sage who had predicted a twelve-year drought. With the drought came famine in place of the affluence described by Megasthenes. In an effort to combat the drought, Chandragupta, in 301 BCE, abdicated in favour of one of his sons, Bindusara, and he withdrew with the Jainist sage to a religious retreat in India's southwest. There, according to legend, while appealing to God for relief from the drought, he fasted to death .

BUDDHIST EMPEROR ASHOKA

Indusara, ruled for twenty-five years. He warred occasionally, reinforcing his authority within India, and he acquired the title "Slayer of Enemies." Then in the year 273 BCE, he was succeeded by his son Ashoka (Ashoka), who in his first eight years of rule did what was expected of him: he looked after the affairs of state and extended his rule where he could. Around the year 260 Ashoka fought great battles and imposed his rule on people southward along the eastern coast of India — an area called Kalinga.

The sufferings created by the war disturbed Ashoka. He found relief in Buddhism and became an emperor at least a little different in values from his father, grandfather and others. He was a Buddhist lay member and went on a 256-day pilgrimage to Buddhist holy places in northern India. Buddhism benefited from the association with state power that Hinduism had enjoyed — and that Christianity would enjoy under Constantine the Great.

Like Jeroboam and other devout kings, Ashoka was no revolutionary. Rather than India changing politically, Buddhism was changing. In the years to come, Ashoka mixed his Buddhism with material concerns that served the Buddha's original desire to see suffering among people mitigated: Ashoka had wells dug, irrigation canals and roads constructed. He had rest houses built along roads, hospitals built, public gardens planted and medicinal herbs grown. But Ashoka maintained his army, and he maintained the secret police and network of spies that he had inherited as a part of his extensive and powerful bureaucracy. He kept his hold over Kalinga, and he did not allow the thousands of people abducted from Kalinga to return there. He announced his intention to "look kindly" upon all his subjects, as was common among kings, and he offered the people of Kalinga a victor's conciliation, erecting a monument in Kalinga which read:

All men are my children, and I, the king, forgive what can be forgiven.

Ashoka converted his foreign policy from expansionism to that of coexistence and peace with his neighbours — the avoidance of additional conquests making his empire easier to administer. In keeping with his Buddhism he announced that he was determined to ensure the safety, peace of mind and happiness of all "animate beings" in his realm. He announced that he would now strive for conquest only in matters of the human spirit and the spread of "right conduct" among people. And he warned other powers that he was not only compassionate but also powerful.

Ashoka's wish for peace was undisturbed by famines or natural disasters. His rule did not suffer from the onslaught of any great migration. And during his reign, no neighbouring kings tried to take some of his territory — perhaps because these kings were accustomed to fearing the Maurya monarchs and thinking them strong.

The resulting peace helped extend economic prosperity. Ashoka relaxed the harsher laws of his grandfather, Chandragupta. He gave up the kingly pastime of hunting game, and in its place he went on religious pilgrimages. He began supporting philanthropies. He proselytized for Buddhism, advocating non-violence, vegetarianism, charity and tenderness to all living things.

Ashoka had edicts cut into rocks and pillars at strategic locations throughout his empire, edicts to communicate to passers-by the way of compassion, edicts such as "listen to your father and mother," and "be generous with your friends and relatives." In his edicts he spread hope in the survival of the soul after death and in good behaviour leading to heavenly salvation. And in keeping with the change that was taking place in Buddhism, in at least one of his edicts Ashoka described Siddhartha Gautama not merely as the teacher that Siddhartha had thought of himself but as "the Lord Buddha."

Ashoka called upon his subjects to desist from eating meat and attending illicit and immoral meetings. He ordered his local agents of various ranks, including governors, to tour their jurisdictions regularly to witness that rules of right conduct were being followed. He commanded the public to recite his edicts on certain days of the year.

Ashoka's patronage of Buddhism gave it more respect, and in his empire Buddhism spread. More people became vegetarian, and perhaps there was some increase in compassion toward others. Ashoka served harmony by pleading for tolerance toward Hindus and Jains. He worshiped no jealous god, and mindful of the close ties between Buddhism and Hinduism he claimed that the Brahmin's creed deserved respect, and he included Brahmins among his officials.

Not all Brahmins returned Ashoka's kindness. They were displeased with Ashoka's campaign against their sacrificial slaughtering of living creatures. But Ashoka's opposition to such sacrifices did please many among India's peasantry, whose flocks had long been plundered by local rulers seeking animals for their sacrifices.

Ashoka sent missionaries to the kingdoms of southern India, to parts of Kashmir in the northwest, to Persia, Egypt and Greece, but as Christians were to learn, old habits are not easily broken. Buddhism outside his kingdom took root only on the island of Lanka.

Work, taxation, class relations, government bureaucracy and village politics changed little, all of which — like Ashoka's authority — were considered the natural order of things. Whether prostitution had ended is unknown. In religion, old habits continued among Buddhists, as they looked to Brahmins to conduct those rites associated with births, marriages and deaths. Ashoka attempted to resolve differences among the Buddhists — as the Christian emperor Constantine would among the Christians — but conflicts among the Buddhists remained and would grow.

In the final years of his reign, Ashoka withdrew from public life, and in 232 BCE — after thirty-seven years of rule — he died. During the reign of his heirs the empire begin to split apart, including the breaking away of Kalinga. Why this happened is unknown. Buddhist writings suggest that decay had come before Ashoka's death. Some scholars attribute the decline to economic pressures: revenues from taxing agriculture and trade that were inadequate in maintaining the large military and army of bureaucrats. Perhaps palace politics reduced the ability of Ashoka 's heirs to govern. Perhaps Ashoka's heirs inherited from Ashoka a pacifism that discouraged their using force in keeping the empire together. Whatever the cause or causes, regions within the empire asserted their independence, and the empire disintegrated while the Maurya family, in Pataliputra, continued to rule.

COLLAPSE OF THE MAURYA EMPIRE

n 185 BCE, the rule of the Maurya family ended when an army commander-in-chief, Pusyamitra Sunga, murdered the last Maurya king during a parade of his troops. Pusyamitra's rise to power has been described, perhaps inaccurately, as a reaction by Brahmins to the Buddhism of the Maurya family. Nevertheless, the influence of state power on religion continued, with Pusyamitra supporting orthodox Brahminism and appointing Brahmins to state offices. And, with Pusyamitra's rule, animal sacrifices returned that had been prohibited under Ashoka and his heirs. Other matters outlawed by the Maurya also returned, including musical festivals and dances.

Then came invasions. Perhaps the collapse of the Maurya Empire signaled to outsiders that India was now vulnerable — much as division after Alexander's death had brought an assault by Celts.

The first of the great invasions began roughly two years after Pusyamitra took power. The king of Bactria, Demetrius, followed the footsteps of Alexander through the Khyber Pass and extended his power into the northern Indus Valley, where he began what was to become a series of wars between the Greeks and Indians.

The Greeks brought with them a better coin than was being used in India, which contributed to regional and inter-regional trade. They brought with them ideas in astronomy, architecture and art that spread through India, and with the new art came new depictions of Hindu gods and a new image of the Buddha.

Between the years 155 and 130, a Greek named Menander (known to Indians as Milinda) ruled in India's northwest. He sent his army into the Ganges Valley as far as Magadha's capital, Pataliputra. But, failing to capture that city, he returned to his kingdom in the northwest. In Pataliputra the Sunga dynasty, created by Pusyamitra Sunga, continued its rule.

Like Ashoka, Menander converted to Buddhism. This conversion may have facilitated the passage of Buddhist ideas west to Bactria and from Bactria farther west. The Greeks in India helped in spreading ideas westward.

The road between India and Bactria and India had become a bridge to and from the West. To the Indus Valley came ideas from Zoroastrianism, and in India arose the belief in a savior who at the end of time would lead the forces of light and goodness in a final victory against of the forces of darkness and evil.

SCYTHIAN AND KUSHAN INVASIONS

Pushed upon by a Chinese resurgence, those whom the Chinese called Xiongnu pushed on the Indo-European speaking tribes whom the Chinese called the Yüeh Chih — a people also called Kushans. The Kushans pushed on Scythians, who left their homeland in Central Asia and pushed into an area southeast of the Caspian Sea, an area to become known as Parthia. From 141 to 128 BCE the Scythians were able to push into lush, agricultural Bactria, against the Greeks there, who were already weakened by warfare. Soon thereafter, the Kushans invaded Bactria. Then around 50 BCE, the Parthian empire — which in Persia had replaced the power of the Seleucid dynasty — invaded northwestern India. And also invading India were the Scythians from Bactria.

The last of the Greek kings in India, Hermaeus, tried unsuccessfully to defend his rule from these attacks. In the Indus Valley, Greeks, Scythians and Parthians fought into the first century CE, and the Scythians extended their rule into north-central India and south along India's western coast, to the Gulf of Cambay. They ended Greek rule in India but maintained the Indo-Greek culture, some of which they had acquired in Bactria. In India, the Scythians became known as *Sakas*. Like other conquerors, the Sakas kept the local royalty as their subordinates. And Saka rulers became known as *Satraps* or *Viceroys*.

In the middle of the first century CE, another tribe of Kushans left Bactria and pushed into northwest India. After a generation or more a Kushan named Kanishka became the greatest of the Kushan kings. He expanded his rule from Bactria to the centre of the Ganges valley and south along the Indus River to the Arabian Sea, and like the Saka rulers he absorbed lesser kings and made them sub-rulers.

TRADE, PROSPERITY AND CULTURAL DIFFUSIONS

The centuries of invasions were dark times for much of India, but not so for the southern part of the sub-continent, which was peopled by Dravidians. Unlike other Dark Ages, during the period of invasions into India much of its roads and ports were maintained. Southern India benefited from expanded economic and cultural contacts with the world outside India and an expanded trade with West Asia and the Roman Empire. The south had become the most prosperous part of India. Leaving southern ports were ivory, onyx, cotton goods, silks, pepper and other spices, and from the Roman empire the Indians imported tin, lead, antimony and wine.

Indian ships sailed south to Lanka and then east to Southeast Asian ports, where Indian merchants sold cotton cloth, ivory, brass wear, monkeys, parrots and elephants to Chinese merchants, who transported their goods by sea to China. From Southeast Asian ports Indian merchants acquired spices that they traded elsewhere. Trade between India and China passed also across Central Asia by camel caravan, across what would become known as the great northern silk route, China sending musk, raw and woven silk, tung oil and amber westward into India.

Accompanying this seagoing trade, wave after wave of Indians emigrated. These colonists reached Lanka, the coast of Burma, what is now Thailand and Cambodia, the Malay Peninsula, Java, Sumatra and Borneo, and a few reached Taiwan and the Philippines.

In India, meanwhile, the increase in India's trade led to the rise of bankers and financiers among the Indians, and these men of wealth gave support to monarchies and landlords short on cash. Families in banking and commerce extended their enterprises into as many urban centres as they could, in India and abroad. And the increase in trade brought a rise in intellectual activity among the Indians - as it had among the Greeks. Science and the arts flourished, stimulated too by ideas that the Greeks brought from Bactria.

KANISHKA'S EMPIRE AND BUDDHISM

Like tribal people before them -- and like the Germans who would invade the Roman Empire -- Kanishka and the Kushans adopted aspects of the civilization they had conquered. Kanishka's empire prospered economically, and it is said that to his court, from all over Asia, the wealth and wisdom of Kanishka attracted merchants, artists, poets and musicians. Like other barbarian rules, Kanishka found Buddhism more accessible than Hinduism. Kanishka became a patron of Buddhism, and Buddhists would rank him as one of their own and with Ashoka and Menander as a great king. Kanishka would remain attached to warfare for the remainder of his life, while his attachment to Buddhism remained an ideal separate from the struggle over power.

Kanishka was eclectic in religion. He appears also to have been inclined toward the Persian cult of Mithras, to Zoroastrianism, and to have also worshiped Greek and Hindu deities. Buddhism dominated in the cities of Kanishka's empire and in Kanishka's court, while through his empire Brahmin families maintained orthodox Hinduism.

Kanishka is said to have been attempting to reconcile Hinduism and Buddhism. And he convened a Buddhist council in Kashmir -- much as the emperor Constantine would call a council of Christians - in hope of resolving conflict that had developed among Buddhists: between Mahayana Buddhism, meaning the Great Vehicle, and Hinayana Buddhism, the Little Vehicle. Hinayana Buddhism was mainly in the southern half of India.

Chapter 8

Foregin Elements

LATERAL CULTURE

The term culture refers to a state of intellectual development or manners. The social and political forces that influence the growth of a human being is defined as culture.

Indian culture is rich and diverse and as a result unique in its very own way. Our manners, way of communicating with one another, etc are one of the important components of our culture. Even though we have accepted modern means of living, improved our lifestyle, our values and beliefs still remain unchanged. A person can change his way of clothing, way of eating and living but the rich values in a person always remains unchanged because they are deeply rooted within our hearts, mind, body and soul which we receive from our culture.

Indian culture treats guests as god and serves them and takes care of them as if they are a part and parcel of the family itself. Even though we don't have anything to eat, the guests are never left hungry and are always looked after by the members of the family. Elders and the respect for elders is a major component in Indian culture. Elders are the driving force for any family and hence the love and respect for elders comes from within and is not artificial. An individual takes blessings from his elders by touching their feet. Elders drill and pass on the Indian culture within us as we grow.

"Respect one another" is another lesson that is taught from the books of Indian culture. All people are alike and respecting one another is ones duty. In foreign countries the relation between the boss and the employee is like a master and slave and is purely monetary whereas in Indian culture the relation between the boss and the employee is more like homely relations unlike foreign countries.

Helpful nature is another striking feature in our Indian culture. Right from our early days of childhood we are taught to help one another in need of help and distress. If not monetary then at least in kind or non-monetary ways. Indian culture tells us to multiply and distribute joy and happiness and share sadness and pain. It tells us that by all this we can develop co-operation and better living amongst ourselves and subsequently make this world a better place to live in.

Indian culture is rich and diverse and as a result unique in its very own way. Our manners, way of communicating with one another, etc are one of the important components of our culture. Even though we have accepted modern means of living, improved our lifestyle, our values and beliefs still remain unchanged. A person can change his way of clothing, way of eating and living but the rich values in a person always remains unchanged because they are deeply rooted within our hearts, mind, body and soul which we receive from our culture.

The culture of India is one of the oldest and unique. In India, there is amazing cultural diversity throughout the country. The South, North, and Northeast have their own distinct cultures and almost every state has carved out its own cultural niche. There is hardly any culture in the world that is as varied and unique as India. India is a vast country, having variety of geographical features and climatic conditions. India is home to some of the most ancient civilizations, including four major world religions, Hinduism, Buddhism, Jainism and Sikhism.

A combination of these factors has resulted into an exclusive culture- Indian culture. Indian culture is a composite mixture of varying styles and influences. In the matter of cuisine, for instance, the North and the South are totally different. Festivals in India are characterized by colour, gaiety, enthusiasm, prayers and rituals. In the realm of music, there are varieties of folk, popular, pop, and classical music. The classical tradition of music in India includes the Carnatic and the Hindustani music.

India, a place of infinite variety, is fascinating with its ancient and complex culture, dazzling contrasts and breathtaking physical beauty. Among the most remarkable features of India, is the arts and culture in particular. The Indian culture has persisted through the ages precisely for the reasons of antiquity, unity, continuity and the universality of its nature. Thus within the ambience of Indian culture one can identify 'Indian Music', 'Indian Dance', 'Indian Cinema', 'Indian Literature', Indian Cuisine' 'Indian Fairs and Festivals' and so on.

Indian culture treats guests as god and serves them and takes care of them as if they are a part and parcel of the family itself. Even though we don't have anything to eat, the guests are never left hungry and are always looked after by the members of the family. "Respect one another" is another lesson that is taught from the books of Indian culture. Helpful nature is another striking feature in our Indian culture. Indian culture tells us to multiply and distribute joy and happiness and share sadness and pain. It tells us that by all this we can develop co-operation and better living amongst ourselves and subsequently make this world a better place to live in.

Nowadays the Indian Culture has crossed the geographic boundaries and has extended globally. Whoever May it be an Indian or a person from any other country, attracted from the exuberant Indian Culture and traditions.

HISTORY OF INDIA'S CULTURE

Ancient civilization in India reveals marvelous facts about our heritage. It is a eye opener as to how kingdoms ruled and how people went about life in a logical way. Though medieval, it is actually amazing to find how people transacted and went about building dams and tended to the chief occupation which was agriculture. Dance and rituals were always a part of Indian culture and this was the chief mode of entertainment.

Indian culture is also about respecting elders, honoring

heroes and cherishing love. It is a land of aspirations, achievements and self reliance. Indian culture has a very high level of tolerance and hence the advent of so many external cultures was not restricted.

Adaptation to any culture or embracing a religion was always the democratic culture. Indian history is about war heroes during Indus valley civilization and the initial time when currency was coined.

Indian history talks a lot about self reliance especially in terms of food and agricultural produce. This was the great effort put in by the farmers and support received through irrigation. The modern agriculture also shows a lot of indigenous methods of preserving the produce. The Chola dynasty, the great King Emperor Ashoka and the secular era of Emperor Akbar will always be green in our memory. Several books are written on the rich Indian culture wherein the saints preserved the Vedas and scriptures.

There are shlokas and mantras i.e. chants that can evoke positive energy and revoke enthusiasm in life. The rich culture of yoga as a part of life and the goodness of ayurveda has now got an universal lifestyle approach. Our roots are strong and despite the westernization and access to technology, the distinct Indianness is still maintained whilst celebrating Diwali or observing the Shravan fast. This is also believed to be a land of Lord Rama which is Ayodhya or the birthplace of Sri Krishna is considered as Mathura. The birth of Sikh religion and the reverence felt by all Indians is still intact. Indians are extremely secular and especially in the metros there is seamless blending of Indians during Xmas and Id.

Attires in Indian culture : Ethnic charm is exuded in simple outfits in India. The tropical climate is well adapted to the range of muslins and cottons. The mixed variety in cotton goes from viscose, polycot and also cotton silk which has a sheen of its own. Attires are very much about the region and climate. The Himalayan costume is suited for the environment where the dress is a blanket wrap in red and black secured with a ethnic pin. The ornaments or jewelry is a festive adornment with a big red bindi to complete the outfit.

The sari happens to be the most versatile drape with its amazing styles of draping and design. The sari is the traditional dress of India which also modifies as per material, drape and style with each region. This has also gone up to international drape style followed by ranking designers on the ramp shows. The chungari sari of the south has the tie and dye pattern that finds its counterpart in the bandhi print of Gujarat. There are embroidery types that seem to be the intrinsic talent of certain regions.

The cardigans and shawls are hand-woven from the North especially the Himachal and Arunchal belt. This displays the rich handicraft culture of India. The modernization in winter wear is seen with details like pockets, zippers, blends of fabrics and easy feel wear. The gota work of Rajashtan and Punjab is skilled golden zari strips woven or fixed on to the main garment like a sari or the dupatta. The most comfortable dress is the salwar kameez that radiates Indianness and is also comfortable.

The south Indian Kerala set-saree is the beautiful print in cream and golden which can be teamed with coloured blouses. The navvari sari or the nine yard drape of Mahrasthra is usually found in leaf green colour that is symbolic of the newly married bride. The colours also seem to be in mauve, red or blues and the sarees happen as Narayan peth, paithani and various other Belgaum prints.

The padavai is the ghagra choli for young girls in the south that is incomplete without the gold jewelry especially the kaashi gold chain and jhumki earrings. This is also modified as ghagra choli is simple cottons for daily wear in the villages and designed as the lehenga choli in designer wear in the metros.

VALUES IN INDIA

Tradition in India is about values that transcend down generations automatically. These are genetic traits and simplicity is the main ingredient. Ancient culture believed in a lot of dogmas and rituals that can be termed as false beliefs and Indians are an intelligent lot to traverse these paths and modify the social requirements. Indians are highly flexible in the sense they would like to imbibe the changes dictated by western influence and yet clearly affirm their belief in traditions.

It is customary to respect elders and touch their feet as to seek their blessings. Occasions or festivals demand a lot of participation in terms of rangoli drawing, diyas and an array of yummy treats made in the authentic variety as per the caste and geography. Hindu rituals are a lot about song and dance and each family has a natural way to adjust to these formats. It is a ritual to pray to the Goddess of learning Ma Saraswathi to achieve success. Similarly business people always insist on drawing the Swastika which marks prosperity and worship the Goddess of wealth.

With the advent of technology and women emancipation there is a trend to mingle free with the western concepts of dress, belief, work and also get into a secular concept. But one can feel a distinct Indianness and most of our brethren abroad miss their homeland. Indians all over the world are known for their hospitality and high level of tolerance. Their adaptation power is high and hence they are able to scale heights in the international arena. Putting oneself on the global map, Indians are seeking new vistas of communicating their beliefs and tradition. The gift of health and well being through yoga and meditation is a great source of Vedas in the rich Hindu tradition which has actually benefited the world.

The values in India is about living life with a zest and observing the belief that there is one God prevailing despite so many religions.

Respecting elders, understanding cross culture traditions, free mingling to accommodate tolerance, staying interested in rural welfare are the values of India. The artifacts, cuisine handicrafts, attire and lifestyle of the rural folks is still followed and preserved by Indians.

YFAMILY CULTURE OF INDIA

Family is about joy and sharing. In India, the family culture is all about love and patience. A girl weds into a family and adjusts herself seamlessly to the rituals, routine and cuisine. Of late, one can see a lot of love marriages i.e. cross border mingling which is also being accepted by the elders in the family.

Association with religious beliefs and sects is also followed by families as many families believe in a particular Guru or saint who guides them in their spiritual path. Families are also getting nuclear owing to independent lifestyle preference and also the concept where in both husband and wife is working and has demanding careers. This is quite common in metros where families are independent in their upbringing and yet love and respect the elders who reside separately. The earlier homes housed themselves together in very large families where one can actually see three or four generations put up together.

Certain families observe a matriarchal concept i.e. the groom resides in the house of the bride or also follows a tradition as per the bride's ancestors. Generally India is patriarchal in the sense the children get the surname of the father and the wife changes her surname to follow that of the husbands.

It is also a tradition in certain families that the wife changes her maiden name but again this concept is also changing. Indian families are very accommodating and willing to accept change. It is a concept to observe the karva chauth or the raksha bandhan with great aplomb. There is an occasion for gifting and seeking the blessings of elders. It is important to respect and hold certain family traditions which are unique in terms of cooking, rituals and beliefs. Families give a lot of importance to lighting the diya in the evening and also each person in family has a habit of doing the puja in his own way.

Metros are also seeing a lot of family value in celebrating birthdays and anniversaries by observing the rituals and also entertaining outdoors. The Indian culture has imbibed the right mix of western influence and yet maintaining the ethnic family tradition. There is more love in every family while blowing candles on the birthday cake and also lighting the diya to observe an Aarti for the birthday person.

SOCIETY, ART AND CULTURE

The kings ruled according to Dharmasastras. Agriculture was the main occupation Trade and commerce flourished. Karshapana and Suvarnas were the approved currency. The vedic scholars received royal patronage. Prakrit language improved.

The Saptasataka, Brihatkatha and the Katantra, a book on Sanskrit grammar, are the important literary works of the Satavahana period. The fine painting at Amaravathi and Nagarjunakonda caves belong to this period. The Satavahana rulers built beautiful temples, Monasteries. Rock cut caves, stupa and prayer halls.

After the fall of the Mauryan Empire, the history of the Andhras, as a continuous account of political and cultural events, commences with the rise of the Satavahanas as a political power. According to Matsya Purana there were 29 rulers of this dynasty. They ruled over the Andhradesa including Deccan for about 400 years from the 2nd century B.C. to beyond the 2nd century A.D. Satavahanas were also called Salivahanas and Satakarnis.

In the 3rd century B.C., Simukha, the founder of the Satavahana dynasty, unified the various Andhra principalities into one kingdom and became its ruler (271 B.C. - 248 B.C.). Dharanikota near Amaravati in Guntur district was the first capital of Simukha, but later he shifted his capital to Pratishtana (Paithan in Aurangabad district). Satakarni II, the sixth ruler of the dynasty (184 B.C.) was an able ruler who extended his kingdom to the west by conquering Malwa. According to inscriptional evidence, he extended the boundaries of his realm far into central India across the Vindhyas, perhaps up to the river Ganges. He ruled for a long period of 56 years. The long reign of Satakarni II was followed successively by eight rulers of whom none can be credited with any notable achievement.

It was the accession of Pulumavi I that brought renewed strength and glory to their kingdom. He struck down the last of the Kanva rulers, Susarman, in 28 B.C. and occupied Magadha. The Satavahanas thus assumed an all-India significance as imperial rulers in succession to the Nandas, Mauryas, Sungas and Kanvas. The kings, who succeeded him, appear to have been driven, by the Sakas, out of Maharashtra back to their home land in Andhra. The only silver lining in that murky atmosphere was the excellent literary work, Gathasaptasati, of Hala, the 17th Satavahana king.

It was during the time of Gautamiputra Satakarni, the 23rd ruler of this dynasty, who ascended the throne in A.D.62, their kingdom made a sharp recovery of the lost territories from the western Kshatrapas. A Nasik record describes him as the restorer of the glory of the Satavahanas. His kingdom included the territories of Asika, Assaka, Mulaka, Saurashtra, Kukura, Aparanta, Anupa, Vidarbha, Akara and Avanti, and the mountainous regions of Vindhya, Achavata, Pariyatra, Sahya, Kanhagiri, Siritana, Malaya, Mahendra, Sata and Chakora, and extended as far as seas on either side.

Though some of the mountains mentioned in the inscription cannot be identified at present, it is clear that Gautamiputra's kingdom covered not only the peninsular India, but also the southern parts of Gujarat, Rajasthan, Madhya Pradesh and Orissa.

He passed away in A.D.86, and his successors witnessed the dismemberment of their far flung empire. Pulumavi II succeeded Gautamiputra and ruled for 28 years. In spite of serious efforts put forth by him to safeguard the frontiers of his vast empire, the closing years of his reign witnessed the decline of the Satavahana authority. Yajnasri Satakarni's accession to the throne in A.D.128 brought matters to a crisis. He came into conflict with the Saka Satrap, Rudradamana, and suffered defeat, and consequently, lost all his western possessions. However, he continued to rule till A.D.157 over a truncated dominion. His ship-marked coins suggest extensive maritime trade during his days. With him passed away the age of the great Satavahanas and by the end of the 2nd century A.D., the rule of the Satavahanas was a matter of past history.

There were different opinions about their capital. Some argue that Srikakulam in Krishna district was their capital.

Evidences show that Dharanikota in Guntur district, Dharmapuri in Karimnagar district and Paithan in Aurangabad district of Maharashtra State were used as capitals at various periods. The Deccan, during this period, was an emporium of inland and maritime trade. The region between the rivers of Godavari and Krishna was full of ports and throbbing with activity. There was plentiful currency to facilitate trade and the Telugus entered upon a period of great industrial, commercial and maritime activity.

Buddhism flourished throughout the period and at the same time the rulers were devoted to Vedic ritualism. They constructed several Buddhist Stupas, Chaityas and Viharas. The Stupa at Amaravati is known for its architecture par excellence. Satavahanas were not only the able rulers but were also lovers of literacy and architecture. The 17th ruler of this dynasty, Hala was himself a great poet and his"Gathasaptasati" in Prakrit was well received by all. Gunadhya, the minister of Hala was the author of"Brihatkadha".

The decline and fall of the Satavahana empire left the Andhra country in a political chaos. Local rulers as well as invaders tried to carve out small kingdoms for themselves and to establish dynasties. During the period from A.D.180 to A.D.624, Ikshvakus, Brihatphalayanas, Salankayanas, Vishnukundins, Vakatakas, Pallavas, Anandagotras, Kalingas and others ruled over the Andhra area with their small kingdoms. Such instability continued to prevail until the rise of the Eastern Chalukyas. Important among them were the Ikshvakus. The Puranas mention them as the Sriparvatiyas. The present Nagarjunakonda was then known as Sriparvata and Vijayapuri, near it, was their capital. They patronised Buddhism, though they followed the vedic ritualism. After the Ikshvakus, a part of the Andhra region north of the river Krishna was ruled over by Jayavarma of Brihatphalayana gotra. Salankayanas ruled over a part of the East Coast with Vengi as their capital.

Next to rule were the Vishnukundins who occupied the territory between the Krishna and Godavari. It is believed that their capital was Indrapura, which can be identified with the modern Indrapalagutta in Ramannapet taluk of Nalgonda district. By A.D.514, the land north of the Godavari, known, as Kalinga became independent. The area south of the Krishna fell to the share of the Pallavas, who ruled from Kanchi. The Vakatakas occupied the present Telangana. This state of affairs continued with few changes up to the beginning of the 7th century A.D.

Buddhism continued, though in a decadent form during this period. Mahayanism gave wide currency to the belief that the installation and worship of Buddha and Bodhisattva images, and the erection of stupas conferred great merit. The Madhyamika School of thought in Mahayana was propounded by Nagarjuna. Sanskrit came to occupy the place of Prakrit as the language of inscriptions. The Vishnukundins extended patronage to architecture and sculpture. The cave temples at Mogalrajapuram and Undavalli near Vijayawada bear testimony to their artistic taste.

The period of Andhra history, between A.D.624 and A.D.1323, spanning over seven centuries, is significant for the sea-change it brought in all spheres of the human activity; social, religious, linguistic and literary. During this period, Desi, the indigenous Telugu language, emerged as a literary medium overthrowing the domination of Prakrit and Sanskrit. As a result, Andhradesa achieved an identity and a distinction of its own as an important constituent of Indian Cultural set-up. This change was brought by strong historical forces, namely, the Eastern and Western Chalukyas, the Rashtrakutas and the early Cholas. Kakatiyas came to power during the later half of this period and extended their rule over the entire Telugu land with the exception of a small land in the northeast. Arts, crafts, language and literature flourished under their benevolent patronage.

SCULPTURE IN SATAVAHANA EMPIRE

ANCIENT SCULPTURES OF SATAVAHANA EMPIRE

The rulers from Satavahanas dynasty are also known, as the Andhras. It was a dynasty, which ruled in Southern and

Central India starting from around 230 BCE. Satavahanas were the first ancient dynasty of Maharashtra. The rulers from this dynasty had occupied a major part of southern India, which included modern Maharashtra, Andhra Pradesh and parts of Gujrath and Karnataka states. Satavahana Empire noted for artistic development and lasted for almost five centuries but eventually collapsed. Many other kingdoms arose in the ruins of Satavahanas.

There exists a controversy about the ending time of the dynasty but the most liberal estimates suggest that it lasted about 450 years. The regime of Satavahanas is praised for establishing peace in the country. There were onslaughts of foreigners on their regime after the decline of Mauryan Empire.

The glory of the Satavahanas is rightly reflected from the tradition of art and architecture, which was evolved and developed by them. The sculpture of this period is mostly of architectural accomplishment.

Many famous places in Andhra like Goli, Jaggayapeta, Ghantasala, Bhattiprolu, Amaravati and Nagarjunakonda have revealed the remains of stupas and sculptures. Among these, the stupa at Amaravati had a dome structure, which is 20 feet high, with its four rectangular offsets. It was surrounded with a railing having 192 feet diametre and 600 feet circumference and it stood 13 or 14 feet high above the pavement. The Amaravati sculptures show some of the traces of the influence of the Gandhara and the Mathura schools to some extent. And no doubt they are of -as Sir John Marshall has pointed out,

"...great originality, freedom of treatment", and" spontaneous exuberance...".

The characteristics of Satavahanas sculptures can be illustrated from the following explanation- The theme of nature and related things are most charmingly depicted through the art of carving with emphasizing on vigour, activity and grace. The erotic sculptures are less in numbers but can be marked with their presence. Speciously, the female figures are carved sensuously and the erotic appeal of the figures and situations is felt easily. One more important stage of development in sculptural history is marked during this period. The Amaravati

School has started the practice of depicting the Buddha as a divine being and receiving worship. The iconic presentation of Buddha was common till this period. Indeed, it is said that the Amaravati school of art," struck a quite novel and unique chord in the symphony of Indian plastic art".

An another centre of showing the Satavahana art is Nagarjunakonda. The sculptural tradition of Amaravati seems to continue at the art of this place. The Buddhist themes dominate the entire picture of artistic creations, although some scholars have evidences to show the influence of the Naga tradition on the art. The mastery of the Satavahanas can be noted from the sculptures at Nagarjunakonda. Throughout the sculptures the main themes is of showing various episodes revolving around the Buddha and his life. But the outstanding example of the sculpture of that ages and art of Satavahanas is the depiction of the Enlightened Buddha.

The images of Buddha are mainly in the `sthanaka` i.e. standing or `asana` i.e. sitting position and marvelously portray a serene oval face of Buddha with a moderately built body. The images in sitting position shows striking similarity with each other`s in carving rounded shoulders. In many images, the right hand of Buddha is held up to give a symbolic gesture of `abhaya` means protection- or `pravachana` means preaching. The famous chaitya hall built at Karle is considered as another example of the magnificence of the Satavahana architecture. The hall is more than 124 feet long, 46 feet broad and 46 feet high.

It also marked with construction of the Garbhagriha, the Pradakshina and the Mantapa. Light and air into the Chaitya hall must have entered only through the doorway. With it, the elegant Chaitya window in which the wood work of sculptures has remained till today. The construction of all the monuments is responsible for the" soft luminous atmosphere" inside it.

The art of Satavahanas can be marked at a Chaitya at Kanheri; the remains of a brick Chaitya at Chandravalli and of a stupa at Sannati have also been discovered in Karnataka. Some historians strongly believe that art schools like the Kshatrapa, the Vakataka, Kalachuri, Chalukya, Pallava,

Pandya, etc had a direct obligation to the art of the Satavahanas. In the field of carvings and paintings also the Satavahanas art was marked, in the caves of Ajanta the painting was started with the Satavahanas. Sculpture of Buddha in cave 10 is shows Buddha as seated on a cushion and wearing red robe. On his forehead a chandan mark in noted. He is shown as surrounded by standing monks and householders.

Some of the Scholars have been wrongly attributed to the Satavahana period; as per them these sculptures from Ajanta seem to belong to a later date, perhaps to the 6th century A. D. But no doubt, the Satavahanas created a tradition in the art of painting from Ajanta. One can transport oneself into that glorious age of Satavahanas by visiting these places.

SATAVAHANA DYNASTY

Indian family that, according to some interpretations based on the Puranas belonged to the Andhrajati (?tribe?) and was the first Deccanese dynasty to build an empire in daksinapatha (southern region). The Satavahanas (also called Andhra and Shalivahan) rose to power in Maharashtra around 200 B.C. They remained in power, for about 400 years. Almost the whole of present day Maharashtra, Madhya Pradesh and South India were under Satavahana rule. Paithan in Maharashtra, formerly called Pratishthan, was the capital of the Satavahanas. The founder of the Satvahanas was Simuka. But the man who raised it to eminence was Satakarni I. Sri Yajna Satakarni was the last great king in this dynasty. After him, the empire began to decline.

Gautamiputra Satakarni was the famous king during the Satvahana dynasty. He defeated the Sakas (Scythians), Yavanas (Greeks) and Pahlavas (Parithans). His empire extended upto Banavasi in the south, and included Maharashtra, Konkan, Saurashtra, Malwa, west Rajasthan and Vidharbha. His son, Vasishtiputra, ruled at Paithan on the banks of Godavari.

Two other cities, Vaijayanti (in North Kanara) and Amravati (in the Guntur district), attained eminence during the Satvahana period. Kings succeeding Gautamiputra lost many of their territories. But the power of Satvahanas revived under Sri Yajna Satakarni, who was the last great king. After him, the empire began to decline.

The Satavahanas inaugurated the Shalivahana Shaka. Satavahanas were very able rulers. Their empire was divided into provinces called Aharas, each under an Amatya (minister). They had a large army. They were lovers of literature and architecture. Prakrit was the court language. Women took part in assemblies. The Karle caves in Maharashtra were built during this period. Some caves of Ajanta were also built during this period. The construction of 29 galleries of Ajantha Caves continued until 650 AD.

Vasishthiputra Pulumavi, Vasishthiputra Satakarni, Yadnyashri Satakarni are some other Satavahana rulers who succeeded Gautamiputra Satakarni. However, the glory of the Satavahana power began to recede after Yadnyashri -Satakarni.

COINS OF SATAVAHANAS

Satavahanas is one of the most celebrated dynasty of ancient India. Satavahanas ruled over large area of modern western and southern India (Maharashtra, Gujarath, Andhra Pradesh, Karnataka and Goa states). The kings of this dynasty were great patrons of art and architecture. They built many beautiful stupas in Krishna River Valley. The impressive stupa of Amrawati was built by them. The railing were carved out of white marble and dome was also covered with marble slabs creating a breathtaking example of ancient stupa building art. The railing were exquisitely carved with various scenes from the life of Buddha.

The figures themselves are slim with elegant features and display striking difference in style from the northern India. The Amarawati stupa represent a new school of art which is named after it. Unfortunately this stupa is in ruins today and the railings have been taken away for dispay in British Museum, London and Goverment Museum, Madras. Shown above is a casing slab from Amarawati stupa on which the miniature of the stupa is carved. This marvellous sculpture might allow us to imagine the grandeur of this great stupa.

This dynasty also have unique distinction of issuing the coin with the portrait of ruler. No other native ruler or indegenous dynasty issued portrait type coins till one of the Satvahana ruler, Vashishtiputra Shri Pulumavi issued the portrait type coins (shown below). Most the coins minted by Satavahanas were made of lead or copper. For some coins they have used potin (an alloy of lead and copper) and Billon (an alloy of silver and copper).

Numismtic studies played crucial role in deciphering history of Satavahana dynasty. Some of the rulers who otherwise find no mention in Puranas (the contemporary texts which provide Satavahana chronology) are known only from their coinage. Satavahan coins do not possess high degree of artistic beauty but their silver portrait coins, essentially minted in Kshatrapa fabric are unique in style. Some of the physical traits depicted on these coins (eg. curly hairs, long ears, their lips etc) suggests their Dravidian origin, and thus might be their real portraits rather the stylized version. Most of the Satavahana coins have elephant, lion, horse, or chaitya on obverse while reverse side shows `Ujjain symbol', a cross with four circles at the end. Shown below are examples of some of the Satavahana coins.

- Vashistiputra Shree Pulumavi
- Satavahana Dynasty
- 78-114 AD
- Silver Drachm or Dramma,
- Weight: 2 gms
- *Obverse*: Kings bust looking right, depicting nice and elabourate hair style, large ear rings and legend Rano Vasithiputasa Siri Pulumavisa
- *Reverse*: Satavahan royal emblem, hill or six hilled Cahitya, sun, moon, water and complete legends Arahanaku Vahitti makanaku Tiru Pulumaviku
- *Reference*: Mitchiner South India, 1998: 146
- *Extremely Rare*: This dynasty came into existance soon after disintegration of Mauryan empire (i.e. after death of Great Ashoka).

Satavahana dynasty was founded by Simuka (or Chimuka) in 232 BC but it was his son (or nephew?) Satakarni I who made Satavahanas as most formidable power of western and southern India.

With the help of powerful Maharathi chieftains (ancestors of Marathas), he brought a large part of southern and western India under his control and later celebrated this victory with Ashwamedha yagna (horse sacrifice ceremony). Shown below is early Satavahana coin which is issued in the family name of Satakarni.

The obverse legends readRano Siri Satakarnisa which was struck in Northern Deccan (mostl likely modern Vidarbha region of Maharashtra).

- Satakarni
- 30-95 AD
- Billon Karshapana
- *Obverse*: Elephant, trunk raised
- *Reverse*: Ujjain symbol
- *Weight*: 3.7 gm
- *Reference*: MAC#4941

After his death, India was invaded by many foreign powers like Shakas (Scythias), Yavanas (Greeks) and Pahalavas (Parthians). At this stage, Gautamiputra Satakarni took control of dynasty and crushed the foreign invaders. It was Gautamiputra who scored a decisive victory over Kshatrapa (Shaka or Scythian) ruler of central India, and thus built the largest empire of Satavahanas, covering almost whole of Malva (central India), western and southern India. Gautamiputra restruck the Nahapana's silver coins with his name and royal emblem for circulation in his empire. Very likley he did not issue his own silver currency.

Gautamiputra Shri Yagna Satakarni was another formadible ruler of this dynasty, who took pride calling himself `Destroyer of Shaka, Yavana and Pahalava'. Centres of art and commerce like Amrawati (in Andhra Pradesh) and Vaijayanti (Karnataka) flourished during his reign. He was followed by his son, Vashishtiputra Pulumavi who had his capital at Pratishthan (modern Paithan in Maharashtra state) on the banks of Godavari river. It was Pulumavi who issued the portrait type coins.

Thus he has distinction of being THE FIRST NATIVE RULER who issued PORTRAIT TYPE COINS in India. His silver coins show his bust on obverse, looking right, having nice and elabourate hair style, large ear rings.

The obverse Legend are in Brahmi script (Sanskrit Prakrit language), begining at XII position, which reads Rano Vasithiputasa Siri Pulumavisa. The reverse depicts, Satavahan royal emblem, hill or six hilled Cahitya, sun, moon, water and legends in Southern Brahmi script (Telugu Prakrit language), begins at XII position Arahanaku Vahitti makanaku Tiru Pulumaviku.

Pulumayi was followed by his brother Vashishtiputra Satakarni, who married daughter of Rudradaman I of Kshatrapa dynasty (described below). Although, this alliance did not stop Rudradaman to score a fantastic victory over Vashishtiputra which gave tremendous blow to Satavahana power and prestige. Shri Yajna Satakarni followed and tried to revive power of Satavahans, but he turned out to be the last great king of this illustrious dynasty. Soon after his death, Satavahana empire collapsed and 456 years of Satavahana rule (totally 30 kings ruled) came to an end.

- Satakarni IV
- 154-164 AD
- Potin unit (Half Karshapana ?)
- *Obverse*: Elephant
- *Reverse*: Ujjain symbol
- *Weight*: 1.8 gm

Many dynasties emerged on the ruins of Satavahana empire. Vakatakas rose to power in Vidarbha region (eastern Maharashtra), Abhiras (king Ishwarsena) occupied Nashik and nearby region of western Maharashtra. Chutukulananda (another line of Satkarnis) occupied most of the western Karnataka with a capital at Vaijayantipura (Banwasi). The main imperial line of Satavahanas ruled in small fertile valley of Krishna river, which eventually succeeded by Vishnukundins.

COINS OF KSHATRAPAS

The western and central part of India consisting of Saurashtra and Malwa (modern Gujrat and neighbouring Maharashtra, Rajasthan and Madhya Pradesh states) was ruled by rulers known as *Ksatrapa* or *Kshatrapas*. This prosperous region was goverend by 27 independent Kshatrapa rulers for about 350 years. The term*Kshatrapa* is considered to be Sanskritized version of old Persian word 'Ksatrapavan', protector of land or viceroy.

The Shaka-Pahalava kings of present day Iran and Afghanistan ruled over a large area and governers of the provinces of these empire were known as 'Satraps or Ksatrapas'. It is believed that the early Kshatrapa rulers which belonged to Kshaharata family, occupied north-western and central India adjoining Mathura and possibly ruled as viceroys of Kushans (this is a controversial issue).

But very soon they acquired enough power to become independent rulers. Although, they retained name Kshatrapa, they were indeed independent rulers as some of the later rulers even proclaimed themselves *Mahakshtrapas*, the great Kshatrapas. Since the later Kshatrapas ruled mainly in Saurashtra and Malwa region (western India), they are called Western Kshatrapas to distinguish them from early rulers (Kshatrpas) who ruled near Mathura. The early Ksatrapas became independent rulers by carving out a principality on the ruins of Satavahana empire. These kings have minted some of the most fascinating silver coins of Indian numismatic history. The life-like portraits of the rulers of early rulers suggests that different dies were made as king grew older, clearly indicating the high degree of care taken while minting their coinage. These remarkable series of silver coins became extremely popular not only in the western provinces directly goverend by Kshatrapa rulers but also in the adjoining regions, possibly whole of northern and western India.

The rulers of neighbouring empires/kingdoms like Satavahanas, Guptas and many successive dynasties those followed Kshatrapas, minted their coinage in Kshatrapa style, providing proof of the immense popularity of Kshatrapa coinage. Apart from aesthtic nature, this series has turn out to be very crucial in deciphering the early history of India. These coins with complete name of ruler, his father's name and date of issue, provided historians necessary evidence for determination of geneology of not only the Kshatrapa rulers but also immensely helped in deciphering the duration of reigns of their contemporary rulers in adjoining empires.

- Nahapana as Kshatrapa
- 119-124 AD or 41-46 Saka Years
- Silver *Dramma*
- *Obverse*: Bust of King, Greek Legend
- *Reverse*: Arrow and thunderbolt, Legends in Kharoshti and Brahmi
- *Weight*: 2.2 gm
- *Reference*: MAC#2682-2684

This dynasty attained great power under king Nahapana who conquored a large part of western and central India which was part of satavahana empire. This brought him in direct conflict with the greatest Satavahana emperor, Gautamiputra Satakarni. Gautamiputra squarely defeated Nahapana and reoccupied the lost territories in 124 AD. In spite of his defeat, Nahapana strengthened his hold over remaining territories and his succesors in time became paramount rulers of western India. Nahapana was founder of the Kshatrapa monetary system and was the first Kshatrapa who minted portrait type silver coins. His coins show his diademed bust with Greek legends on obverse, which is the reminiscent of Indo-Greek coinage. The reverse show arrow and thunderbolt with legends in Prakrit (in heavily Sanskritized form) written in *Kharoshti* and *Bramhi* scripts. The legends in Kharoshti reads, *Rano Chaharatasa Nahapanasa* while legends in Brahmi reads *Rajana Kshaharatasa Nahapanasa*. Shown above is a nice example of his coinage.

Chastana followed Nahapana and established himself at Ujjain and ruled large part of western India. His grandson Rudradaman (130-150 AD) was perhaps the greatest Shaka ruler of ancient India. Rudradaman entered into matrimonial alliance with the great Satavahanas of Deccan and later even defeated them, extending his kingdom from Marwad to Konkan (from Rajasthan to Maharashtra). His achievements are carved at Junagadh rock inscriptions.

Rudrasen II (256-278 AD) was 19th ruler of Kshatrapa family and minted prodigious number of coins, exclusively as Mahakshatrapa. This indicate the prosperous period of Kshatrapa dynasty. Unlike the early Ksatrapa rulers, the later rulers had no Greek legends on obverse and reverse had legends written only in *Brahmi. Kharoshti* script was primarily used in norht-western parts of India and since later Kshatrapas dominion was confined to western India where *Brahmi* script was used, *Kharoshti* was withdrawn from the coins. Similarly, all the coins of later Kshatrapas bear the chaitya or three arched hill and river symbol on reverse of their coins, instead of thunderbot and arrow. This coin of Rudrasen bears *Bramhi* inscription which reads, *Rajanah Ksatrapasa Viradamaputrasa Rajno Mahakstrapasa Rudrasensa,* on reverse, which can be translated as King Kshatrapa Viradaman's son King Mahakshatrapa Rudrasena.

- Rudrasen II as Mahakshatrapa
- 256-278 AD
- Silver *Dramma*
- *Obverse*: Bust of King
- *Reverse*: Hill and river
- *Weight*: 2.2 gm
- *Reference*: MAC#2722-2741

Bhratadaman was Rudrasen's son who ruled from 278 to 295 AD and minted very similar coins as that of other Kshatrapa rulers. His brother Vishwasen was the last ruler of the Kshatrapa descent, who was replaced by Rudrasimha. Rudrasimha was not related to the royal family. This new family could not keep the control of this kingdom and soon the Gupta emperor Vikramaditya conqured and incorporated the Kshatrapa Kingdom in his mighty Gupta empire. Shown below is a fine example of his coin.

- Vishwasen
- 294-304 AD
- Silver *Dramma*

- *Obverse*: Bust of King
- *Reverse*: Hill and river
- *Weight*: 2.3 gm
- *Reference*: MAC#2780-2795

THE MAITRAKAS OF VALABHI

In Saurashtra (modern Gujrat), Bhattaraka established a new independent kingdom during decline of Gupta empire. This new kingdom of Valabhi was ruled by Maitraka family for next 350 years. All the coins issue by Valabhi rulers were in the name of Bhattaraka, who took a title of *Senapati*, army general.

The coins of this dynasty are minted in kshatrapa style depicting bust of ruler(highly stylize in the later issues) on obverse, while reverse depict the trident (*shastra* or weapon of Lord Shiva) with or without side arm. The legends are present on reverse written in *Brahmi* script, which reads *Rajno Mahakshatrapa Paramaditya Bhakta Mahasamanta Sri Sarva Bhattarakasa*.

- Bhattaraka (title: Senapati)
- 470-800 AD
- Silver *Dramma*
- *Obverse*: Bust of King
- *Reverse*: Trident with curved prong
- *Weight*: 1.9 gm
- *Reference*: MAC#4894

COINS OF POST-GUPTA DYNASTIES

Skanda Gupta put up the brave struggle against barbaric Huns to protect India and even won decisive battles against them. But he turned out to be the last great Gupta emperor. Battling the barbaric tribes of Huns and internal uprising of Pushyamitras who were Gupta feudatories, made the Gupta empire weak.

Budha Gupta was the last Gupta emperor. By sixth century AD Gupta empire was completely disintegrated and Huns, Toramana and his son Mihirgula had firmly established themselves in Sialkot region (modern Pakistan). At this stage Yasodharman who belonged to a family which were feudatories of Gupta, emerged and bravely defended Gupta territory against tyrant Hun ruler, Mihirgula. Maukahri, another feaudatory family also rose to distinction and bravely carried on the struggle against these foreign invaders. But the next dynasty of significance in post-Gupta India was Vardhanas of Thanesar, rulers of which brought disintegrated Gupta empire together and later even managed to revive those glorious days of Vikramaditya

Post-Gupta era clearly show decline in artistry in coinage. Except few, most rulers hardly paid any attention towards their coinage. Unlike Gupta and Kushan emperors who used their coinage for propaganda and minted fine specimen of numismatic arts, post-Gupta successors rarely experiemnted with their coinage.

Most of the time post-Gupta rulers copied motifs from earlier Gupta coinage (a fine example of such type is shown above, where the stylization of the image of Laxmi is clear) and introduced very few novel iconographic features and motifs.

Often, the great ruler of dynasty issued a specific type of coin which was minted by his successors without making any change, sometimes even the name. Thus often coinage of whole dynasty was struck in name of one (or two rulers) with identical motifs except the later coinage is debased compared to the earliest. Interestingly, many of these post-Gupta rulers had great tastes and they undertook construction of some of the most beautiful temples of India with fantastic architecture and breathtaking sculptures. But, why their coinage received almost no attention is still a mystery. Some major dynasties of Post-Gupta era which introduced interesting coinage are discussed below.

THE VARDHANAS OF KANNAUJ AND THANESAR

Vardhana dynasty assumed substantial power and prestige during rule of Prabhakar-vardhana, who was of later

Gupta lineage. His son Harsha-Vardhana brought up whole of northern India under his command and made Kanyakubj (modern Kannauj) as capital of his sprawling empire.

Harsha-Vardhana is the greatest king in post-Gupta history of India who revived the glorious days of Gupta emperors. Harsha-Vardhana took a title of Siladitya and later received embassies from China. Harsha was a staunch Hindu (worshiper of Shiva) but it did not stop him from patronizing Budhism.

He organized the greatest religious gathering of ancient India called *Mahamokshaparishad* at Prayag (Allahabad) which was attended by famous Chinese traveller and scholar Hiuen Tsang. Apart from 20 kings, thousands of Buddhist, Hindu and Jain priests and scholars attended this religious meeting. At the end of this meeting, Harsha started distributing his personal belongings which he kept doing till he was left with nothing! At this juncture, this great emperor wore second-hand clothes and paid visit to various shrines of his empire.

Harsha, a grandson of Gupta princess, had an ambition to emulate his great-great Grandfather, Samudragupta. And that he did it in style. He was a capable general and fantastic administrator. He was also a man of very sophisticated tastes. Some of the finest intellectuals of early period like Bana (who wrote *Harsha Charita*), Mayura, Divakara and Hiuen Tsang adorned his court.

Harsha died in 646 AD and with his death the empire collapsed and fragmented into various smaller kingdoms. I shall soon introduce image of his coin.

THE IMPERIAL PRATIHARAS

By ninth century, the supremacy of northern India was taken over by another illustrious dynasty called Pratiharas which claimed descent from Lakhamana, brother of Lord Rama.

The greatest king of pratihara dynasty was Bhoja I who took control of Kanyakubj (modern Kannauj) in 836 AD and created an empire which was similar in size of his predecessor, Harsha-Vardhana. He built a city Bhojpal (modern Bhopal, capital of Madhya Pradesh state) which was named after him. He was successful general and managed to defeat many of his powerful neighbours including the Gaudas of Bengal. Like Harsha-Vardhana, Bhoja too was a great patron of art and literature and famous poet Rajashekhar was in his court. He received foreign travellers like Sulaiman and Al Masudi who left account of their travels to India. Both talk highly of his superior cavalry and his fine administration.

- Bhoja I
- 836-885 AD
- mperial Pratihars
- Silver drachm
- *Obverse*: *Aadivaraha,* Anthropoid boar representing incarnation of Vishnu
- *Reverse*: Fire altar and two attendants (Stylized), legends in *Brahmi.*
- *Weight*: 3.9 gm
- MNW#336-348

Pratihara dynasty ruled for another 200 years although their dominion was never to the extent of during Bhoja's rule. In 1018, Kannauj then ruled by Rajyapala Pratihara was sacked by Mahmud of Gazni and that was beginning of the end of this illustrious dynasty of north India.

Shown above is a coin minted by the great Pratihara king Bhoja I. The obverse show *Aadivaraha,* boar like incarnation of Lord Vishnu while reverse of the coin show stylized fire altar and two attendant.

The deity *Aadivaraha* is supposedly holding earth by his snout. The vigour and strength of Aadivaraha's image on these coin amply show die engraver's knowledge of scultptures of that era. Altar and attendant motif was borrowed from Sassanaian coins which possibly came in India due to trade from Sassanian ruled Persia.

The coins of Bhoja were immencely popular in medieval period and were extensively copied by his successors. All the kings of Pratihara dynasty minted exact same coin which were introduced by Bhoja I. Although the coins of later rulers of Pratihara dynasty were more stylized and heavily debased.

THE HINDU SHAHI OF KABUL

During 717 to 920 AD the Kabul valley, Zabul and Gandhara, till river Sindhu or Indus, (modern Afghanistan and Pakistan) was occupied by Turko-Hephthalic kings. Because of spread of Hinduism in these kingdoms, these dynasties were popularly known as 'Hindu Shahis of Kabul and Gandhara'. At this time Arabs united under banner of Islam and made many advances on Shah of Kabul and Ratbil of Zabul.

Ratbils succumbed to muslims after brave struggle in 870 AD. Shah of Kabul, a proud desecendent of Great Kushan emperor, Kanishka, maintained his kingdom till the end of ninth century and later replaced by Kallar or Lalliyas who founded Hindu Shahiya dynasty of Udabhandapura (Ohind or WaiHind or Und).

- Samanta Deva
- Hindu Shahi of Kabul
- 850-1000 AD
- Silver jital
- *Obverse*: Recumbent Bull
- *Reverse:* Horseman with spear in his hand
- Ohind (Udabhandapura) Mint
- *Weight*: 3.3 gm
- MNW#1585, T14, D45

This Brahmanical Shahi of Afganistan and Punjab (modern Pakistan) minted interesting coins, called 'bull and horseman' type coins which were later adopted by many post-Gupta dynasties including all Rajput kings (an example of Chauhan dynasty is shown below). Interestingly, these coins were also widely used as prototype by all muslim conquerors and rulers of North-west part of India which include Mahmud of Ghor. These coins were first minted by Spalapati Deva in mid-ninth century.

Later on the Samanta Deva coinage was used as prototype for increasingly debased coinage struck by many dynasties. Shown above is a fine example of coin of this dynasty. The reverse of these well-executed silver coins display a recumbent bull partly draped with an ornamental cloth and stamped with the mark of trident on his rear flank. Above is the legend, "Shri

Samanta Deva". On the obverse is a horseman who holds a long spear with legend "Bhi" on left margin.

THE KALACHURIS OF TRIPURI OR DAHAL

- Gangeyadeva
- Kalachuris of Tripuri
- 1019-1042 AD
- Gold quarter stater
- *Obverse*: Stylized Laxmi sitting
- *Reverse*: Name of king in *Devnagri* script
- *Weight*: 0.97 gm
- Scarce

Disintegration of Pratihara empire signaled emergence of new dynasties.

The feudatories of old empires took up a difficult task of defending India against new foreign invaders, Turks. In tradition of great Vikramaditya (Chandragupta II) who killed Shaka ruler,a foreighner in his own city, these new kings too took titles 'Vikramaditya or new Shahasankas. One notable king was Gangeyadeva of Kalachuris who did considerable justice to his title of Vikramaditya.

He brought large part of Gangetic plain under his command and cemented friendships with strong neighbours by matrimonial alliance thus bringing the glorious traditions of Harsha and Bhoja days. He had his capital at Tewar or Dahala which is located near modern city of Jabalpur in Madhya Pradesh.

On his death his son Lakshmi Karna did fine job but after him the power was passed on to next major dynasty of northern India, Gahadvala. After decline of Gupta dynasty, gold coins simply disappeared from India. Indeed very few dynasties minted silver coins of high purity. Almost the entire monetary system of northern India (a similar trend is noticable in south too) was based on billon (a alloy of silver and copper) coins either derived from Hindu Shahi of Kabul and Indo-Sassanian type silver coins.

It was Gangeyadeva who brought the gold coinage in vogue in Northern India which became so popular again (the reson was obvious, they were copies of Gupta!) that many other dynasties followed the suit. Shown above is coin of Gangeyadeva which depict goddess of wealth, Laxmi seated on lotus. Although it is highly stylized version of Laxmi shown on Gupta gold coins, the well proportional limbs, narrow waist, deep naval, well developed breasts and graceful appearance still remind that Gupta enfluence was not lost even almost 500 years after their decline.

COINS OF RAJPUT DYNASTIES

By tenth century the Kshatriyas or warriors of northern India, who were descendents of post-Gupta rulers, took up a name for themselves, Rajputs, sons of Kings (derived from Sankrit word Rajputra).

These warriors depending upon lineage, divided into various clans. Each clan had a distinct lineage and kingdom. These Rajput rulers often fought among themselves to assert the supramacy, but none could built an empire. Instead, the northern, central and western parts of India was divided among many of these rulers into kingdoms of various sizes.

This was the major factor which prompted the Islamic invaders to pour in India, mainly from Afghanistan and central asia, as there was no central authority left to cahllenge them. Most of these Rajput rulers minted coins of similar fabric. Their gold coins were almost always had stylized Laxmi on obverse, the design of which was essentially derived from Gangeyadeva coinage (originally from Gupta coins), while reverse had name of the ruler in Devnagri script. The weight of these gold coins was maintained to be four and half *Masha,* which is equivalent to 3.6 gms.

The silver coinage was almost entirely copied from Bull-Horseman type coin of Hindu Shahi of Kabul (an example of which is shown above) except the name of ruler was changed. Unfortunatley, no ruler (Vigraharaja may be an exception) made any serious attempt to introduce new motifs or design on their coinage, nor any monetary reforms were introduced. The debasement of coinage was widesprad and artistry was perhaps lowest in entire history of India.

THE KACCHAVAHAS (KACCHAPAGHATA) OF NARWAR

- Vira Simha Ram
- 1120-1121 AD
- Rajput Kingdom of Narwar
- Gold Stater
- *Obverse*: Laxmi holding various objects, sitting
- *Reverse*: Name of king in Devnagri *Shrimad Vira Simha Ram*
- *Weight*: 4.9 gm
- *Reference*: Deyell#153
- Extremely Rare

Narwar is located in northern part of modern Madhya Pradesh state in central India. This kingdom has roots in mythology. It was the capital of legendary king, Raja Nala who find his name in the great Sanskrit epic, Mahabharata (the story of Nala and his queen Damayanti is told even today). This town was called Nalapura (named after King Nala) until the 12th century.

In 10th century, this kingdom came to prominence when the Kacchawaha Rajput rulers occupied the Narwar fort, which stands on a steep scarp of the Vindhya (mountains of central India) Range. From the 12th century onward, Narwar was held successively by Kacchwaha, Parihar and Tomar Rajputs until its capture by the Mughals in the 16th century. It fell to the Maratha chief Mahadaji Shinde (Sindhia) in the early 19th century and remianed part of Shinde kingdom till independence.

THE RATHORS (GAHADVALA) OF BANARAS AND KANNAUJ

Gahadavala dynasty was established by Chandradeva who belonged to Rathor clan of Rajput warriors. It was during rule of Govind Chandra Rathor, grandson of Chandradeva, this dynasty reached it's pinnacle of power. Govind Chandra occupied most of the Gangetic valley consisting of modern Bihar and Uttar pradesh states. He had his capital at Banaras and it was a prosperous kingdom. At this juncture a rival empire was established at the western boundry of Gahadavalas. This kingdom was by another clan of warrior Rajputs, Chauhans (Chahmanas).

The grandson of Govind Chandra, Jai Chandra (Jai Chand) was the last Gahadavala ruler. According to legends, Jai Chandras daughter was abducted by King of Chauhan dynasty, Prithviraja which added bitterness to long standing rivalary. When Mahmud of Ghor (or Ghur) invaded India, Rathors and Chauhan, the two most prominent dynasties of northern India, could not put up a joint struggle against foreign invader. Ghori defeated both Prithviraja Chauhan and Jai Chandra Rathor separately and later killed them. Shown below is a coin of greatest ruler of this dynasty, Govindchandra Rathor. Like Kalachuris, even Gahadavalas minted gold coins showing highly stylized version of Laxmi depicted on Gupta gold coins. The reverse of the coin has name of the ruler Govind Chandra. All the rulers of this dynsty minted coin in the name of Govind Chandra.

- Govindchandra
- Gahadavala Dynasty
- 1114-1154AD
- Gold stater
- *Weight*: 3.8 gms
- *Obverse*: Stylized Laxmi sitting
- *Reverse*: name of king in Devnagri script
- Ref:Deyell#145

THE CHAUHANS (CHAHAMANS) OF SAMBHOR, AJMER AND DELHI

- Vigraharaja IV
- 1153-1163 AD
- Chauhan of Sambhor and Ajmer
- Gold Stater
- *Obverse*: Lord Rama holding bow wandering in forest
- *Reverse*: Legend in *Devnagri, Shrimad Vigraha Raja Deva*
- *Weight*: 4.3 gm
- Extremely Rare

In middle of 11th century AD Tomara chieftains founded the famous city of Delhi (named after goddess *Dhillika*) which was later taken over by Chauhana, a Rajput warrior clan. Vigraharaja IV was the greatest ruler of Chauhan dynasty who enlarged his dominion over large part of northern India. It was Vigraharaja who took control of Delhi from Tomara. His kingdom consisted of modern states of Delhi, Rajasthan and Madya Pradesh.

His capital was located at Sakhambari or Sambhor (the ancient name of this town is Stambhapura) which is located near Ajmer city in Rajasthan. Vigraharaja minted very interesting coins. Shown above is gold coin of this great king of Chauhan dynasty. This coin is very special as the obverse of coin show Lord Rama, hero of epic *Ramayana* wandering in forest. According to legend, Lord Rama was sent to forest for 14 years, this very scene is depicted in this coin. Rama holding bow in his left hand is surrounded by trees and other animals. A bird like creature (possibly a peacock) is shown in left hand corner.

This is very interesting coin and represent ONLY numismatic representation of this favourite deity of Hindus. This unique coin is also extremely rare and was unknown till recent discovery of perhaps 5-6 specimen (nobody knows the exact number) in 90s. The obverse also show the legend *Shri Ra Ma* writen in Devnagri script. The reverse shows name of King Vigraharaja in Devnagri script.

Vigraharja's illustrious nephew, Prithviraja III came into conflict with grandson of Govind Chandra, Jaya Chandra (Jai Chand). The rivalary between these two most powerful dynasties of northern india weakened both the kingdoms. And this opportunity was cleaverly exploited by Mahmud of Ghor. He defeated first Prithviraja Chauhan in second battle of Tarain (near Delhi). Prithviraja was captured alive, but soon Mahmud blinded him and had him executed. Soon Mahmud invaded Banaras, capital of Gahadavalas, captured Jai Chandra and tortured him to death. Prithviraja was the last Hindu king of Delhi and his death marked new era in indian history. Never again the throne of Delhi was accupied by another Hindu ruler.

Shown below is silver coin of this gallant Rajput warrior who inspired scores of legends some of which are very popular even today.

AGE OF GUPTAS GUPTA DYNASTY, GOLDEN AGE OF INDIA

By the fourth century A.D., political and military turmoil destroyed the Kushan empire in the north and many kingdoms in the south India. At this juncture, India was invaded by a series of foreigners and barbarians or *Mlechchhas* from the north western frontier region and central Asia. It signaled the emergence of a leader, a Magadha ruler, Chandragupta I. Chandragupta successfully combated the foreign invasion and laid foundation of the great Gupta dynasty, the emperors of which ruled for the next 300 years, bringing the most prosperous era in Indian history.

The reign of Gupta emperors can truly be considered as the golden age of classical Indian history. Srigupta I (270-290 AD) who was perhaps a petty ruler of Magadha (modern Bihar) established Gupta dynasty with Patliputra or Patna as its capital. He and his son Ghatotkacha (290-305 AD) have left very little evidences of their rule and did not issue any coins of their own (although there have been reports of coins of Shrigupta which need more thorough studies). Ghatotkacha was succeeded by his son Chandragupta I (305-325 AD) who strengthened his kingdom by matrimonial alliance with the powerful family of Lichchavi who were rulers of Mithila.

His marriage to Lichchhavi princess Kumaradevi, brought an enormous power, resources and prestige. He took advantage of the situation and occupied whole of fertile Gangetic valley.

Chandragupta I eventually assumed the title of *Maharajadhiraja* (emperor) in formal coronation. Most probably Chandragupta I never minted gold coins of his own, although some historians believe that gold coins depicting king (Chandragupta) and queen (Kumardevi) are minted by him. It is very likely that these coins were minted by their illustrious son, Samudragupta. Shown below is very nice example of this controversial coin where Chandragupta and Kumardevi are shown (without halo).

Chandragupta is offering a ring (or putting *Sindur*) to his queen Kumardevi. *Chandra* in Brahmi script is written below left arm of King while *Shri-Kumardevi* is written near right hand of queen. Reverse of coin shows goddess Ambika, sitting on Lion. The legend on reverse reads*Lichchavyah,* which suggests that indeed, Samudragupta took pride in being son of Lichchavi princess. His affection towards his parents is amply demonstrated while issuing this superb (commemorative?) gold coin. This coin is a rare and very special in Indian numismatics.

- Kumardevi and Chandragupta I
- (Minted by their son Samudragupta)
- 335-370 AD
- Gold Dinar
- *Weight*: 7.8 gm
- *Obverse*: King and queen
- *Reverse*: Goddess Ambika (Durga) sitting on lion
- *Reference*: Altekar#1
- Rare

SAMUDRAGUPTA (335-380 AD)

Samudragupta was perhaps the greatest king of Gupta dynasty. His name appear in Javanese text 'Tantrikamandaka', and Chinese writer, Wang-hiuen-tse refers that a ambassador was sent to his court by King Meghvarma of Sri Lanka, who had asked his permission to build a Buddhist monastery at Bodh Gaya for the monks traveling from Sri Lanka. But the most detailed and authentic record of his reign is preserved in the rock pillar of the Allahabad, composed by Harisena. Samudragupta enlarged the Gupta Kingdom by winning a series of battles till he was a master of northern India.

Soon he defeated the kings of *Vindhyan* region (central India) and Deccan. He although made no attempt to incorporate the kingdoms of south of Narmada and Mahanadi rivers (southern India) into his empire.

When he died his mighty empire bordered with Kushan of Western province (modern Afganistan and Pakistan) and Vakatakas in Deccan (modern southern Maharashtra). Samudragupta was a staunch Hindu and after all his military triumphs, he performed the *Ashwamedha Yagna* (Horse sacrifice ceremony) which is evident on some of his coins.

Ashwamedha Yagna gave him the coveted title of *Maharajadhiraj*, the supreme king of kings. His greatest achievement can be described as the political unification of most of the northern India or *Aryavarta* into a formadible power.

- Samudragupta
- 335-370 AD
- Gold Dinar
- *Weight*: 7.6 gm
- *Obverse*: King sacrificing at altar
- *Reverse*: Laxmi sitting
- MAC#4773 ff

Most certainly, Samudragupta is the father of Gupta monetary system. It is very likely that, the Kushan gold coins were circulating in the north and central India (possibly in the eastern India too), the dominion which comprised of Samudragupta's empire.

It was these Kushan coins which were the source of inspiration for Samudragupta. When he introduced the first Gupta coinage, they were of the same weight standard as that of Kushan. The Kushan rulers had adopted Roman standard and minted their coins as 8 gms unit which were called as *Dinara*, derived from Roman name for their gold coins, *Denarius Aurius*.

Thus, the Gupta gold coins were also named as Dinara and referred by that name in most contemporary literature. Interestingly, this obviously foreign weight standard (122.9 grains) was not very satisfactory for the rulers, thus a conscious effort was made by later Gupta rulers to mint coins in Indian weight standard, popularly called *Suvarna*. The Suvarna weight standaard suggests coin of 144 grains or approximately

9.2 gms of gold. Finally, it was Skandagupta who succeed in minting Gupta gold coins in Suvarna standard (commonly called as heavy type gold coins).

- Samudragupta
- 335-370 AD
- Gold Dinar
- *Weight*: 7.6 gm
- *Obverse*: Uncaparisoned horse standing to left before yupa (a sacrificial post), Yupa has pedestal in two steps. A pennon fly from Yupa, top over the horse. The mane of the horse is probably plaited with a string of golden beads. Letter Si is under the horse, standing for Siddham.The legend reads Rajadhirajah Prithvimavitva divam jayatyaha-ritavajimedhah.
- *Reverse*: Crowned the chief queen (Mahashi) standing not nimbate, (most coins have queen nimbate), holding in her right arm a chauri over right shoulder and in her left hand a towel, hanging by her side. A lotus is under her feet. Suchi, a sacrificial appear before queen. The legend reads Ashwamedha-parakramah
- *Reference*: Altekar plate VI, 3; BMC plate V 9, MAC#4787
- Rare

Samudragupta paid considerable attention and left an extensive coinage. Samudragupta minted seven distinct types of coins: standard type (shown above), the archer type, Battle Axe type (refers to his military activities), Ashwamedha type (Commemorating the horse sacrifice ceremony), tiger slayer type, King and queen type (shown above) and Lyrist types (shown below).

All Gupta emperors minted splendid gold coins which have evoked widespread admiration for their technical and sculptural finesse. Most Gupta gold coins weighed close to 8 grams and had Shri-Laxmi (goddess of wealth) on reverse side of the coin. Both the weight standard and the concept of presence of deity on coins is almost certainly borrowed from the late Kushana gold coinage.

The symbols, phrasing of Sanskrit legends (written in*Bramhi* script), size, weight and gold content in their coins appears to have been meticulously planned and executed. The coin shown above depicts Samudragupta, a tall man with sharp features making an offering at an altar with his right hand. Below his left arm his name *Samudra* is written while legends at edge of coin reads*Samara Sata Vitata Vijayo Jita Ripurajito Divam Jayati* (the invincible king who had won hundred battles). The legends are in Sanskrit written in *Brahmi* script. On reverse is Shri-Laxmi (the goddess of wealth) seated on throne. This is the earliest issue of Gupta gold staters.

- Samudragupta
- 335-370 AD
- Gold Dinar
- *Weight*: 7.6 gm
- *Obverse*: King, standing looking left, holding battle-Axe (Parashu) with his left hand, resting right hand on hip. A dwarf looking upto him and standard at the left of flan. Brahmi legend 'Samudra' below his arm. The legend around '
- *Reverse*: Goddess Laxmi nimbate, enthroned holding cornucopiae and a bouquet of flower, symbol to left, to right the Brahmi legend 'Krtantaparasuh'
- *Reference*: BMC plate IV, 8-9; Altekar plate V, 6
- Rare

Beyond doubt Samudragupta was a great military general, but apart from that, his personal accomplishments are equally remarkable. He showed great magnanimity towards all those kings who were defeated.

His polished intelligence and good knowledge of scriptures won him many admirers. He gathered a galaxy of poets and scholars and took effective actions to foster and propagate religious, artistic and literary aspects of Indian culture.

He had good proficiency in music and was perhaps an accomplished Lyrist (Lyre or *Veena* is a musical instrument). This fact is amply demonstrated in his lyrist type coins. Most king took pride in trumpeting their bravery but Samudragupta is the only king in whole of Indian history who showed softer side of his personality (Kumargupta, his grandson, have copied this type and minted few Lyrist type gold coins, which are exceedingly rare). These coins are unique, very special and rare. Shown below is this coin where Samudragupta is shown playing Lyre, a kind of (harp like) string musical instrument. The legends on obverse in margin reads *Maharajadhiraja Shri Samudragupta*. The legends are in Sanskrit, written in *Brahmi* script.

- Samudragupta
- 335-370 AD
- Gold Dinar
- *Weight*: 7.9 gm
- *Obverse*: King playing *Veena* or Lyre
- *Reverse*: Laxmi sitting
- MAC#4788-90
- Rare

VIKRAMADITYA OR CHANDRAGUPTA II (380 TO 413 AD)

It is very apt to say, like father like son. Samudragupta's son, Chandragupta II tried to be better than his father, and most historians agree, he was certainly successful. Vikramaditya is THE LEGENDARY emperor of India. More stories/legends are associated with him than any other ruler of India. It was during his (and his son Kumargupta) reign, India was at the pinnacle of prosperity and opulence. Although named after his grandfather Chandragupta, he took a title of Vikramaditya, which became a synonym for sovereign of tremendous power and wealth. This title was later taken up by scores of other sovereign rulers of India. Chandragupta minted prodigious number of gold coins. Even today, the largest number of Gupta coins found in various hoards are minted during his rule, a solid evidence of prosperity of his reign.

- Vikramaditya or Chandragupta II
- 375-414 AD

- Gold Dinar
- *Weight*: 7.77 gm
- *Obverse*: King holding Bow, looking right
- *Reverse*: Laxmi sitting on lotus
- MAC#4796 ff
- Rare

Vikramaditya succeeded his father Samudragupta (possibly there was another prince, or his elder brother who ruled briefly, and according to legends slayed by Shakas), and carried on the policy of 'world conquest' of his predecessors. Political marriages occupied a prominent place in foreign policy of Gupta emperors. He married princess Kubernaga, daughter of Naga Chieftains and later gave his daughter Prabhavati in marriage to Rudrasena of powerful family of Vakatakas of the Deccan (modern Maharashtra).

His most significant and well celebrated military achievement being total destruction of Kshatrapas, the Shaka (Scythian) rulers of Malawa and Saurashtra, the western India (modern Gujrath and neighbouring states). He scored a fantastic victory over the Kshatrapa rulers and incorporated these provinces into his increasing empire. The cool courage he showed in fight with Shakas and killing their king in their own city entitled him the epithets *Shakari*(destroyer of Shakas) or *Sahasanka*. He has also been credited for the era, popularly known as *Vikram Samvat* which commence in 58 BC. This era has been used by major Hindu dynasties and still in use in modern India.

- Vikramaditya or Chandragupta II
- 375-414 AD
- Gold Dinar
- *Weight*: 7.77 gm
- *Obverse*: King holding Bow, looking right
- *Reverse*: Laxmi sitting on lotus
- MAC#4796 ff
- Rare

Vikramaditya's reign was perhaps THE most prosperous and progressive reign in the ENTIRE Indian history. The contemporary Chinese traveller and Buddhist monk Fa-hein was struck with the prosperity of subject during Gupta rule. He has admired the royal palaces and houses for dispensing charity medicine. He speaks highly of system of Government.

Shown above is a beautiful example of his coin where King is hoding bow, looking right. It is a rare coin as most of his coin depicts him looking left. Shown below is another example of Vikramaditya's gold coin which shows him holding bow and arrow but looking left. *Chandra* (literally means moon) is written on obverse (below his arm). Also one can read *Gupta* on left side of coin. On reverse Laxmi is depicted, seated cross legged on lotus.

- Vikramaditya or Chandragupta II
- 375-414 AD
- Gold Dinar
- *Weight*: 7.77 gm
- *Obverse*: King holding Bow, looking right
- *Reverse*: Laxmi sitting on lotus
- MAC#4796 ff
- Rare

Vikramaditya minted seven distinct types of coins: Sceptre/standard type, Archer type, Chatra type, Chakravikrama type, horseman type, lion-slayer type and couch type. Shown below is another beautiful specimen of Vikramaditya where he is shown alying a lion, an absolute beauty!

- Vikramaditya or Chandragupta II
- 375-414 AD
- Gold Dinar
- *Weight*: 8.01 gm
- *Obverse*: King is barebodied, a crest jewel on the forehead, curly hair falling on neck. He holds bow in right hand and strings it to ear by left hand to shoot at lion standing in front of him. The legend around read *Narendrachandrah prathitaranorane jayatyajayyo bhuvi sinhavikramah*
- *Reverse*: Goddess Abmika-Laxmi nimbate, seated on lion couchant to left, holding lotus in her left hand and noose in her right hand. The legend reads

Simhavikramah
- Reference: BMC Plate 114, pl IX3 obverse; Altekar Bayana Plate
- Finest animated style, broad flan
- Very Rare in such condition

KUMARGUPTA I OR MAHENDRADITYA (415-455 AD)

Vikramaditya was succeeded by his able son Kumargupta I. He maintained his hold over the vast empire of his forebears, which covered most of India except southern four states of India. Later he too performed the Ashwamedha Yagna and proclaimed himself to be *Chakrawarti*, king of all kings. Why he did not mint coins commemorating this event is not clear. Kumargupta also was a great patron of art and culture; evidence exist that he endowed a college of fine arts at great ancient university at Nalanda, which flourished during 5th to 12th century AD.

Numismatic evidence suggests that during his reign the Gupta empire was at its zenith. His reign also saw tremendous creativity and thus a lot of variety in Gupta coinage. Kumargupta minted 14 distinct types of Gold coins, the largest of all Gupta rulers. Many of them, like Rhinoceros-slayer, Apratigha (parents crowning him as ruler) and Kartikeya or Peacock rider type (shown below) are unique in entire Indian numismatic history. He also minted two coin types, Tiger-slayer (shown below) and Lyrist, which his grandfather, Samudragupta minted briefly. These two types were discontinued during the reign Chandragupta.

- Kumargupta I
- 415-455 AD
- Two Gold Dinars
- *Obverse*: King shooting the tiger
- *Reverse*: River goddess Ganga, feeding grapes to peacock
- *Weight* (#1): 10.26 gm with mount
- *Reference*: BMC Gupta#244, Altekar#1706ff
- *Weight* (#2): 9.75 gm with mount

- Reference: BMC Gupta# 243, Altekar# 1739ff
- From the 'Bayana Hoard'
- Very Rare

Shown above are two of the finest known coins of Kumargupta. On obverse, king is shown wearing short sleeved coat, *Dhoti,* turban, earrings, necklace, armlets, wristles and trampling tiger by his right foot. He is shooting at it with his bow held in right arm, left hand drawing the string of the bow. The tiger is shown falling backwards with gaping mouth. The legends on obverse reads *Srimama Vyagrahabala Parakramaha,* his majesty having the strength and valor of a tiger.

The reverse show goddess, nimbate, standing, slightly bent on *Makara,* the mythic crocodile, holding behind her a lotus with long stalk, in her left hand. She is shown feeding a peacock with fruit (very likely the grapes). The goddess is identified as river Ganga who is shown wearing a *sari,* bodice, earrings, necklace, armlets etc. The Legends written in Brahmi reads his official name, *Kumarguptodhiraja.* This tiger slayer type of coins are very rare and considered to be the master pieces of craftsmanship and truly represents the glory of Gupta empire and their brave emperors. Both the coins were recovered from the famous Bayana hoard.

- Kumargupta I
- 415-455 AD
- Gold Dinars
- *Weight*: 8.3 gm
- *Obverse*: Kumaragupta, nimbate, standing left, feeding peacock from fruit bunch held in his right hand
- *Reverse*: Karttikeya, nimbate, seated on his peacock, Paravani, left, sprinkling incense with his right hand on altar to right, and holding spear in his left hand.
- *Reference*: BMC Guptas 250, (same reverse die); Altekar pl. XIII, 11; Bayana 1697
- From the 'Bayana Hoard'
- Very Rare

A hoard of at least 1821 (there were perhaps some more) gold coins belonging to Gupta dynasty was discovered in

February 1946 near village Bayana in the Bharatpur princely state. It was first noticed by small boys scavenging for brass shell casings. These shells were of bullets fired by hunting party of *Maharaja* (King) of Bharatpur, Col. His Highness Shri Brajendra Sawai Maharaja Brajendra Singhji Bahadur Bahadurjung, who was fond of hunting wild life. This hoard was eventually acquired by Maharaja and a selection of coins from this hoard (mostly rare and beautiful coins) were picked up by Maharaja for making jewelry for members of Royal family. Rest of the coins of the hoard were graciously handed over to the first president of Modern India, Dr. Rajendra Prasad, who himself was a distinguished scholar of Indian history and philosophy. Now, the coins from this hoard can be seen in the National museums of India, New Delhi, Prince of Wales Museum, Bombay and Lalit Kala Bhavan in Varanasi. All the coins from this hoard were catalogued by Dr. Anant Sadashiv Altekar, which remains the best reference book for Gupta gold coins. The two beautiful coins shown above are from the bracelet of the Queen of Bharatpur (either wife or aunt of Maharaja). The original bracelet had 9 (or 8) coins.

ROLE OF FOREIGN ELEMENTS

Long before Alexander reached the gates of geographical India, the people of the subcontinent enjoyed a sporadic cultural interaction with their immediate western neighbours through the "lateral valleys" of Makran and the mountain passes of Hindukush, which were major land-routes.

The complex nature of Indian culture makes it almost impossible to trace the traits left by the "foreigners" in that remote past. In a diverse and culturally rich country like India, there remains very little difference between culture and civilization. The cultural life of a land consists of social behaviour of the inhabitants as manifested in their typical custom and usages, its spiritual emancipation enriched by the advancements of ethics, philosophy and religion, its aesthetic experiences and technical abilities expressed through the medium of fine arts and other aspects of higher pursuits of intellectual life.

The book examines in some detail the traces that the westerners left upon three major aspects Indian culture, viz. social life, fine arts and religion. It is an attempt to present a picture of the cross-fertilization of ideas in an age of Indian history when it came in contact with the geographical external ethnic elements.

In this we have dealt with certain aspects of culture of ancient India from c.600 BC to AD 320. The complex nature of Indian culture makes it impossible to trace the traits left by the foreigners in that remote past. In a diverse and culturally rich country like India of the ancient times there remains very little difference between civilization and culture.

The cultural life of a nation consists of social behaviour of its inhabitants manifested in their typical customs and usages, its spiritual emancipation enriched by the advancement of ethics, philosophy and religion, its aesthetic experiences and technical abilities expressed through the medium of fine arts and other aspects of higher pursuits of intellectual life. I have examined in some detail the traces that the westerners left upon three major aspects of Indian culture, viz., social life, fine arts and religion.

When started the study several years ago on this subject, I had thought to make an attempt to trace the history of how India enriched her culture as a result of the contacts with the foreigners, who came over and over again and made India their home. So I had the title of my work as Foreign Influence on Indian Culture. But as gradually my work progressed, I realised that the topic was too ambitious and its scope was too wide as it would have meant to trace the influence of all the foreign tribes on all the aspects of Indian culture, which would not have been possible for me to do justice in a few years time. Consequently, I limited my studies to the western influences on some aspects of ancient Indian culture to make the study more complete.

I have planned the work in the following manner: First, the period of the study has been defined. I have chosen this period as it witnessed the succession of foreign invasions and immigration from the west and those people had brought with them completely new and different traditions of social institutions, techniques in fine arts and theistic ideas. India finds herself faced with difficult situations as the invaders and settlers had many uncommon cultural traits than hers. How India had adjusted to their culture as circumstances necessitated is a highly fascinating history.

India finds herself faced with difficult situations as the invaders and settlers had many uncommon cultural traits than hers. How India had adjusted to their culture as circumstances necessitated is a highly fascinating history.

It relates how the indigenous and the foreign tribes tried to solve the first clashes of inconsistency which later on had subsided down to give way to co-operation and mutual understanding. This happy co-ordination is one of the chief virtues of Indian civilization.

References in literature about India's contact with the west in this period have come down to us. It was in this epoch that the Indians absorbed the spiritual thinking, saw the incursions of the sophisticated Persians from Achaemenid Iran, the proud and energetic Greeks and Bactrians, the more savage yet remarkably adaptable Scythio-Parthians and the versatile Kushans in the heart of their motherland. It was in this period that we find India becoming conscious about lands beyond her geographical boundary and her horizon stretching out towards the west.

I have given a brief political outline as a background of the whole picture. In the following sections I have dealt with the land and the sea-routes to and from the west to India, as those routes were followed in those ages. I have based my discussion of these routes on contemporary sources, chiefly Indian.

In the second chapter I have discussed the available Indian literary sources for the purpose. How and in what sense the term Mleccha (meaning a foreigner) has been used in the contemporary Indian literature is discussed in an independent section of this chapter. Some of the Indian tribes who had settled in the ages preceding in the bordering regions had been actually influenced deeply by the foreign contacts in this period and were branded as Mlecchas as well. They contributed considerably in enriching Indian culture. So I have included several of them in my study.

In the third chapter, the western impacts on ancient India's social system have been included. The reason for presenting a study of social life first is that, before an external influence is felt on any other spheres of culture of a land, society in general faces its impacts first of all, and it is more susceptible to new things while other aspects of culture are rather conservative.

The Indian society is comprised of many institutions and systems, such as, the distinction of the castes, the various samskaras (customs) which the people followed, and common ways of life. The foreign impact is rather obvious on some of those social institutions while on the others it is not quite clear. I have taken into account only those aspects of social life on which the alien traits are somewhat pronounced.

After causing certain changes or renovations in the society, the newly arrived forces find their way to the realm of fine arts. They rejuvenate the visual and plastic expression and add new innovations to sphere of music, dance and drama. They add new varieties to the already existing set-motifs of the minor arts; refresh the stereo-typed skill of the traditional artists, artisans and craftsmen. In the fourth chapter, I have presented a study of all these influences in the realm of fine arts. It is a gripping history of how the new-comers made themselves and their skill prominent through the chisel and brushes of the native artists and artisans.

The foreign impacts take longest time to react on the sphere of religious life of a people. It seems that the human mind is more conservative in his theistic dogmas and anything that is new or branded with an exotic colouring is accepted only after a prolonged time-tested persistence. Religion is the last to yield before a fresh surge of foreign ideas. Society may accept new ways in it's everyday life, that is, the styles may change in dress and costume, new dishes may be added to the culinary art, and acceptance of new modes and mediums of expression in it's feelings in fine arts becomes obvious, yet it adheres to it's philosophical and religious beliefs of hoary past. For in India of the past, as has been said, the art was the "hand-maid of religion"; any adjustment and inter-change of ideas in the realm of religion was bound to tint her artistic expressions too.

The fifth and the last chapter of the book deals with the study of the western influences on the religious beliefs of India. I have discussed the possible influence on the Brahmanical religion in a more detailed manner.

In separate sections, I have dealt with the various prominent sects that flourished during this period. The Mahayana Buddhism has been left out from this study as its main development does not come in the period and it is commonly accepted that Jainism got hardly influenced by any external doctrine.

During this period of study general disturbances and calamities fell over the land. One can easily imagine that the successive foreign invasions of the Achaemenid Iranians, Hellenistic Greeks and especially of the Bactrian Greeks, the barbarous Schythio-Parthians and the Kushans aroused a feeling if insecurity in the mind of the common people. It was heightened up by the bitter strife in between the followers of Gautama Buddha, Mahavira and the orthodox adheres of the earlier Vedic traditions. It seems, that in this period when the political sky of India was clouded with transitional uncertainties, the common people, irrespective of their faiths, viz. Vedic, Buddhist or Jaina, greeted any government that provided a shelter to them. e.g., be it Indo-Hellenistic, Schythian or Kushan, be the ruler a man with cosmopolitan outlooks, a devout Buddhist or a Brahmana, a Kshatriya, even a Vratya.

It is only natural, that some humanitarian authorities took the leading role and tried to create a happy harmony amongst the diverse centrifugal forces. Fortunately enough some of the great kings of this period-Asoka, Menander, Kanishka and Rudradaman were personalities of this rank. Indeed, the contemporary agriculturists, business guilds, artists, artisans, doctors, astrologers, priests, officials, clerks, literati-all belonging to commoner's class had welcomed the golden rule of these kings which do not make any difference between the races, the castes and faiths. It appears from the literary references that the followers of the Gautama Buddha were somewhat more liberal in accepting the foreigners into their fold. But as their contribution towards culture was indiscriminately utilized by the Hindus, Buddhists and Jainas alike no classification have been made to define Brahmanical culture or Buddhist culture. Hence no distinction has been made either to describe a picture of a Hindu society or a Buddhist society, and Brahmanical art and Buddhist art. The archeological remains of this period are mostly Buddhistic, and it had cast a profound influence on the Hindu art and architecture of the period that followed. Therefore what the Buddhists accepted from the foreigners was adopted and applied by the Hindus.

The subject is very fascinating. This book is not in anyway conclusive. It is just an attempt to present a picture of culture interaction of an age of the history of our land when it came in contact with the others. The brief account that has been given is at least sufficient to show how receptive and full of vitality our people of these ages were. This could be just an opening for a fuller study of all the aspects of India's culture. For a comprehensive study of this nature it is absolutely imperative to know many classical languages like Old Persian, Hebrew, Greek, Latin etc., and I have contended myself only with English translations. Though some of these aspects have been studied by other great scholars, I have tried to present a little more complete picture of the various aspects in this book and at many places I have suggested some new interpretations.

CULTURAL TRANISMISSION

The process of transmitting cultural elements through literary translation is a complicated and vital task. Culture is a complex collection of experiences which condition daily life; it includes history, social structure, religion, traditional customs and everyday usage. This is difficult to comprehend completely. Especially in relation to a target language, one important question is whether the translation will have any readership at all, as the specific reality being portrayed is not quite familiar to the reader.

We shall discuss some of the problems a translator encounters while translating a text from one language to another in the Indian context.

A name is a linguistic cultural element, and an author uses it for its associative value. It resists translation; therefore its evocative value is lost.

In the Indian culture, people show respect to their elders by addressing them in plural. A simple he/she cannot be substituted, because then the idea behind the use of plural address would be lost. So, in addressing an elder person, either choice-retaining the plural form or replacing it by a simple "you"-will lead to ambiguity.

It seems artificial here for family members to greet one another with "good morning," "have a nice day," etc., to apologize, or to express gratitude by saying "thank you."

Regarding social relationships, most Indians used to live with their extended families. A need to address each relative arose. For this reason, there are different words in all Indian languages to refer to each relation. There are words to address a wife's mother or father, a wife's sister or brother, a husband's sister or brother, a mother's sister or brother, and so on. This concept (practice?) of the extended family living together is unheard of in western countries; therefore, the English language lacks the corresponding terms.

One may say that this extended-family lifestyle keeps many family values alive. In some texts, awareness of the society's or the family's values must be stressed; the linguistic manifestations of these values cannot be translated into a language where the audience is unfamiliar with these values.

Dress code or ornaments used and the symbols behind each of them also pose a problem for a translator. Here some of the ornaments are meant for only a woman whose husband is alive. A widow has certain restrictions. This idea of widowhood is non-existent in western countries. The pain behind this widowhood cannot be conveyed to such an audience.

Regarding food habits, the very flavour behind a food or its significance is untranslatable to an audience who has never heard of it. For instance, certain foods are prepared only during certain festivals, and such foods remind Indian readers of the season or some religious story. This is not experienced by an audience of a different culture.

Customs and tradition are part of a culture. Be it a marriage or a funeral, be it a festival or some vows, the story and the significance or hidden symbolism behind it become a stumbling block for a translator. For instance, in a Christian marriage, the exchange of kisses is part of the ceremony. In an Indian context, this would be totally inappropriate! Even expressing feelings in public is outrageous here.

Beliefs and feelings change from culture to culture. The colour white may represent purity and black may represent evil in the Indian context, but it may not be the same in another culture. What is considered a good omen, whether an event, an animal or a bird, may not symbolize the same thing in another culture.

Religious elements, myths, legends, and the like are major components of any culture. They present major hurdles in translating a text. This sensitive issue demands the translator's full attention.

Lastly, geographical and environmental elements are also part of one's culture. For instance, snow is a part of the Eskimos' life. There are different words to identify different kinds of snow in their language. In India, people have no idea of snow, and there are no words to describe different kinds of snow. Another example: the Chinese language has different words for different types of ants; in the Indian languages all kinds of ants are just ants!

CONCLUSION

Cultural transfer requires a multi-pronged approach. It is concerned with the author's relationship to his subject matter and with the author's relationship to his reader. These should be reflected in a good translation. The translator must transmit this special cultural quality from one language to another.

Most translations are intended to serve, however imperfectly, as a substitute for the original, making it available to people who cannot read the language in which it was written. This imposes a heavy responsibility on the translator.

Awareness of history is an essential requirement for the translator of a work coming from an alien culture. Thorough knowledge of a foreign language, its vocabulary, and grammar is not sufficient to make one competent as a translator. One should be familiar with one's own culture and be aware of the source-language culture before attempting to build any bridge between them.

If the reality being represented is not familiar to the audience, the translation stumbles and becomes difficult to read. The translator would have to consider whether similar or parallel language resources exist in the literary subculture of the target language. In translations of a culture rich in literature, the question of relevance to the projected audience is more significant to the translator than to the original author. A translator has to look for equivalents in terms of relevance in the target language and exercise discretion by substituting rather than translating certain elements in a work. Even with all the apparent cultural hurdles, a translator can create equivalence by the judicious use of resources.

EFFECT OF FOREIGN CULTURE

Foreign language learning is comprised of several components, including grammatical competence, communicative competence, language proficiency, as well as a change in attitudes towards one's own or another culture. For scholars and laymen alike, cultural competence, i.e., the knowledge of the conventions, customs, beliefs, and systems of meaning of another country, is indisputably an integral part of foreign language learning, and many teachers have seen it as their goal to incorporate the teaching of culture into the foreign language curriculum. It could be maintained that the notion of communicative competence, which, in the past decade or so, has blazed a trail, so to speak, in foreign language teaching, emphasising the role of context and the circumstances under which language can be used accurately and appropriately, 'fall[s] short of the mark when it comes to actually equipping students with the cognitive skills they need in a second-culture environment'. In other words, since the wider context of language, that is, society and culture, has been reduced to a variable elusive of any definition—as many teachers and students incessantly talk about it without knowing what its exact meaning is—it stands to reason that the term communicative competence should become nothing more than an empty and meretricious word, resorted to if for no other reason than to make an "educational point." In reality, what most teachers and students seem to lose sight of is the fact that 'knowledge of the grammatical system of a language has to be complemented by understanding (sic) of culture-specific meanings.

Of course, we are long past an era when first language acquisition and second or foreign language learning were cast in a "behaviouristic mould," being the products of imitation and language "drills," and language was thought of as a compendium of rules and strings of words and sentences used to form propositions about a state of affairs. In the last two decades, there has been a resurgence of interest in the study of language in relation to society, which has led to a shift of focus from behaviourism and positivism to constructivism to critical theory. Yet, there are still some deeply ingrained beliefs as to the nature of language learning and teaching—beliefs that determine methodology as well as the content of the foreign language curriculum—which have, gradually and insidiously, contrived to undermine the teaching of culture.

One of the misconceptions that have permeated foreign language teaching is the conviction that language is merely a code and, once mastered-mainly by dint of steeping oneself into grammatical rules and some aspects of the social context in which it is embedded-'one language is essentially (albeit not easily) translatable into another'. To a certain extent, this belief has been instrumental in promoting various approaches to foreign language teaching-pragmatic, sociolinguistic, and communicative-which have certainly endowed the study of language with a social "hue"; nevertheless, paying lip service to the social dynamics that undergird language without trying to identify and gain insights into the very fabric of society and culture that have come to charge language in many and varied ways can only cause misunderstanding and lead to cross-cultural miscommunication.

At any rate, foreign language learning is foreign culture learning, and, in one form or another, culture has, even implicitly, been taught in the foreign language classroom-if for different reasons. What is debatable, though, is what is meant by the term "culture" and how the latter is integrated into language learning and teaching. Kramsch's keen observation should not go unnoticed:

> Culture in language learning is not an expendable fifth skill, tacked on, so to speak, to the teaching of speaking, listening, reading, and writing. It is always in the background, right from day one, ready to unsettle the good language learners when they expect it least, making evident the limitations of their hard-won communicative competence, challenging their ability to make sense of the world around them.

The teaching of culture is not akin to the transmission of information regarding the people of the target community or country-even though knowledge about (let alone experience of) the "target group" is an important ingredient. It would be nothing short of ludicrous to assert that culture is merely a repository of facts and experiences to which one can have recourse, if need be. Furthermore, what Kramsch herself seems to insinuate is that to learn a foreign language is not merely to learn how to communicate but also to discover how much leeway the target language allows learners to manipulate grammatical forms, sounds, and meanings, and to reflect upon, or even flout, socially accepted norms at work both in their own or the target culture.

There is definitely more than meets the eye, and the present paper has the aim of unravelling the "mystery," shedding some light on the role of teaching culture in fostering cross-cultural understanding which transcends the boundaries of linguistic forms-while enriching and giving far deeper meaning to what is dubbed "communicative competence"-and runs counter to a solipsistic world view. I would like to show that the teaching of culture has enjoyed far less "adulation" than it merits, and consider ways of incorporating it not only into the foreign language curriculum but also into learners' repertoire and outlook on life. The main premise of this paper is that we cannot go about teaching a foreign language without at least offering some insights into its speakers' culture. By the same token, we cannot go about fostering "communicative competence" without taking into account the different views and perspectives of people in different cultures which may enhance or even inhibit communication. After all, communication requires understanding, and understanding requires stepping into the shoes of the foreigner and sifting her cultural baggage, while always 'putting [the target] culture in relation with one's own'. Moreover, we should be cognisant of the fact that '[i]f we teach language without teaching at the same time the culture in which it operates, we are teaching meaningless symbols or symbols to which the student attaches the wrong meaning'.

THE HISTORY OF CULTURE TEACHING

As will become evident, the role of cultural learning in the foreign language classroom has been the concern of many teachers and scholars and has sparked considerable controversy, yet its validity as an equal complement to language learning has often been overlooked or even impugned. Up to now, two main perspectives have influenced the teaching of culture. One pertains to the transmission of factual, cultural information, which consists in statistical information, that is, institutional structures and other aspects of the target civilisation, highbrow information, i.e., immersion in literature and the arts, and lowbrow information, which may focus on the customs, habits, and folklore of everyday life. This preoccupation with facts rather than meanings, though, leaves much to be desired as far as an understanding of foreign attitudes and values is concerned, and virtually blindfolds learners to the minute albeit significant aspects of their own as well as the target group's identity that are not easily divined and appropriated (ibid.) All that it offers is 'mere book knowledge learned by rote'. The other perspective, drawing upon cross-cultural psychology or anthropology, has been to embed culture within an interpretive framework and establish connections, namely, points of reference or departure, between one's own and the target country. This approach, however, has certain limitations, since it can only furnish learners with cultural knowledge, while leaving them to their own devices to integrate that knowledge with the assumptions, beliefs, and mindsets already obtaining in their society. Prior to considering a third perspective, to which the present paper aspires to contribute, it is of consequence to briefly sift through the relevant literature and see what the teaching of culture has come to be associated with.

As Lessard-Clouston (1997) notes, in the past, people learned a foreign language to study its literature, and this was the main medium of culture. '[I]t was through reading that students learned of the civilization associated with the target language' (Flewelling, 1993: 339, cited in Lessard-Clouston, 1997). In the 1960s and 1970s, such eminent scholars as Hall (1959), Nostrand (1974), Seelye ([1974] 1984), and Brooks made an endeavour to base foreign language learning on a universal ground of emotional and physical needs, so that 'the foreign culture [would appear] less threatening and more accessible to the language learner'. In the heyday of the audiolingual era in language teaching, Brooks 'emphasized the importance of culture not for the study of literature but for language learning', as Steele has observed. Earlier on, Brooks (1960) in his seminal work Language and Language Learning had offered sixty-four topics regarding culture interspersed with questions covering several pages. These 'hors d' oeuvres', as he called them, concerned, inter alia, such crucial aspects of culture as greetings, expletives, personal possessions, cosmetics, tobacco and smoking, verbal taboos, cafes, bars, and restaurants, contrasts in town and country life, patterns of politeness, keeping warm and cool, medicine and doctors [...]

In a sense, his groundbreaking work was conducive to a shift of focus from teaching geography and history as part of language learning to an anthropological approach to the study of culture. What is important is that, by making the distinction between "Culture with a Capital C"-art, music, literature, politics and so on-and "culture with a small c"-the behavioural patterns and lifestyles of everyday people-he helped dispel the myth that culture (or civilisation or Landeskunde, or what other name it is known by is an intellectual gift bestowed only upon the elite. Admittedly, the main thrust of his work was to make people aware that culture resides in the very fabric of their lives-their modus vivendi, their beliefs, assumptions, and attitudes-rather than in a preoccupation with aesthetic reflections or high-falutin ideas. As Weaver insightfully remarks, the commonly held notion of culture is largely concerned with its insignificant aspects, whereas our actual interaction with it takes place at a subconscious level.

Many, if not most, people think of culture as what is often called "high culture"-art, literature, music, and the like. This culture is set in the framework of history and of social, political, and economic structures....Actually, the most important part of culture for the sojourner is that which is internal and hidden..., but which governs the behaviour they encounter. This dimension of culture can be seen as an iceberg with the tip sticking above the water level of conscious awareness. By far the most significant part, however, is unconscious or below the water level of awareness and includes values and thought patterns.

Following Brooks, Nostrand developed the Emergent Model scheme, which comprised six main categories. The first, culture, regarded value systems and habits of thought; society included organizations and familial, religious, and other institutions. The third category of conflict was comprised of interpersonal as well as intrapersonal conflict. Ecology and technology included knowledge of plants and animals, health care, travel etc., while the fifth category, individuals, was about intra/interpersonal variation. Finally, cross-cultural environment had to do with attitudes towards other cultures.

As Singhal notes, '[i]t is evident that one would have to be quite knowledgeable in the culture under study to be able to present all of these aspects accurately to second language learners'. Since the 1960s, a great many educators have concerned themselves with the importance of the cultural aspect in foreign language learning, with Hammerly, Seelye (1984) and Damen being among those who have considered ways of incorporating culture into language teaching. In the 1970s, an emphasis on sociolinguistics led to greater emphasis on the situational context of the foreign language. Savignon's study on communicative competence, for example, suggested the 'value of training in communicative skills from the very beginning of the FL programme'. As a result, the role of culture in the foreign language curriculum was enhanced, and influential works by Seelye and Lafayette appeared. The audiolingual method was replaced by the communicative approach, and Canale and Swain claimed that 'a more natural integration' of language and culture takes place 'through a more communicative approach than through a more grammatically based approach'. In addition, teacher-oriented texts now included detailed chapters on culture teaching for the foreign language classroom, attesting to the predominant goal: communication within the cultural context of the target language.

It is only in the 1980s that scholars begin to delve into the dynamics of culture and its vital contribution to 'successful' language learning. For example, Littlewood advocates the value of cultural learning, although he still 'keeps linguistic proficiency as the overall aim of communicative competence' (ibid.). Also, there are many insightful comparisons made between behavioural conventions in the L1 and L2 societies which are culture-specific and which could be said to impede understanding: the use of silence, frequency of turn-taking, politeness (Odlin, and so forth Furthermore, in the 1980s and 1990s, advances in pragmatics and sociolinguistics laying bare the very essence of language, which is no longer thought of as merely describing or communicating but, rather, as persuading, deceiving, or punishing and controlling, have rendered people's frames of reference and cultural schemata tentative, and led to attempts at 'bridg[ing] the cultural gap in language teaching'.

On the assumption that communication is not only an exchange of information but also a highly cognitive as well as affective and value-laden activity, Melde holds that foreign language teaching should foster 'critical awareness' of social life—a view commensurate with Fairclough's critical theory. More specifically, when the learner understands the perspectives of others and is offered the opportunity to reflect on his own perspectives, 'through a process of decentering and a level of reciprocity, there arises a moral dimension, a judgmental tendency, which is not defined purely on formal, logical grounds'.

To this end, the learner needs to take the role of the foreigner, so that he may gain insights into the values and meanings that the latter has internalised and unconsciously negotiates with the members of the society to which he belongs. Beside Melde, Baumgratz-Gangl (1990) asserts that the integration of values and meanings of the foreign culture with those of one's "native culture" can bring about a shift of perspective or the 'recognition of cognitive dissonance' (Byram, Morgan et al.), both conducive to reciprocity and empathy.

What is more, Swaffar acknowledges the contribution of culture when he says that, in order to combat, as it were, 'cultural distance', students must be exposed to foreign literature with a view to developing the ability to put into question and evaluate the cultural elements L2 texts are suffused with.

Kramsch also believes that culture should be taught as an interpersonal process and, rather than presenting cultural facts, teachers should assist language learners in coming to grips with the 'other culture' She maintains that, by virtue of the increasing multiculturality of various societies, learners should be made aware of certain cultural factors at work, such as age, gender, and social class, provided that the former usually have little or no systematic knowledge about their membership in a given society and culture, nor do they have enough knowledge about the target culture to be able to interpret and synthesize the cultural phenomena presented.

From all the above, it is evident that, much as the element of culture has gained momentum in foreign language learning, most educators have seen it as yet another skill at the disposal of those who aspire to become conversant with the history and life of the target community rather than as an integral part of communicative competence and intercultural awareness at which every "educated individual" should aim. As has been intimated above, the present paper takes a third perspective, in claiming that cultural knowledge is not only an aspect of communicative competence, but an educational objective in its own right.

Nevertheless, cultural knowledge is unlike, say, knowledge of mathematics or Ancient Greek, in the sense that it is an all-encompassing kind of knowledge which, to a certain extent, has determined—facilitated or precluded—all other types of "knowledge." Rather than viewing cultural knowledge as a prerequisite for language proficiency, it is more important to view it as 'the community's store of established knowledge', which comprises 'structures of expectation' with which everyone belonging to a certain group is expected to unconsciously and unerringly comply.

A corollary of this third perspective is to view the teaching of culture as a means of 'developing an awareness of, and sensitivity towards, the values and traditions of the people whose language is being studied'. It goes without saying that to foster cultural awareness by dint of teaching culture means to bring to our learners' conscious the latent assumptions and premises underlying their belief and value systems and, most importantly, to show that our own culture predisposes us to a certain worldview by creating a 'cognitive framework.... [which] is made up of a number of unquantifiables [my emphasis] ....embrac[ing] ...assumptions about how the world is constructed' (ibid.).

But this cognitive framework is, to a great extent, maintained and sanctioned through the very use of language, which is arguably 'the most visible and available expression of [a] culture'. As will be shown, though, language and culture are so intricately related that their boundaries, if any, are extremely blurred and it is difficult to become aware of—let alone question—the assumptions and expectations that we hold. It should be reiterated that language teaching is culture teaching, and what the next chapter will set out to show is that, 'by teaching a language...one is inevitably already teaching culture implicitly' and gaining insights into the foreign language should automatically presuppose immersion in the foreign culture, in so far as these two, language and culture, go hand in hand.

LANGUAGE AND CULTURE

In this section, we will briefly examine the relationship between language and culture and see why the teaching of culture should constitute an integral part of the English language curriculum. To begin with, language is a social institution, both shaping and shaped by society at large, or in particular the 'cultural niches' in which it plays an important role.

Thus, if our premise is that language is, or should be, understood as cultural practice, then ineluctably we must also grapple with the notion of culture in relation to language. Language is not an 'autonomous construct' but social practice both creating and created by 'the structures and forces of [the] social institutions within which we live and function'. Certainly, language cannot exist in a vacuum; one could make so bold as to maintain that there is a kind of "transfusion" at work between language and culture. Amongst those who have dilated upon the affinity between language and culture, it is Duranti who succinctly encapsulates how these two interpenetrate:

> to be part of a culture means to share the propositional knowledge and the rules of inference necessary to understand whether certain propositions are true (given certain premises). To the propositional knowledge, one might add the procedural knowledge to carry out tasks such as cooking, weaving,

farming, fishing, giving a formal speech, answering the phone, asking for a favor, writing a letter for a job application.

Clearly, everyday language is "tinged" with cultural bits and pieces—a fact most people seem to ignore. By the very act of talking, we assume social and cultural roles, which are so deeply entrenched in our thought processes as to go unnoticed.

Interestingly, 'culture defines not only what its members should think or learn but also what they should ignore or treat as irrelevant'. That language has a setting, in that the people who speak it belong to a race or races and are incumbents of particular cultural roles, is blatantly obvious. 'Language does not exist apart from culture, that is, from the socially inherited assemblage of practices and beliefs that determines the texture of our lives'.

Nineteenth-century sociologists, such as Durkheim, were well aware of, and expatiated upon, the interdependence of language and culture. For Durkheim, children master their mother tongue by dint of making hypotheses as to the possible circumstances under which it can be used, and by learning probabilities.

For example, a child sees a canary and is culturally conditioned to associate certain features and attributes of the bird with the actual word canary. And most importantly, the extent to which the child will internalise the relationship (or lack thereof) between the word canary and its referent in the world is contingent upon 'social adulation' (Landar, 1965: 225). If he is taken for a walk and sees a sparrow and says, "canary," he will be corrected, learning that 'competence counts' (ibid.). In other words, '[s]socioculturally structured associations have to be internalized' (ibid.)—and, as often as not, these associations vary from culture to culture. Rather than getting bogged down in a 'linguistic relativity' debate, the tenets of which are widely known, some consideration should be given to the claim that 'language is not merely the external covering of a thought; it is also its internal framework. It does not confine itself to expressing this thought after it has once been formed; it also aids in making it'.

Fairly recently, many ethnographers such as Buttjes (1990), Ochs & Schieffelin (1984), Poyatos, (1985), and Peters & Boggs, (1986) have attempted to show that 'language and culture are from the start inseparably connected' (Buttjes, 1990: 55, cited in Lessard-Clouston, 1997). More specifically, he summarises the reasons why this should be the case: language acquisition does not follow a universal sequence, but differs across cultures; the process of becoming a competent member of society is realised through exchanges of language in particular social situations;

- Every society orchestrates the ways in which children participate in
- Particular situations, and this, in turn, affects the form, the function and
- The content of children's utterances;
- Caregivers' primary concern is not with grammatical input, but with the
- Transmission of sociocultural knowledge;
- The native learner, in addition to language; acquires also the
- Paralinguistic patterns and the kinesics of his or her culture.

The implications of Buttjes' findings for the teaching of culture are evident. Language teaching is culture teaching and teachers do their students a great disservice in placing emphasis on the former, to the detriment of the latter. As Buttjes (1990: 55-56) notes, 'language teachers need to go beyond monitoring linguistic production in the classroom and become aware of the complex and numerous processes of intercultural mediation that any foreign language learner undergoes...'. To hark back to the relationship between language and culture; Samovar, Porter, & Jain (1981: 24) observe:

Culture and communication are inseparable because culture not only dictates who talks to whom, about what, and how the communication proceeds, it also helps to determine how people encode messages, the meanings they have for messages, and the conditions and circumstances under which various messages may or may not be sent, noticed, or interpreted... Culture...is the foundation of communication.

Moreover, given Duranti's (1997: 24) definition of culture as 'something learned, transmitted, passed down from one generation to the next, through human actions, often in the form of face-to-face interaction, and, of course, through linguistic communication', it is patently obvious that language, albeit a subpart of culture, plays a pivotal role. Bourdieu has emphasised the importance of language not as an autonomous construct but as a system determined by various socio-political processes. For him, a language exists as a linguistic habitus (see Bourdieu, 1990: 52), as a set of practices that imply not only a particular system of words and grammatical rules, but also an often forgotten or hidden struggle over the symbolic power of a particular way of communicating, with particular systems of classification, address and reference forms, specialized lexicons, and metaphors (for politics, medicine, ethics) (Bourdieu, 1982: 31, cited in Duranti, 1997: 45).

At any rate, to speak means to choose a particular way of entering the world and a particular way of sustaining relationships with those we come in contact with. It is often through language use that we, to a large extent, are members of a community of ideas and practices (ibid.). Thus, as a complex system of classification of experience and 'an important window on the universe of thoughts' (Duranti, 1997: 49); as a link between thought and behaviour; and as 'the prototypical tool for interacting with the world' (ibid.), language is intertwined with culture. In the past, language and culture were lumped together as if they automatically implied each other. Wilhelm von Humboldt, an eminent diplomat and scholar, once wrote:

The spiritual traits and the structure of the language of a people are so intimately blended that, given either of the two, one should be able to derive the other from it to the fullest extent...Language is the outward manifestation of the spirit of people: their language is their spirit, and their spirit is their language; it is difficult to imagine any two things more identical (Humboldt, 1907, cited in Salzmann, 1998: 39).

On the other hand, Sapir (1921: 215) asserts that '[l]anguage, race, and culture are not necessarily correlated', only to admit later on that '[l]anguage and our thought-grooves are inextricably interrelated, are, in a sense, one and the same' (ibid.: 217-218), thus oscillating between a view of language and culture as being autonomous and separate from each other and one of linguistic determinism, whereby language affects and shapes human thought. According to his lights, '[c]ulture may be defined as what a society does and thinks. Language is a particular how of thought' (ibid.: 218). In addition, Hall (1981: 36) aligns himself with Humboldt and Bourdieu in dubbing language 'one of the dominant threads in all cultures'.

In a similar vein, Bruner (1996: 3) says that '[a]lthough meanings are "in the mind," they have their origins and their significance in the culture in which they are created'. And he adds, 'human beings do not terminate at their own skins; they are expressions of a culture' (Bruner, 1990: 12). Furthermore, we could envision the possibility of 'certain linguistic features mak[ing] certain modes of perception more prevalent or more probable' (Henle, 1970: 18).

Index